EMOTIONAL FITNESS

A workout plan to master your emotions,
conquer your goals, and live the life of your dreams

Corey Corpodian

ISBN (Print): 978-1-7333232-0-8
ISBN: (Ebook) 978-1-7333232-1-5

Cover Designer: Michelle Fairbanks
Cover photographer: Mayra Cardenas
Page Designer: Jose Pepito Jr.
Editing: ArtofStorytellingOnline.com
Illustrator: Aliosa Tran Phan

First Edition: 2019

www.UnleashSuccess.com
www.MasterEmotionalFitness.com/step1

DEDICATION

This book is dedicated to anyone out there struggling to survive or wanting more out of life. You are not alone. There is hope. This is your roadmap.

CONTENTS

Part I
Awareness

Part II
Where Emotional Fitness Gets Results

Part III
Emotional Fitness Mastery

The Emotional Fitness Guide and Course
(For Free!)

Many of the exercises in this book require you to write down a few things and refer back to them often. To help you get the most out of this book, I created a **free** online tutorial and course complete with downloadable worksheets, bonus video content, and a daily journal workbook to help you master Emotional Fitness.

Although it's not required, I highly recommend you access the free course and worksheets to help you maximize your success with the content of this book. Visit the following address to sign up:

www.MasterEmotionalFitness.com/step1

Once you sign up, you'll find the material in the same order as the chapters and sections of this book to help you easily master Emotional Fitness. There's additional bonus content beyond what is shared in this book, and I'll be adding more bonus content over time. Make sure to visit the website address below and get free instant access to it now! See you inside!

Visit the link to get free access to your

Emotional Fitness bonus materials now:

www.MasterEmotionalFitness.com/step1

How Emotional Fitness Leads to Success

It is not death that a man should fear, but he should fear never beginning to live.

—Marcus Aurelius

What is the difference between success and failure? Why do some achieve all their goals and dreams while others struggle to even survive? Whatever your goals, whether it is to have financial success, professional accolades, good health, a great body, or great relationships, there are common strategies for achieving success. But do any of these strategies guarantee success? Is that even possible? My lifelong obsession has been to learn how to be successful. While some people want success in one area—business, relationships, fitness—I wanted to know how I could be successful in *every* area of life. In this journey, I found that at its most basic level, the ability to control our mental and emotional states is the difference between those who achieve their biggest goals and those who do not. This book is a step-by-step guide to help you train your Emotional Fitness, so you no longer struggle to survive and instead begin to live the life of your dreams today.

Success Strategies that Work until They Don't

There's a famous urban legend about the first time Bill Gates and Warren Buffet sat down to dinner. Someone asked them, "What is the number one key to success?"

At the same time, they answered, "Focus!"

And just like that story, when I was a kid, everyone told me, "Corey, you have to set goals and stay focused if you want to be successful." They said I had to be laser focused on my goals. I listened intently to the advice of those around me who had built success. I found the fastest way to build success was to model them. I would set a goal and be laser focused. And it worked! I thought, *This makes sense. It's like a GPS system where you type in the exact destination. In order to get to where you want to be, you have to know exactly where you want to go.* Our goals are just destinations in life's GPS system.

Every year, people set New Year's resolutions or goals to make their new year a success. There is no doubt that setting goals help people become more successful. In fact, one Dominican University of California study shows people who physically write down their goals are 42 percent more likely to achieve them. And yet 80–92 percent of people fail to keep their New Year's resolutions.[1]

While setting clear goals and staying focused is needed to be successful, it doesn't always guarantee success. Lots of people want to be the MVP of their sports team, the top seller in their company, or the savvy entrepreneur who makes a million dollars, but few actually achieve these dreams. Didn't other people set the same exact goal? Didn't they focus on it? Why did one person succeed while everyone else failed?

Multiple Routes to Success

As I grew older, I noticed that some people were more successful than others, even though they all had the same goal. Some people achieved their goals fast, while others didn't achieve them at all.

Why? When we enter our destinations into the GPS, what do we see? *Multiple routes!* Some take the long way with many detours, and some take the shorter, faster path. We want the best route to success: the fastest and shortest route. To find the best route, you have to have the BEST strategy. If only we had the best strategy, how could we NOT be successful?

All of us know someone who wants to lose weight or save money. And yet they don't know how to find the best strategy. You could literally Google and find hundreds of *free* trainings, videos, and articles online. With weight loss, you almost have to work harder to avoid posts about a new diet or workout program. They are everywhere. And still, people struggle to succeed. Even worse, they fail.

That's because knowing the BEST strategy is not enough. *Knowing is not enough. Knowledge alone is not power. Action is Power.*

You have to take real action to get real results. And the more action you take, the more successful you become. We see the positive benefits of taking more action everywhere. Want better grades? Study more. Want a better body? Workout more often. Want more money? Make more sales calls. As you take more action, you find better strategies, and your successes multiply. Taking massive action with the best strategy is critical to success and works most of the time, but it does not guarantee success. Let me give you an example.

Massive Action with the Best Strategy Still Led to Failure

Growing up, I moved around a lot. My sisters and I were all born in different states. I probably moved thirty times before I was eighteen. I went to four different high schools in three states in my freshman year alone. In 2001, the US economy had just been hit by the "dot-com" bubble. We had to move because my dad's business failed, and we declared bankruptcy. It was "grab everything and run to any job" to survive. The financial stress of not knowing where the next paycheck was coming from caused a lot of problems in my family.

However, as usual, my parents recovered. By 2003, they were doing well again as they took advantage of the real estate boom in Las Vegas. They were taking *massive action with the best strategy.* They were flipping homes, buying apartments, and making hundreds of thousands of dollars—and even over a million one year. The strategy was hands down the best. Everyone we knew was making mountains of cash, including my family. We were buying boats, a third car—it was like it would never end. But we all know how this story ends.

In 2008, the housing market collapsed in the worst economic crisis in over a century. With all our eggs in one basket, my family lost everything. Again. We went from building a multi-million-dollar custom home to zero. My parents did everything right: they were using the best strategy in the world, and it still failed. The best strategy seemed like the best, until it wasn't.

I learned one very important lesson during this time. As human beings, we can survive almost anything. Our brains have evolved and are literally designed to make us adapt and survive. But surviving and succeeding are two very different things.

If setting goals, focusing intensely, finding the best strategy, and then taking massive action still don't guarantee success, how do other people achieve it? How do others become successful when the odds of success are so low? I knew it couldn't just be luck. I wouldn't figure out the real key to success until years later. In fact, I thought I was doing everything I was supposed to do to be successful. I followed the blueprint for success but still ended up failing.

The Blueprint

A lot of people are taught a blueprint on how to live a successful and happy life: go to school, get a good job, have kids, work thirty years, and retire. Do this and you will live a happy and successful life. Don't do this and you will struggle.

That was the blueprint I was given. I was born and bred in a middle-class family and told, "Get good grades, go to college, become a doctor or lawyer, and then you will be successful." I did exactly what I was told. I thought in my head that if I followed this blueprint, I would be successful and happy. That was the goal for life, right?

There was one problem. My vision of success and happiness did not match the results I was getting from the blueprint I was following. And when your expectations don't meet the reality you live in, that's when you feel unhappy . . .

My Blueprint for Success Actually Led Me to Failure

Success without fulfillment is
the ultimate failure

—Tony Robbins

It all started when I was a kid. I wanted to have a lot of money so I could have the freedom to do what I wanted and not have to move every year. People would always say, "Money doesn't buy happiness." And as a kid I always thought, *That's what people without money say, because I never saw anyone crying in a Ferrari.* Only years later would I understand that money doesn't buy happiness or sadness, it merely magnifies what you feel already.

There are a lot of ways to earn money, but as a kid, I also wanted to do something that helped people. I didn't care to be a lawyer, and at eleven years old, being a doctor around sick people all day sounded horrible. My orthodontist at the time, Dr. White (great dentist name), was awesome. He had video games in his office, traveled often, and only worked three to four days a week. Well, being an orthodontist fit my blueprint-—lawyer or doctor.

I set a clearly defined goal to become an orthodontist. I thought this would give me money and make me happy. I focused intensely on this goal, never wavering. I did everything I thought I needed to do to be successful. I graduated high school a year early as valedictorian, finished college in three years, spent four years in dental school, and completed three more years in orthodontic residency. I was driven by the vision of success. I thought that once I became an orthodontist, I would make millions of dollars and life would be perfect. After more than a decade of dedication, hard work, and relentless sacrifice, I woke up at twenty-seven years old with my lifelong dream accomplished: I was a board-certified orthodontist.

Something BIG Was Missing

On paper, I was a "success," but something really big was missing. I had been depressed for eight years. After ten years of hard work, I expected to find a pot of gold at the end of the rainbow, but there was no gold. In fact, it was worse than no gold. Instead, I had $850,000 in student loan debt!

I hated my job. Like, I f*cking hated it. I had been hypnotized by a fantasy of success and living the life of my dreams. It was a fantasy that wasn't real. The economy changed and I realize now that I never stopped to ask myself if that life was what I really wanted. *I got lost in the idea of success.*

With so much debt, I had to keep working just to pay my bills. What was once a dream truly looked like a prison sentence. Would I really have to work this job every day of my life for the next thirty years? Where was the freedom, passion, love, excitement, and enjoyment of life? At twenty-eight years old, being "successful" with no fulfillment really felt like the ultimate failure, and ending my life sounded better than living the life I'd created for myself.

Rock Bottom

Family has always been the most important thing to me. I was used to leaning on my family for support. Unfortunately, they had their own issues to deal with. My family struggled financially and filed for bankruptcy again. Then my parents got divorced. The family unit, my support system, was destroyed. I felt numb to the world.

With nothing else in my life going right, I turned to the gym. I had been working out since high school, but now the gym was my meditation, my way to relieve stress. It was my sanctuary. I set a goal to participate in a men's physique competition and won first place. I was nationally qualified and went to larger competitions in Las Vegas to compete for my pro card. I was still depressed, but this was helping me cope with life, albeit poorly. It gave me a goal, a reason to keep going.

Life was moving along. I probably never would have changed if not for a divine intervention. Around the time my family was going through a rough time and after my last competition, I decided to get a doctor's checkup and full physical exam. I hadn't had one in years and figured I should use the insurance I was paying for. And thank God I did.

My doctor noticed a small mole on my chest. I had it my whole life, but it had changed, and she was concerned. After a biopsy, we found out it was skin cancer—melanoma, which is highly aggressive. At first, I wanted to postpone the surgery as I was trying to become a pro physique competitor. The magnitude of it didn't hit me until I asked how long I could wait. They said I had to do it now. If I waited six months, I would lose half my chest. A year or more, and they couldn't predict how far it might go. Had

I waited another year or two to go to the doctor, I don't know if I would be here.

I was in shock. The mole was smaller than my pinky nail. How could this tiny mole be so deadly? There was no time to wait. Luckily, they caught it early. A week later, I was in a surgeon's office having it taken out. With cancer, you have to remove more than just the cancerous part to make sure not even one cancerous cell is left behind. They took out roughly larger than a golf ball sized chunk out of my chest. To make sure they removed all the cancer cells, they test the removed mass of tissue. I didn't breathe until test results came back post-surgery—no more cancer cells. I couldn't work out for months, and without the sanctity of my gym for stress relief, I went deeper into depression and felt there was nothing to live for.

All my dreams of success were nowhere to be found. Happiness was something I hadn't felt in years. Hearing people say how "successful" I was supposed to be and how happy I "should" feel only made it worse. I felt like I should be happy but wasn't, and I couldn't figure out why. I felt completely alone and miserable. I felt like I had completely failed at the biggest goal of all . . . enjoying life.

"Death is not the greatest loss in life. The greatest loss is what dies inside us while we live."

—Norman Cousins

Getting cancer was a wake-up call, one I desperately needed. Facing my own mortality made me realize that our time on earth is limited. **Memento Mori** means *remember that one day you will die.* I received my *memento mori* at that doctor's visit, and I didn't want to waste this precious life. I had to change and start living the life I wanted. Facing death often makes us reflect on our lives and look at our successes and our failures. And that's when I realized the real key to success. It's not who has the best strategy. Because no matter who you are, at some point, you are going to fail. I had one of the best strategies, but I still failed at life.

As Mike Tyson said, "Everyone has a plan, until they get punched in the face." It's as true in boxing as it is in life. On your path to success, when your GPS hits an obstacle, what do you do? Do you turn around and go home? Do you give up? Or do you STEP UP?

It was after cancer that I discovered the real key to success, Emotional Fitness. Emotional Fitness gives you the ability to handle failure and reroute your GPS to success.

You see, people may have all of the above —defined goals, a clear why, great strategies, hard work—and still they are not guaranteed success. Many people still fail. Maybe they experience success for a time and then life kicks them back down. Or they have success in one area of life, like business, but might have a drinking problem, weight problem, or poor relationships. Maybe they have great relationships but are horrible with money.

What was the ultimate secret and strategy for success? What would guarantee success in every area of life? During my time of profound failure, I realized the key to success is not based on how you handle success, but on how you handle failure.

"Get knocked down seven times, get up eight."

—Chinese proverb

What about getting knocked down a hundred times, a thousand times, even ten thousand times? How many times can you get knocked down and still get back up?

How many obstacles on your GPS route to success can you hit before you give up? Are you able to keep pushing forward with the same enthusiasm, focus, confidence, energy, and courage as before? Most people stop after one to three failed attempts. How do you handle complete failure in life? The answer lies in how you handle the emotions of failure. And in that, I found the most important and final key that would guarantee my success: Emotional Fitness.

Why Emotional Fitness?

You see, **we are motivated in life by our emotions**. We want to feel certain emotions and avoid others. We then take actions that will either give us *positive feelings*, such as happiness, pride, importance, love, and success, OR help us avoid *negative feelings*, such as disappointment, anger, sadness, stress, and fear.

Emotions are the fuel that drives us to our goals, and they can also be the very reasons we stop trying. We get a job to *feel* financially secure. We work out to *feel* confident and healthy. We risk rejection talking to that guy or girl to *feel* love. In the end, we want to *feel* happy, successful and fulfilled. But we also want to avoid feelings. We don't want to feel the fear of being hurt, of not being good enough, of failing, and so we stay in our comfort zone.

Emotional Fitness is the ability to control your emotions instead of letting them control you. If you control your emotions, then you control the very fuel that drives you to action. You control how you feel at any moment. You can create a life you've always wanted.

I began to train my mind and emotions. Each and every day I would train my Emotional Fitness and that's when everything changed . . .

How Emotional Fitness Changed My Life

Over the course of six months, I changed everything in my life. I was accomplishing goals at an incredible speed. I doubled my income while working less. I became a motivational speaker and spoke to hundreds, and eventually thousands, of people. I bought my dream beach house, met my girlfriend, and developed some amazing relationships. In six months, I looked in the mirror and felt happy and successful. I started a podcast called Unleash Success. I traveled the world, to Australia, Thailand, Vietnam, Bali, Costa Rica—the list goes on. I had more money, love, freedom, time, enjoyment, fulfillment, and purpose in my life than ever before. I was literally living the life of my dreams and it was all because of Emotional Fitness.

People started asking, "How did you do it?" I didn't call it Emotional Fitness in the beginning. I told them I was training my mind. I started sharing how I was doing it. At first, some people reacted with, "*This is just more of that positivity BS. 'Just think positively and your life will be great.' It doesn't work.*" They were right. Positivity alone isn't enough. People read a positive quote or book or go to a weekend seminar on how to think positive. They might feel better for a day, or a week, or even a month and then go back to their normal selves. Why? Why wasn't just being positive enough?

For as long as I can remember, I've been going to the gym at least four to five times a week. If you give up lifting weights and working out for a few weeks or a month, you'll notice right away how weak you have become. In order to stay strong physically, you have to keep a consistent routine. You can't work out for eight hours one day and expect to be fit for six months. I realized it was the same for our minds and Emotional Fitness. You can't just do a program for a weekend or a week and expect to remain emotionally strong six months down the road. You need a daily program. I began to formulate in my mind a step-by-step system for training my mind and emotions to keep them strong. Thus, Emotional Fitness was born.

Whey We Need Emotional Fitness Now More than Ever

We've all read about the number of suicides by famous people over the past few years, from actor Robin Williams, to celebrity chef Anthony Bourdain, to fashion icon Kate Spade, to Tim Bergling, the world famous DJ known as Avicii—the list goes on. The World Health Organization (WHO) puts the number of deaths by suicide at one million per year globally, which translates to one suicide every forty seconds. In the US, there are more than 45,000 suicides per year, which is more than double the number of homicides (~19,250). This number is up 30 percent since 1999, and it's the second leading cause of death among 10–34 year olds. Men are 3.5 times as likely to die by suicide than women. And in 2017, there were an estimated 1.3 million suicide attempts. How are this many people in so much pain mentally that they choose to end their own lives?

[5]If you or anyone you know is suffering from a serious mental illness, contact the toll-free National Suicide Prevention Lifeline at 1–800–273–TALK (8255), or text the Crisis Text Line (text HOME to 741741).

Mental health issues are at an all-time high in the US, as well. In 2016, nearly one in five US adults—or 44.7 million people—lives with a mental illness.[5] And that's only for the people who come forward. These numbers are staggering. According to the Centers for Disease Control and Prevention (CDC), many factors contribute to suicide, including relationship problems, financial issues, substance abuse, and a recent major life crisis. Many of these mental health illnesses arise from our inability to control our emotional state. When the demands on a person exceed their resources and coping abilities, their mental health can be affected.

In this book, I want to help you gain back control of your emotional state so that you can handle any adversity without it negatively affecting your mental health. Two quick examples show how simple physiological changes create biochemical reactions that positively affect our mental health. Psychological scientists Tara Kraft and Sarah Pressman of the University of Kansas found in a recent study that smiling during brief stressors can help to reduce the intensity of the body's stress response, regardless of whether a person actually feels happy.[2] Another study from James Blumenthal, a Duke psychologist, showed that regular aerobic exercise had a similar effect as the antidepressant sertraline (trade name Zoloft) to treat major depressive disorder. Science is finally catching on to the ability we have to control our emotional state and mental health. All I ask is you keep an open mind as I show you how you can actually change the biochemical processes in your brain.

The inability to control our emotions can manifest itself in other ways, such as violence. We're all well aware of the dramatic increase in mass shootings in the US. From Orlando to Las Vegas, the numbers are horrifying. In fact, there's been a 20 percent increase in homicides over the past two years.[3, 4] Why is there such an increase in violence?

We're living in a challenging time of great change. While technological advances make life easier, we now face one of the most difficult challenges ever as a species. When we are not spending every waking moment trying to survive, we are left with our thoughts and emotions. The vast interconnectedness of social media and the internet often leaves us feeling like we are missing something and lonelier than before. Our inability to understand and control our emotions has led to an epidemic where mental health issues, suicide, and violence are on the rise.

I share these staggering statistics to show how important the need to manage our emotions has become. We need guidance on how to stay consistently in our best emotional health. But surviving life and succeeding in life are two different things. Emotional Fitness doesn't just help those who are suffering to get better; it also helps those who want more out of life to achieve their goals. It gives you the ability to reroute yourself to achieve even more success in life faster than ever before. Emotional Fitness gives you the tools to create your dream life.

Why is Emotional Fitness different from other programs?

Unlike other self-help books that suggest positivity as the answer, (*"Just think positively and everything else will fall into place"*), this book is about training your mind and taking daily actions that lead to specific goals in the real world. Emotional Fitness trains your mind to help get you measurable results in the real world. And it doesn't matter where you start, because Emotional Fitness is about training and growing. Just like physical fitness, you can be the skinniest or fattest person, and you can grow into a body-builder over time. With Emotional Fitness, even if you are starting at zero, you can still master it. There is NO limit to your ability. Some say our Emotional Intelligence, like our IQ, is fixed based on our genetics. Emotional Fitness has no limits. It only requires training.

As human beings, we are the most dominant species on Earth because our greatest evolutionary skill is the ability to *adapt* to any circumstance and survive. Just as we can adapt and transform our bodies, we have the same power to adapt and transform our minds and emotions. But permanent transformation requires daily practice. You have to train every day. At first, it's intensive, and then it becomes part of your daily thought process. By using Emotional Fitness, I've trained my mind and rewired my brain to think differently. At first it was tough, but now it's easy and automatic. As a result of training my own Emotional Fitness, I've achieved exponential results in my relationships, my goals, in wealth building, and every other area of my life.

I've structured this book in a very deliberate fashion. Most people go through life letting others impress bad habits upon them, such as negative thinking, disempowering beliefs, and poor values. Letting others dictate how you live your life is a sure way to fuck up your life. Instead, I will guide you step-by-step through consistently more intensive exercises.

In Part I, I will show you the world through a different lens, one with Emotional Fitness in mind. This first part of the book is to help build your awareness of Emotional Fitness and yourself. In Part II, we dive deep into how exactly Emotional Fitness empowers you to achieve your goals so you can go further, faster. Finally, in Part III, we climb the Emotional Fitness Pyramid of Mastery, where I will help you rewire your brain, build habits, and train your emotions with specific exercises to help you create the person you want to be, so you can live your dream life in every way.

In this book, your beliefs about life and who you are might be challenged. Your initial reaction may be, "This doesn't work," or, "This is just too difficult." All I ask—whatever you believe about change, mindset, and emotions—is to please try and come in with an open mind. After you are done reading, you can go back to what you believe or not. This is going to challenge the norms of society and challenge the status quo about what's possible.

We live in a world undergoing great change. The things many of us face in our lives are more intense than they've ever been before. Whether you simply want to have joy and a fulfilling life for yourself and your loved ones, or you want to be the next Elon Musk and become a multi-billionaire changing the way we live in this world, you need Emotional Fitness.

Welcome to the journey!

Part I

Awareness

Awareness is the greatest agent for change.

—Eckhart Tolle

Chapter 1

Understanding Emotions

Anyone can be angry—that is easy. But to be angry with the right person, to the right degree, at the right time, for the right purpose, and in the right way—that is not easy.

—Aristotle

What Are Your Emotions?

Every day, we experience all different kinds of emotions—happiness, contentment, surprise, anger, hope, disappointment, joy, hopelessness. There are over 3,000 words to describe emotions in the English language. **Emotions motivate us and are the fuel for every action we take.** Emotions are the juice of life. We pursue a goal out of the desire to either feel certain emotions, like happiness, or avoid certain ones, like worry. Emotions are the reason we accomplish our goals, but they also can be the very things that stop us. Often, we're controlled by these emotions without even being aware that they are playing us. We react to these emotions and try to deal with them. How many times in the last month have you felt angry, upset, sad, worried, afraid, frustrated, or even just stressed? Stress and worry have become so common that people experience these emotions daily. In turn, emotions like stress can cause headaches, high blood pressure, more worry, overeating, as well as indulgence in stress-relieving substances, like drugs and alcohol (and even comfort food). All of these negative emotions arise inside our minds. From that same place in our minds, however, also arise positive, empowering feelings, such as happiness, purpose, fulfillment, love, confidence, courage, and hope.

Each emotion has a distinct purpose and gives us the readiness to act. Throughout the evolution of our brains, emotions were imprinted onto our nervous system to keep us alive. Just like breathing, emotions are at times unconscious. You don't have to think about them; they just happen. This is because each emotion at its core creates a physiological response that directs us towards survival. This was the purpose of emotions—to keep us alive!

Emotions helped us survive in pre-modern eras when sabretooth tigers, other wild animals, and death lurked around every corner. However, our minds have not evolved as fast as civilization. While we no longer experience daily near-death experiences, our emotional responses have yet to catch up. Thus, when we experience certain emotions, they still run the same programming to our brain to help us survive. Unfortunately, this programming that is meant to keep us alive is not wired to help achieve success, love, and happiness. What once helped us now can cause us extreme emotional pain.

For example, stress was meant to trigger a flight or fight response to survive. Fear would trigger you to assess a situation and flee death; anger would help you survive an attack. But now people are stressed when their coffee is cold, upset they wake up late, angry that there is traffic, afraid they missed their favorite TV show, etc. What once helped us survive has now caused problems of violence, depression, and debilitating anxiety in modern society. More importantly, surviving and succeeding in life are two very different things. And our emotional responses were not originally designed to make us successful or fulfilled. But what if we can change these responses? What if we can rewire our brains to respond differently? Let's first understand where emotions come from, then learn how we can change them.

Where do Emotions Come From?

All emotions are impulses to act. Emotion comes from the Latin verb *motere*, meaning "to move." Adding the prefix *e* means to "move away." It's easy to see how emotions move us when we look at children who act on impulse. Kids will say and do anything. According to Paul Ekman of the University of California in his work, *Only in Adults*, we only see this disconnect between emotions felt and the obvious reaction in adults. Paul Ekman is a psychologist whose research dramatically changed the way we think about emotion.

The Discovery of Universal Emotions

In 1967, Ekman was a young researcher and journeyed to Papua New Guinea to study the Fore people. It was one of the most isolated places on Earth. The society had very limited outside influence or exposure to modern Western culture, which made them perfect subjects for Ekman's research. Ekman studied these tribes in an effort to prove that all humans share a universal set of basic emotions.

In 1972, Ekman published his research, along with Wallace Friesen, showing that the isolated Fore tribes used exactly the same set of facial expressions to express emotions as every other Western and non-Western culture that had been studied. Ekman called these expressions the six basic emotions. They were Fear, Anger, Surprise, Disgust, Sadness, and Happiness. These core emotions create the base from which all other emotions arise. While sadness is a basic emotion, depression is an extreme form of sadness. Anxiety is boiled down to the fear of what might happen. From these base emotions, a myriad of other emotions, such as joy, ecstasy, rage, anxiety, stress, and regret can be felt.

Over the years, Ekman pioneered the research in psycho-physiological studies of emotion, especially how emotions express themselves in our bodies. By 1978, he developed the Facial

Action Coding System, or FACS, to identify and label all human facial expressions. In 2009, he was named one of the 100 most influential people by *Time* Magazine. Over fifty years of research and knowledge from Ekman has shaped the very way we view human emotion and its effect on our physiology.[5, 6, 7] From Ekman's Research and other studies, we discovered that the emotions we feel play a unique role biologically with a specific purpose. As science advances, we learn through studying the nervous system that each of the basic emotions prepares the body for a different kind of response.

The Six Core Emotions

1. **FEAR** induces biological support for fight or flight! What comes with that is a greater heart-rate acceleration. When fleeing danger, fear shifts blood flow to be diverted away from the periphery and redirected toward the large skeletal muscles, like the legs, for helping you run away.

2. **ANGER** creates an increase in heart rate, muscle tension, blood flow to the hands, and a rush of hormones, such as adrenaline, which gives increased strength, energy, and decreased sensitivity to pain, making you ready to "fight." A very interesting difference between anger and fear is the increased blood flow to the hand muscles, which provide support when grabbing a weapon or hitting an enemy during a fight.

3. **SURPRISE** raises the eyebrows and opens the eyes wide to allow for increased attention and alertness, which is needed in the event you need to focus on a threat and make a quick decision. When someone surprises you around the corner, your first reaction is to assess whether you are in danger. Your increased attention gathers that

it's either an intruder and you should run for help, or that it's just a friend and all is well in the world.

4. **DISGUST** seems to evolve early with our senses to reject or shut out an unpleasant environmental object. Facially, you will see the upper lip curled to the side as the nose wrinkles slightly (possibly to close the nostrils) in reaction to a noxious odor or poisonous food. In today's world, the feeling of disgust from something someone did can create the same facial expression and is universal.

5. **SADNESS** slows down metabolism and thus creates a drop in energy and excitement for life. This commonly happens around the loss or death of a loved one and may have kept early humans close to home where they were safer. Someone experiencing sadness may withdraw from normal life, which allows them to undergo a deep internal reflection on the meaning of life and the consequences of our actions. As the sadness disappears, we can plan for a better life.

6. **HAPPINESS** is an increased activity in a brain center that inhibits negative and worrisome feelings and fosters an increase in available energy. While other more intense emotions create a concrete physiological shift in temperature, blood flow, or heart rate, happiness only seems to provide a biological buffer that wards off negative emotions. In this state of happiness, you may often experience an overflow of energy and a willingness to strive towards your goals. Being happy makes life better.

In 1986, Ekman's research revealed a seventh universal emotion: contempt.

7. **CONTEMPT** is marked by the corner of the lip pulling back and slightly upwards into a mild sneer. Interestingly, it's also the only asymmetrical universal facial expression. Contempt is a negative judgment of the most severe kind. It is a sense of repulsiveness that is marked by an undeniable air of superiority. It's possible this arose as a warning to others that someone could not be trusted or did not have good intentions toward you.

Contempt seems to have a big significance in the success of our intimate relationships, according to Dr. John Gottman. Gottman evaluated microexpressions in romantic relationships. Microexpressions are brief, involuntary human facial expressions that vary according to emotions experienced. They can occur as fast as 1/25th of a second! They can happen so fast that we may miss them. These microexpressions express Ekman's seven universal emotions: disgust, anger, fear, sadness, happiness, surprise, and contempt. They usually occur in high-stakes situations, where people have something to lose or gain. And unlike regular facial expressions, these emotions can't be faked, as they are involuntary and automatic. In fact, Dr. John Gottman studied thousands of couples in his research lab, nicknamed the "love lab," and now scientists can predict with 94 percent accuracy whether a couple will eventually get divorced. How?

According to Gottman, a partner showing contempt is by far the number-one predictor of divorce. When interviewed for Malcolm Gladwell's bestseller *Blink*, Gottman said, "You would think that criticism would be the worst . . . But if I speak from a superior plane, that's far more damaging, and contempt is any statement made from a higher level."[8, 9, 10]

Why Emotional Responses Differ

Universal emotions have been ingrained into our nervous system through tens of thousands of years of evolution. While initially designed to protect us and help us survive, in the modern age, these emotions express themselves in various ways. In fact, **our perception of how or why we feel these emotions are further shaped by our life experiences, culture, and beliefs.** For example, losing a loved one creates sadness and grief nearly worldwide, regardless of culture. However, how we show our grief, whether specific emotions are displayed or held back, is largely dictated by our culture and beliefs.

The same environmental and evolutionary pressures that once molded our emotional responses have disappeared with the rise of modern civilization. Anger may have been life-saving in the distant past, but now anger coupled with the ease of access to guns has led to a staggering epidemic in the United States, which has seen a horrific rise in the number of mass shootings.

In 2016, the mass shooting at an Orlando nightclub left forty-nine dead and fifty-three wounded. In 2017, the horrifying and deadly mass shooting in Las Vegas on innocent concertgoers left fifty-eight dead and eight hundred fifty-one wounded. This one was particularly hard for me, as some of my friends were at that music festival. No one I know personally died, but some friends of mine suffered losses. The scariest thing for me was that the shooter had looked at another location a week before: The Life is Beautiful Music & Art Festival. Due to a nearby sold-out hotel, he couldn't get "the right vantage point" he wanted. The news of this sent chills down my spine. My youngest sister was at that festival, at the front of the main stage, having the time of her life at twenty-one years old. I could never imagine suffering such a terrible loss, and my heart goes out to those who have suffered.

This is why Emotional Fitness needs to be taught at a young age. And while there are many theories on why people commit these horrific acts, I believe that their inability to handle their negative emotions builds up over time and they commit an unspeakable, horrifying crime. Instead of anger boiling up into a mass shooting, it should be handled without violence. Emotional Fitness bridges the gap between evolutionary pressures that once gave rise to our emotions and how we deal with our emotions in modern society.

Two Minds, One Body

Many scientists argue we have two separate minds: an emotional mind and a rational mind. These two minds combine to construct our thoughts, meaning, and actions. While the rational mind reflects, thinks, and ponders, the emotional mind is impulsive, reactive, and powerfully overriding. The emotional mind is far quicker to act than the rational mind—again an evolutionary advantage for survival. With Emotional Fitness, we train our minds and emotions to act in line with our rational mind's desires instead of against.

The advantage of the emotional mind, according to Goleman, is that the emotional mind can read an emotional reality quickly and tell us who to be wary of, who to trust, and who's in distress. "The emotional mind is our radar for danger," Goleman explains. "If we (or our forebears in evolution) waited for the rational mind to make some of these judgments, we might not only be wrong— we might be dead." Goleman goes on to explain the drawbacks to the emotional mind. "These impressions and intuitive judgments, because they are made in the snap of a finger, may be mistaken or misguided."[11]

Why are we, as human beings, always looking for what could go wrong in a situation? It's because during the development of humans, those who could identify what was "wrong" in a situation—such as escaping a predator or avoiding poisonous fruit— were more likely to survive. Early humans didn't have sharp teeth or venom. They had to rely on their ability to identify what was wrong to survive. However, in today's modern world, always pointing out what's wrong with your life, focusing on the negative, and finding ways to put yourself down can lead to a depressing, pessimistic, and miserable life. As you'll see, always focusing on what's wrong can prevent us from seeing a solution right in front of our eyes. But shouldn't our large, rational minds overpower these emotions and show us the right way? Unfortunately, our rational minds do not always do this. For some people, their rational mind rarely controls their emotions. Why? The answer is that our brains developed in a series of stages, with the deeper levels being more unconscious and primal to help us survive. While the brain is vastly complex, we will simplify the origin of structures and function into three main areas.

The Formation of the Brain Was an Emotional One

First, there was the brainstem, the most primitive part of the brain that controls autonomic functions like breathing, heartbeat, blood flow, and digestion. It does not have to think or learn. You don't have to tell your heart to beat—it just does. The brainstem runs a set of programs automatically for survival.

Second, from this primal brainstem evolved the limbic system. The limbic system is the emotional control center for the brain and is largely responsible for motivation. You will soon learn the unique tie between motivation and emotion in Chapter 5. Here, in the limbic system, two incredible tools formed: learning and memory. With this, emotional imprints began to form. To this day, the limbic system is the main driver of our emotions.

Finally, the third and final layer, the neocortex, evolved, a layer of the brain that is significantly larger in humans than any other species. The neocortex controls conscious thought, comprehension of complex problems, and adds feelings to thoughts. This no doubt made human beings much better at adapting to adversity—our greatest evolutionary advantage—which led us to become the apex predator on Earth. The neocortex allows for strategy and long-term planning. But the neocortex also allows for the subtlety and complexity of emotional life. It gives us the ability to have feelings *about our feelings*. And therein lies the problem with humans.

Our ability to think and ponder, combined with our emotions means we can spiral out of control. This is our greatest strength, but also our Achilles Heel. This is why Emotional Fitness is so necessary. It trains you to control your emotions, instead of thinking about how they control you.

The brain's higher centers evolved around the limbic area. Because of this, emotions are fundamentally intertwined with all parts of the neocortex. Emotional centers have incredible power over the functioning of the brain, including centers for thought.[12] We often possess the intelligence to make a good decision, but our emotions override our rational brain. Indeed, we often hear, *"I don't know what I was thinking. I just panicked . . . I just saw red . . . I just reacted."* These are our emotions at work.

Emotional Hijacking

When we hear people talk about their emotions "getting the best of them" and allowing their emotional mind to control their rational mind, it comes down to a very important structure in the limbic system: the amygdala. This is our last stop on the science of emotion formation before we dive into how to shift our emotional experience. In humans, the amygdala (from the Greek word for *almond*) is an almond-shaped cluster of interconnected structures perched above the brainstem, near the bottom of the limbic ring. The amygdala is the major controller of emotional matters. In fact, in a case study of a young man whose amygdala was surgically removed to control seizures, he lost all recognition of emotion in life and was content to sit alone, not even recognizing family and friends. Without the amygdala, we have no emotional memory and thus no meaning in life.

Joseph LeDoux, a neuroscientist at the Center for Neural Science at New York University, was the first to discover the key role of the amygdala in the emotional brain. While the "thinking brain," the neocortex, is coming to a decision, the amygdala can take control.

The amygdala acts like an alarm system for your brain. It can quickly take over your brain and move you to act faster than the neocortex can think. This is vitally important in a moment of survival. Fear of death signals the amygdala to override all logic because if you spend too much time thinking, you could die. The amygdala yells, "Run for your life!" This survival mechanism can't wait for you to decide and so the amygdala can *hijack the brain* and override your rational mind. It seems any moment where we feel fear, even if it is fear of rejection, our amygdala could hijack our brain and respond illogically with emotion. What if you could rewire your brain to respond differently? We will learn how to control this and reshape our emotional responses using Emotional Fitness in future chapters.

What is probably the toughest realization for people is that emotional memories, and thus involuntary emotional responses, can be made without conscious knowledge. According to LeDoux, the emotional part of the brain can act completely separate and independent from the rational part of the brain. Some emotional reactions and emotional memories can even form without you being consciously aware of it. Not sure why you're afraid of heights, spiders, or small spaces? Not sure why you feel anxiety, stress, or worry when you can't "think" of any reason? It could be you have an emotional memory from an unconscious emotional connection you made, and that emotional response program is running without your conscious awareness. Therefore, if you do not consciously choose to train your Emotional Fitness, the world around you will unconsciously train you, for better or worse.

Why Most Fail to Master Emotional Fitness

Success in school, relationships, business, and health are largely affected by our Emotional Fitness. While the idea that we have the ability to control our emotions and training in these areas is relatively new, there have been many attempts to train emotions, including through seminars and school programs. The problem is that most training programs target the neocortex of the brain, which is more analytical and technical, like reading a book! Most people attempt to train Emotional Fitness by *thinking* about it. However, emotions arise largely in the limbic system, which controls feelings, impulses, and drives. This system learns best through practice and feedback, which will not work as well *unless you engage your body.* This is why you have to actually do the exercises in this book and why I ask you to do them out loud, so that you engage your body, mind, voice, and, yes, the limbic system!

Emotional Fitness Is Much More Than Just Emotional Intelligence

First appearing in a 1964 paper by Michael Beldoch, Emotional Intelligence (EI) was a phrase popularized by author and psychologist Daniel Goleman in a 1995 book "Emotional Intelligence." EI is the ability to recognize one's own <u>emotions</u> and those of others, discern between feelings and label them, and use this information to guide thinking and behavior. Whatever the original intention of EI, it has become a way to focus solely on how emotionally smart a person is, without focusing on results. Many people have powerful emotional intelligence but are not necessarily successful.

People may claim they are self-aware and emotionally intelligent. They talk about their mindfulness, their ability to deeply feel their emotions and connect with themselves. They may even have an *ego* about their self-awareness, as if this ability to dive deep into themselves makes them superior and yet they still struggle to achieve their goals. As you will see, self-awareness is only the first part of Emotional Fitness. Emotional Fitness puts that self-awareness into action to empower you to achieve your goals.

The word *intelligence* comes with certain assumptions: that how smart you are is something you are born with, and that there is a limit to your capability. Unfortunately, these assumptions often transfer over to Emotional Intelligence. As such, some people may know they are an angry person, for example, but feel they cannot change that. It's a given. That's how they were born. There is a place for Emotional Intelligence and studies have shown that it greatly improves life and success. With Emotional Fitness, I've expanded EI from something you simply *learn* to something you actually *do*.

The Benefits of Emotional Intelligence

Studies show that Emotional Intelligence can make a huge difference. As you read through the positive benefits of EI, don't get discouraged if you are not as emotionally intelligent as you want to be. Emotional Fitness gives you the training program so no matter where you start, you can accomplish any level of success.

EI advocate Daniel Goleman analyzed 188 companies, including British Airways and Credit Suisse, and found that 90 percent of the difference between the best leaders versus average ones in senior positions was their Emotional Intelligence as opposed to their IQ. In fact, a 1996 study of senior managers at McClelland, a global food and beverage company, found that those with strong Emotional Intelligence outperformed their yearly earnings goals by 20 percent. Can awareness and emotions really improve your career path and the amount of money you make?

Another study done in 1986 by Martin Seligman and Peter Schulman of the University of Pennsylvania demonstrated that insurance agents who had a "glass half-full" outlook closed more sales than their more pessimistic peers. This was due to their ability to persist despite rejections, a very emotionally fit response.

What about teaching Emotional Fitness to children? A case can be made from a scientific standpoint that helping children improve their self-awareness and confidence, manage their disturbing emotions and impulses, and increasing their empathy pays off not just in improved behavior but in measurable academic achievement. A meta-analysis by Roger Weissberg at the University of Illinois at Chicago looked at 668 evaluation studies of Social and Emotional Learning (SEL) programs for children from preschoolers through high school. In participating schools, up to 50 percent of children showed improved achievement scores, and up to 38 percent improved their grade-point averages. SEL programs also made schools safer: incidents of misbehavior dropped by an average of 28 percent, suspensions by 44 percent, and other disciplinary actions by 27 percent. At the same time, attendance rates rose, while 63 percent of students demonstrated significantly more positive behavior."

The Key Difference between Emotional Intelligence and Emotional Fitness

At the very highest levels, competence models for leadership typically consist of anywhere from 80 to 100 percent of EI-based abilities. As the head of research at a global executive search firm put it, "CEOs are hired for their intellect and business expertise—and fired for a lack of emotional intelligence."[13]

Goleman writes, "Of course an employee who combines self-awareness with internal motivation will recognize her limits but won't settle for objectives that are too easy." This illustrates a key difference between Emotional Intelligence and Emotional Fitness. EI has limits; Emotional Fitness does not. Emotional Fitness does not train you to limit yourself; it trains you to break through limitations. If you feel like your limit is eight hours of work a day, you will never work longer or you'll just crash after, as many people often do. However, entrepreneurs work twelve- to eighteen-hour days, six to seven days a week for years. How? Don't they have a limit? What about how long you can study? American students study for a few hours a night, while Chinese students study for significantly longer because it is part of their culture and they believe that it is necessary for success in life. **Emotional Fitness is about using your emotions to take action to help you get results and accomplish your goals faster.** It is not about limits; it is about training. It's about living your best life mentally, physically, and financially.

IQ is often the measure of success defining what college we go to and what job we get. EI is the knowledge of our emotions, and those who have that knowledge tend to perform better. But knowing is not enough. Knowledge is not power. Action is Power. Emotional Fitness is the key that empowers you to act. Emotional Fitness does not put limits on you. No matter where you are in life, whether you have lost your job, your family, and everything else, and you have no idea where to go, Emotional Fitness can help. Whether you are a stay-at-home mom or dad, a college graduate, or a successful businessperson, Emotional Fitness is for you. With Emotional Fitness, no matter where you start, no matter how weak or strong your current ability, through training you can break through any limit and master it. Just like physical fitness, the more you practice Emotional Fitness, the stronger you get. The exercises in this book are like exercises in the gym and with each rep, you get stronger. Emotions are not just something we are born with, they are something we can learn about and train. Emotional Fitness will give you the edge you need to live the life of your dreams.

Not Just More Positive Thinking Bullshit

This book is more than positive thinking. We've all heard people say, "Just think positive!" We're told to repeat to ourselves, "I'm happy. I'm successful. I'm beautiful. I'm handsome," even when we don't feel that way. We look into the mirror for ten minutes with clenched teeth and an angry "smile" saying, "I'm happy. I'm happy. I'm happy," until we explode, because in the back of our minds we're thinking, *This is so stupid; it will never work!*

These affirmations are supposedly the secret to success. People love to say, "All you have to do is think positively and manifest what you want!" We've all known people who practice this daily and who still do not find real success. Why? Because positive thoughts alone do not automatically translate into results in the world. Does having a positive attitude help? Absolutely. But positive thoughts without real world action leave many of us without the results we want. I've heard people say, "Wish for success in one hand and shit in the other and see what comes first." We need to have the right attitude, but wishing without action won't get us anywhere. **Taking real action is the only way to get real results.**

How do you respond when you lose a client, a job, or even a loved one? Positive thinking alone won't get that back for you. There is real pain out there in the world, and I want to address that, not whitewash it. You may feel upset, angry, disappointed, regretful, sad, or even depressed. Painful things do happen in life, but letting the pain stop you from achieving your goals and dreams is a choice.

Whatever has happened to you, you've already proven you have the strength to survive it, because you are here reading this book right now. Whatever you want to change in your life, you can change. You can rewire your brain to think differently. Through Emotional Fitness and taking action toward your goals, you can have the life you've always wanted, and you can love your life. I won't just tell you, but through this book, I'll show you. I know because I have done it.

We *all* have the power to be aware of our emotions, but we may define them differently and thus take different actions in the world. We all experience the day-to-day small nuisances —we wake up late, our coffee is cold, our dog pees on the carpet— as well as the big life-changing events. Many of us also deal with serious illness, heartbreaks, losing a loved one, bankruptcy, natural disasters, and much more. How do we deal with both minor day-to-day grievances, as well as these larger life-changing events?

That is what Emotional Fitness is all about. Now let's take a look at how these emotions shift our reality and our very experience of life.

Chapter 2

The Power of Story

Stories are the best invention ever created for delivering mental models that drive behavior.

—Daniel Coyle, *The Talent Code*

Now that we understand what emotions are and why we have them, it is important to understand how emotions affect our lives. Emotions are the way in which we experience life, and they help us create our narrative about life or our *story.*

In life, there are the **facts** about what happens and there is our **story** about these facts. For example, it might be a fact that it is eighty-five degrees and sunny outside. The story about this fact is how that makes you feel. Some people might say, "The weather is too hot outside; it makes me uncomfortable." Others might say, "This is perfect beach weather; I love it!"

Another fact might be that you did not receive a promotion. To some the story becomes, "I've worked so hard and my company doesn't appreciate me enough to give me a promotion." Or at least that's what you feel. It might be that they can't afford to give you a promotion even though they do appreciate you. Others might think, "I did not get the promotion, so I will just have to work harder to prove that I am worthy of more."

There are **facts**: what happened without emotions tied to them. And there is your **story**: your interpretation of the facts,

18

why something happened, and how it makes you feel. Our stories become the narratives we tell ourselves that help us relate to the outside world. We constantly tell ourselves stories about who we are to help us understand our relationship with the world and how we interact with it. It is important to note that most people will never even hear or understand this concept. They believe their stories *are* the facts. This is very normal and common. If your story empowers you, use it. If it doesn't help you, lose it. The story you write for yourself creates your reality. If you aren't where you want to be, you have the ability to *rewrite* your story.

Same Facts, Different Stories

I remember reading a story about how two brothers were raised by a single father in a tough neighborhood with little to no money. Their father, who had a criminal record, ended up getting busted for armed robbery and was sentenced to seven years in prison. The brothers were put in the system and unfortunately separated. Years later, they were interviewed. One brother grew up following in his dad's footsteps by committing petty theft and selling drugs. He ended up in jail for armed robbery. When asked why he thought his life turned out like this, he responded, "Look at where I'm from. Look at my dad. How else could I have turned out any different?" This brother used the facts of his family and background to back up his story about how the criminal life was all he knew, and he was bound to end up in it.

Unknown to him, his other brother was living happily married with two kids in the suburbs. He had gone to college and now had a respectable job working in finance. When asked why he thought his life turned out like this, he responded, "Look at where I'm from. Look at my dad. How else could I have turned any different?" This brother used the same facts of his family and background as ways to show that he could never follow in his father's footsteps. He talked about how his father showed him exactly what *not to do* and that he did everything he could to avoid ending up like that.

These two brothers had the same early experience but created very different stories around that past. One followed in his father's footsteps to jail, while the other decided to write a new story for himself.

These brothers are not as rare as you might think. There are numerous stories of two brothers, one in jail and the other who became a success. When facing the same circumstances in life, the difference comes down to the story they tell themselves.

The facts of your upbringing do not create your story, but rather the emotions you tie to that story is what creates your story. Your story is your emotional experience. Two soldiers who witness a brother die in combat may take very different meanings from the experience. The fact is the same: they both witness the same person die in combat. The story one soldier creates is that life is meaningless, we are all going to die anyway, and there's no point to all of it. The other soldier sees the same fact, but his story might be that life is precious, that you never know when your time is up, and so we should do everything we can to live life to the fullest and cherish each day. These are the same facts, but the outcome is a different story.

Is Your Story a Lie?

Are you telling a story to yourself? The answer is yes. We are constantly telling ourselves what we are or are not capable of, what we feel, what we believe we can do. We all to tell ourselves a narrative, as it's the way we relate our conscious self and mind to the world. Your story is your narrative and becomes an interpretation of outward experiences and, in truth, the *reality* of your life. The question is, do you even know you are telling yourself a story? And more importantly, is your story true? Or is it a lie?

Let's look at two different people who tell themselves different stories. How many of us know a person who always has the biggest problems in the world? They wake up five minutes late and they are stressed! Maybe they lose a client at work and they say their career is over! Maybe they argue with their significant other and their life is over!

How many of us know someone who is the opposite? Literally nothing is ever that big of a deal for them. They lose a client, no big deal— *"I'll get the next one!"* They argue with their significant other— *"It's OK; it was my fault. I started it, and I know they love me. It's all good."* They *smile* through life's ups and downs. They just beam positivity. How many of us know someone like this?

How is it that these two people live such different lives? The answer is not in their experience, but in how they interpret it. It's in the story they tell themselves. I learned this lesson the hard way. As I said, when I was growing up, I did all the "right" things: earned good grades, played sports, went to college, and became an orthodontist. But after ten years of school, my massive student debt meant I struggled to survive financially, and I felt trapped under the weight of that debt. I used to look at those years of depression with regret, as a black hole of a life lost and a pain that I wanted to forget. I felt that my life was just fucked up, and it would always be like that. With everything I went through with my family and with skin cancer, it felt like everything in life was going against me. I wanted to give up. I hated my career, and I hated my life. There were times where I thought, *Is this all life has to offer? Is it even worth it?*

That was what I told myself. That was my story. But we all have our own stories. My story is no better or worse than yours. The only thing my story did was put me in a place of desperation for change. Now I look back and see the challenges I overcame, my courage to face fears, and the pain I faced to grow stronger and handle the next stages of my life. And I am grateful for the lessons. I'm grateful for what I went through because it brought me to a place when I finally said, "Enough is enough." I had to change my life. Sure, I wish I could have taken the hint sooner! But after eight years, I finally realized that the facts of my life were not going to change. What could change was the story I told myself.

The first step to Emotional Fitness involves awareness, of both your emotions and your story. Your story either empowers you to achieve your goals or limits you from living life. The language you use, your daily self-talk, determines your story. What happens in the external world is one thing, but how you view that experience is based on your story. One story might be that you are the victim and feel helpless and unable to succeed. The empowering version of that story is that you are a survivor who will stop at nothing to make the world a better place.

The writer of this story? You and you alone. Sure, you may let people influence your thoughts, but you are the one who *lets* them. Your stories about life literally become the reality in which you live. If your story is that life is tough, an uphill battle, and messed up, you will probably find adversity and challenges every single day. For some people, life is a game. Games are fun, and they just want to enjoy the game of life. For others, life may be a game as well, but to them, games are not about fun, they are about winning. And they stop at nothing to win the game of life. Your perspective on life dictates the story of your life, which becomes your reality.

So, what is your story? What is the story you tell yourself?

- "I wasn't a smart kid and that's why I'm not successful."
- "I don't have time for the gym."
- "I was abused as a child, so I am too weak or damaged or in too much pain to create the life I want."
- "I nearly died of cancer and now I'm terrified to take risks in case it affects my health."
- "I was fired from my job, so I will never be successful."
- "I was rejected so many times that now I don't even try because I know that I'll be rejected."

- "My dad said I was a loser and I will always be a loser."
- "I failed when I tried and realized I'm not good enough."

All of these are stories. Sure, the facts of what happened are true. Maybe you didn't get straight A's; maybe you were abused, had cancer, lost your job or your family, and failed when you tried. But let's look at how you end each sentence, the "and that's why I'll never have what I want in life or be successful" part of your thought process. These are merely the meanings you give to your experiences, the story you tell yourself. You must be very careful with the story you tell yourself.

"If you tell a big enough lie, long enough, and loud enough, eventually they will believe it." This quote is from Adolf Hitler. He used this philosophy to do terrible things. He murdered millions of innocent people. I do not use this quote lightly. Its purpose is to understand a simple but important fact. Every day, we tell ourselves a story. Most of the time, we do not even realize we are telling a story.

In fact, the story has become so woven into our reality and our lives that it ceases to exist. It is like a fish in water. A fish is born in water, surrounded by water, and the water is so ubiquitous and so ever-present that, to the fish, the water ceases to exist. We have been raised to tell ourselves a story about what we can or cannot think, say, and do. Over time, our environment shapes our inner story. This inner voice telling our story is usually loud and it repeats that story day in and day out, so we truly believe it. The biggest issues occur when our stories disempower us. Stories like, "I'm not good enough," "I'm big-boned," or "I'll never be loved." If your story is disempowering, why do you hold on to it? Remember, stories are our interpretation of the facts. Change your story and you change your life.

You may question this, and you should. But question your story, as well. This is the first layer of the onion. Questioning your story is the beginning of setting yourself free. The story we tell ourselves is sometimes so unconscious, so hidden, that it usually only shows itself by its lack of results. We want more out of life. We ask ourselves, *How did I end up here? Why didn't I achieve my goals?* Awareness is the first step to becoming Emotionally Fit. You can't change what you don't know you don't know.

Some of you may be asking, isn't my story true? The answer is *yes*. Your stories are completely true. A better question is, "Does your story help you? Does your story empower you? Does your story help you live the life of your dreams?"

You may have a story about how your lack of education stops you from getting a good job, your lack of money stops you from making money, your parents mistreated you and that's why you can't find true love, or you're big-boned and that's why you can't lose weight. Is your story right or wrong? The answer often jolts people because they are so attached to their stories. There is no right or wrong, *only what you believe.* And if your story doesn't empower you to live a happier, healthier, and wealthier life, then why hold on to it? Why not shift your perspective? You have the power to choose.

What stories do you tell yourself? What stories do you use to define yourself? The only way to change your narrative is to begin by being aware. You are the writer of your own story, the director of your own movie. If you don't like the story, rewrite it, or change the channel and watch a different movie.

What is your story? Who are you and why? What do you tell yourself that empowers you, and what do you tell yourself that might limit you? (*To download the free Emotional Fitness workbook for all exercises in this book visit* www.MasterEmotionalFitness. com/step1.)

Write down your story.

_____

_____

_____

_____

_____

_____

_____

_____

_____

_____

_____

_____

_____

_____

_____

_____

Chapter 3

The Emotional Experience

When you change the way you look at things,
the things change the way they look.

—Wayne Dyer

My maternal grandfather passed when I was in high school. It was tough for our family, but we knew it was coming. He was obese—nearly four hundred pounds at one point—and needed open-heart surgery and a pacemaker. For the last ten years I knew him, he was wheelchair-bound. All of her life, my grandmother always found a way to enjoy life. When we lost my grandfather, she didn't sit around moping for long. Within a month, she was going out dancing five nights a week. She was in her sixties and had more of a social life than I did in my teens! At that age, I didn't understand and was upset that she didn't seem to care. I felt like she didn't mourn my grandfather.

Now I admire her courage—yes, *courage*. She lives her life to the fullest despite losing her husband of forty years and never lets anything get her down. Even in her seventies, she still goes out dancing, plays pickleball (a form of tennis played with paddles and a plastic ball) and travels back and forth from Florida to California with her new husband, an amazing man. His name is Wayman: *way man*. Such a perfect name for the man to make my grandmother happy. Wayman, too, finds a way to have a good time and never lets anything get him down.

When I asked Wayman why he's always so happy and loves life, he replied, "I woke up above ground today. There's so much to love in life, and there ain't no point in worrying about things you can't do nothin' about."

Is "real" life hard sometimes? Sure. We experience pain in the form of failure and rejection, as well through the loss of money, time, and love. We lose friends and family throughout the years. I've dealt with pain and lost friends and family members to alcoholism, obesity, diabetes, heart disease, cancer, stroke, and even suicide. Life isn't always happy thoughts and happy experiences. Sometimes, there is real pain in this world.

Pain is a part of life, but suffering from these painful experiences is a choice. Pain happens in a moment, but we can feel the negative disempowering emotions for hours, days, or even years after the event. These lingering emotions are a choice. This is where Emotional Fitness can change your life. It empowers you to make a conscious choice. It gives you the option to keep suffering, or to let it go and become the person you have always dreamed of. It all starts with understanding there are certain things we can change and certain things that we cannot change. Knowing the difference can change your life.

The Emotional Experience

To master Emotional Fitness, we must first understand the emotional experience. When examining the emotional experience, we see there are two main areas: the external world and the internal world. These represent two different aspects of our experience. In order to master Emotional Fitness, we must first understand what part of the experience we can actually *control*. It is only there that we can create change, make a difference, and shift our experience of life.

The **external world** is everything we experience outside of us and our control. External experiences include events, the environment, and other people. Events are things like a promotion, getting fired, traffic accidents, elections, and terrorist attacks. Environment includes things that happen in our surroundings, like the weather (if it's sunny or rainy) or the arrangement of tables at a restaurant. And the biggest thing that we truly do not have control over is other people. We may think we have control over things or people. But in truth, that control is merely influence. You may be able to *influence* the external world. You might manage people and tell them they will get fired if they don't do what you say. It may even feel like control. But ultimately you do not have *direct control* over them. They could choose to come into work or not and you would not be able to force them one way or the other.

When my grandfather passed, I had no control over his health. I had no control over my grandmother's reaction. I could only control myself. Once we understand that we do not have control over the external world, life actually gets so much easier. Stress, worry, and fear start to disappear. If you don't have control, you can't change something. And if you can't change something, why are you worried about it?

Most people *use* external experiences as a way to **blame** why they don't have what they want in this world. It's easy to shift the blame to things outside of your control. After all, if you can't control it, it's not your fault it happened. But doing this does not empower you. If anything, it limits your ability to take action to improve your life. The key to wisdom here is to understand what is and what is not in your control. Take full ownership and responsibility for your life and actions, but do not worry about things outside your control.

Another area that falls into the external world once it happens is past experiences. In the moment, you have control, but once an experience is over, once it's in the past, you no longer have control over what happened. What's done is done. People often blame their current situations or reactions because of what happened to them in the past. It's an easy way out, and it's easier to blame the past because no matter what they or anyone else does, no one can change the past. They become a victim to their past and feel powerless to change their present. Later in this book, we will go over *why* people let their pasts limit them. For now, we move on to the only place we can control, take action, and see results. Because the external world is outside of your control, to train your Emotional Fitness and improve your life, you must focus on the internal world.

The **internal world** is the only place we have control in our lives. Therefore, it is here where we train our Emotional Fitness. Trying to control the external world leads to failure, worry, fear, and frustration. It leads to disappointment, and anger, and wondering why you can't make it better. It's because we have no control over it. Instead we can learn how to control ourselves. By controlling our emotions and our actions, we begin to mold our internal world to reflect what we want to see in life, and, through consistent action, that begins to shape our external world. We can learn how to be Emotionally Fit. Then, no matter what happens in the external world, we not only survive it, we thrive in it.

How We Process Experiences

The **internal experience** is directed by how our minds process information. After any external event, the first thing that happens is our minds focus on some aspect of the experience. Then we put that experience through another filter to give the experience a meaning to us. This finally causes us to react to what happened or act upon our experience, which ultimately produces our behavior in the external world. See the diagram below.

External World vs. Internal World

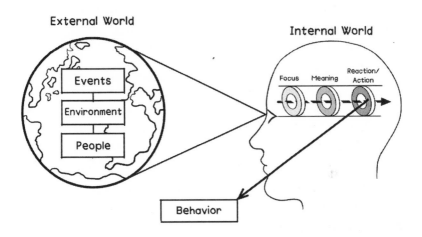

Let me give you a simple example. When I was younger, I could never remember peoples' names. At first, I thought I had a bad memory, but that was complete BS. I was often praised for remembering numerous random facts and memorizing sheets of information for tests after only a few hours. I realize now that I was so focused on how the person presented themselves, trying to see what they were all about and measuring them up, that their name fell on deaf ears. Because I wasn't focused on their name, I could literally *never* remember it. It's as if I never heard it in the first place.

Now when I first meet someone, I say their name back to them, once more in my head, and say it out loud to them again when I say goodbye. I make sure to focus on their name more than anything else. Saying their name three times forces me to consciously think about it and helps me remember names significantly more! This is the first filter of the internal experience and, as you can see, it is directed by our focus.

The Focus System

Have you ever purchased a new car, new outfit, new anything and before the purchase you had never seen that item anywhere before? Then, after the purchase, all of a sudden you see that car or outfit *everywhere*? Is it that suddenly everyone bought the item at the same time as you? Nope.

In your mind, you became focused on the item. For you, it was something that was now *important to focus on*, and so you started noticing it more. The item was always there, but until you thought it was important, you didn't notice it. This is a phenomenon in the brain structure called the Reticular Activating System (RAS). RAS controls how we focus and process information from the outside world. It controls where we direct our attention. Once you buy something, it becomes important to you, so your brain starts to focus on it, allowing you to "suddenly" see it everywhere.

Every day we are overloaded with stimuli, and there is no way to sift through everything, so the brain deletes some from our conscious mind and focuses only on certain areas that we deem *important*. This is an easy trick when it comes to cars or material items, but what are you **not** seeing that might be important in your business, career, finances, health, friendships, or even your intimate relationships because you simply don't focus on them? What's something that helps you that you never noticed because you didn't focus on it? For example, for a while I was practicing gratitude by posting with the #thankfulthursday hashtag on Instagram. I looked through photos or memories of good times and focused on how amazing my life is. I started doing this at times when I didn't feel happy about life, and it helps to remind me about all the good in my life, simply because I started to focus on it.

Once we focus on something, we give it meaning. Sometimes our brain fills in the gaps of what we think we see in order to give it meaning.

Do yuo fnid tihs smilpe to raed?
The pweor of yuor mnid to fcuos on
waht yuo wnat biluds yuor raeltiy.

That's the power of the mind to focus on what it wants to see. Your mind begins to fill in the gaps to create meaning in what you are reading. That meaning may be positive or negative, empowering or disempowering. Seeing a car you just bought everywhere could mean you are excited because you've joined "the club" (empowering), or it could mean you feel less special because you realize everyone else owns the same car as you (disempowering).

Finally, your mind reacts or takes action to the meaning you give this experience. Do you get excited and share with everyone you know that you've got this amazing new car, or do you regret buying this car and feel bummed that you are not as cool, unique, or special as you thought you were? This internal experience is full of choices, and the only person who has control over how you react is *you.*

A young woman had no control over the abuse she suffered as a girl. She had no control over it when it happened, and she has no control over her past now as an adult. What she does have control over is how she processes that event, what meaning she gives to her recovery, and what actions or reactions she has. She can move from victim, to survivor, to someone who thrives. She can find purpose and be of service to others.

A husband and father may have no control over being laid off from his job, over not having enough money, over the lack of new jobs in the challenging economy. He does have control, though, over how he perceives this loss, what he focuses on, the meaning he gives this experience, and the actions he takes. He can give up, or he can step up to the challenge, embrace the opportunity for a new beginning, and make the best of it.

Do you react to experiences as an end or as a beginning? Do you give up or take action? Do you find excuses (even if your complaints are true, they are still excuses), or do you find a way to be successful? Do you give up or do you *step up*?

The Emotional Experience, then, is understanding the nature of both our *internal* and *external* experiences. It involves an experience from the external world that we cannot control and an experience from the internal world where we control what we choose to focus on, whether it brings pain or pleasure, what meaning we give to it, and what action or reaction we choose to take. Our external experiences from the external world filter through our internal world to create our behavior. The internal world is where we can train our Emotional Fitness.

There are exercises throughout this book. It helps to do these exercises right away, while the material is fresh and you are engaged. I encourage you to physically write down your thoughts, as you'll see that it creates a bigger impact. And remember, Emotional Fitness will not work unless you couple the information you're learning with action. So, let's take some action!

Write down all the things that cause problems in your life. This includes everything that causes you to become upset, angry, frustrated, disappointed, or sad. Write down everything that causes you pain.

_____

_____

_____

_____

_____

_____

_____

_____

_____

Now, divide these negative problems into two categories: things that are in the external world and things that are in the internal world.

External Experiences   *Internal Experiences*

_____   _____

_____   _____

_____   _____

_____   _____

_____   _____

You might find that a lot of problems are in the external world. These are out of your control. What's the first thing we change? The first filter of the internal world is your focus.

   If you notice a large number of problems in your life arise from the internal world, that's completely normal. Most people don't know you can change that, but Emotional Fitness teaches you exactly how to do it. Mastering the internal world is the only way to master the external world. This book teaches you how to become Emotionally Fit so that you can master your world!

Spend the next few days adding to your list and dividing your situations into the two categories. This exercise is meant to increase your awareness. You are taking your first steps toward Emotional Fitness.

What if?

I want to tell you the story of Jerry Ryan. He has had his fair share of violence and tragedy. In fact, every day Jerry lives with burning pain rated at an eight out of ten . . . on a good day. When I asked him what it feels like, Ryan said, "It feels like someone poured gasoline down my left side and lit it on fire." When I asked him if it ever goes away, he said no, it is always there.

Let's go into Ryan's backstory a little and learn from a man who against all odds has found purpose, fulfillment, and happiness using Emotional Fitness.

When Ryan was a child, his family moved eleven times in twelve years. He was bullied so much for being the new kid throughout his school years, that when he was in sixth grade, a doctor diagnosed him with an ulcer and actually put him on a diet of baby food to recover. As we all know, kids can be cruel at that age, and Ryan often faced a barrage of insults and jokes from his peers—each one hurting his self-esteem. He started taking martial arts lessons to gain his confidence back, which worked for a time.

When Ryan was thirty, he was attacked at his work in an operating room by someone looking for narcotics. He was attacked from behind, hit over the head, and left for dead. Knocked unconscious, Ryan woke up after three days in a coma. His doctors gave him only a 5 percent chance of survival. When he awakened, his sense of smell and taste was gone, his memory was damaged, and his emotions were out of control.

The attack took Ryan's confidence from him. He was a big guy, and his presence commanded the room. He used to walk around tall, strong, and without fear, but now, after severe brain damage and trauma, even if an old lady walked up behind him, he was scared for his life. He lived in fear every moment of the day. He also suffered significant brain damage, which only made things worse.

At first, Ryan resorted to alcohol and drugs to cope. The stress of his new circumstances triggered arguments and difficulties with his wife, kids, and parents. It took time, but slowly Ryan turned to better ways to manage stress, like yoga, martial arts, weight training, and meditation. All of these modalities helped him tune into himself and give him more awareness of his feelings. They also humbled him. "We all have mental habits that decrease our actual awareness of what's really going on in life. We all need to discover the basic benefits of mindfulness."

Jerry Ryan managed his stress by studying yoga and Tai Chi after his traumatic event, which increased his awareness of mind and body. Taking up these kinds of activities is known to decrease stress and increase health. But what if a person is not physically capable of, say, doing yoga? What if they do not fully recover from their trauma, become confined to a wheelchair, and are never able to walk again? What if they're a veteran, they've lost both legs, and they love playing contact sports? How can someone tell you to master your emotions and take action when the action you love is now an impossibility for you? What if you have cancer and have been given only a few months to live? What if?

I had a speaking engagement recently where I was discussing Emotional Fitness with a group of marines, and one of them posed such a question. What if you have a passion for something and you've lost the physical capabilities to do that thing? What then? I stopped to think about the question. I thought about what I love to do—to speak at events and to be onstage motivating and inspiring people. I thought about how much I love bringing people to the raw edge of human transformation so they can start living the life of their dreams. I thought, *What if I lost my voice? What would I do then?* I knew what I would do instantly. If I couldn't speak, I would write. To me, speaking was only a vehicle to fulfill my passion and purpose. My true passion is inspiring and helping others. If I could no longer physically do it through my voice, I would find a different medium, like writing.

I haven't actually finished telling you Jerry Ryan's story. In 1994, Ryan bought a used vehicle. One day, he was driving to an Easter Sunday celebration with his two sons in the car when the front wheel flew off. The car flipped several times and ended up on the side of the road in a ditch. The roof collapsed on Ryan, crushing his spine. Fumes quickly filled the car. Miraculously, his two sons were relatively unharmed. They quickly dragged their dad out of the car. Because it was Easter Sunday, there were few people on the road, and in 1994, only a few people owned cell phones. Miles away from help, Ryan was on the verge of death. In dramatic fashion, the first person to arrive on the scene was a trauma nurse with a cell phone! She was able to call for help immediately. If it wasn't for that nurse, Ryan surely would have died. In fact, the very doctors who were tasked with saving his life felt it was hopeless. They asked Ryan's wife to pull the plug on him. I cried as Ryan told me his story. His wife defied the doctors, telling them Ryan was a fighter and he would make it. She demanded they do everything they could to save his life. Through tears, Ryan told me, with deep gratitude, "My wife saved my life."

He was alive, but Ryan was now a paraplegic. He is now wheelchair-bound for the rest of his life. He cannot move his legs, can barely move his arms, and can only use one finger. Ryan could've given up, but he didn't. He studied. He became a therapist. And now he helps dozens of people overcome trauma and live a life of purpose.

Ryan's typical day looks like this: He wakes up at 5:30 a.m., while his wife sleeps in. The caregiver gets there at 6:15 a.m. and helps him go to the bathroom, shower, and dress. He is driven to his office. He sees five to six clients. He gets home by around 6:30 p.m. and has three hours to enjoy dinner and relax with his wife. At about 9:30 p.m., a caregiver comes to help him into bed.

What more can life throw at one man?

Ryan could have been angry, resentful, and bitter. He could ask how any human being could do this to another and how *God* could do this to him after everything he had already gone through. Brain damage was one thing; losing the use of his body was another level of an extreme uncontrollable event. He has no control over what happened to him. The only thing he has control over is what he focuses on.

After the accident, Ryan couldn't even do the yoga and Tai Chi he had come to depend upon. Every day, his body hurt. What could he possibly do? All the awareness in the world wouldn't bring his body back or ease his pain.

We complain about having to get up and go to work on Monday, about traffic, about our lukewarm lattes. But what if you weren't able to walk? What if, like Ryan, everything was taken away from you? What would you do? How would you cope? Read the next chapter to find out more about Ryan's transformation. Is it possible to change how we feel? Is it possible to rewire our brains to choose better, more empowering emotions? Is it possible to use Emotional Fitness to build the life of our dreams? Yes, and in the next chapter we'll learn how to use the three Decisions of Destiny.

CHAPTER 4

DECISIONS OF DESTINY

The journey of 1,000 miles begins with a single step.

—LAO TZU

Everything you have ever wanted in life began with a single step. The same thing holds true for everything you did not want. Everything that has gone wrong in your life also began with a step, a misstep. Whatever step we take, whether good or bad, requires a decision. Every day, we are faced with decisions. *Do I snooze the alarm clock? Do I go to work? Do I sit on the couch and watch a movie? Do I work until 3:00 a.m.? Do I get up early to go to the gym? Do I take action toward my goals or get distracted?*

The decisions we make every day affect the kind of life we ultimately live. Each decision can be viewed as a single step in any direction. Imagine how decisions like whether to go to college, take a job, move out of state, or simply go on a date have dramatically changed the course of your life. One step might take you one degree north or south. That one degree after a thousand miles changes your final destination dramatically. Over time, little decisions add up to make huge differences in where we end up.

There are three decisions that we make when we process our experiences of life. This is because every experience from the external world passes through three internal world filters: focus, meaning, and action. This is just how our minds process information and ultimately create our behavior. Each stage involves a choice.

As small or as big as these decisions are, they shape our destiny. For each experience in life, we make a decision, consciously or unconsciously, on

1) What or what not to focus on
2) The meaning an experience has
3) What reaction or action we take

I call these our Three Decisions of Destiny. Each time you make a decision on what to focus on, what that experience means to you, and what action you take, you create your life. Each small decision builds into a bigger one, which affects the direction, and ultimately the destiny, of your life. If you consciously choose what your decisions are instead of simply reacting, then you become the master and decide your destiny.

With Emotional Fitness, we bring to light just how powerful each one of these decisions is in shaping your life. Let's dive in.

Internal World

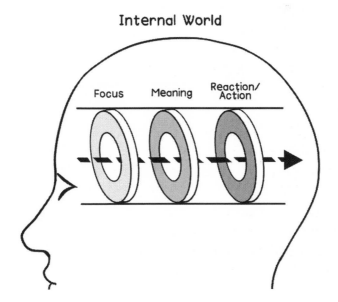

41

Decision One: The Power of Focus

The Power of Focus is the first decision we make. Sometimes we make this decision before we even have an external experience. The Power of Focus is greatly exemplified by John "Jocko" Willink, a retired Navy SEAL commander and current author, motivational speaker, and expert in leadership. As a leader, he is forced to make both easy and tough decisions every day.

When Jocko tells the story of his life as a SEAL commander, he talks about how one of his direct subordinates would regularly pull him aside and tell him about some major problem. Jocko retells the story like this on his popular podcast:

> *He'd say, "Boss, we got this and that and the other thing," and I'd look at him and say, "Good." Finally, one day he was telling me about some issue he was having, some problem, and he said, "I already know what you're going to say."*
>
> *"Well, what am I going to say?"*
>
> *"You're going to say, 'Good.' That's what you always say."*
>
> *When things are going bad, there is going to be some good that comes from it. Didn't get the new high-speed gear we wanted? Good. Didn't get promoted? Good. More time to get better. Got injured? Sprained my ankle? Got tapped out? Good. Got beat? Good. You learned.*[14]

Now on to the next mission. Now on to finding alternatives. Now on to finding a way to survive, because that's what war is really like.

Jocko could have focused on everything that went wrong in the Navy: the mistakes, the delay, the loss, the pain. He could have blamed others, bitched, complained, and got angry. But all that would do is suck the energy from finding a solution. All that would do is waste time. In war, that could get you killed. Instead, Jocko made a different choice, to find the good in every situation. He shifts what he focuses on to find something that is good about the problem. This simple decision to always find something good made him one of the greatest leaders in command. That's the Power of Focus.

Our first Decision of Destiny is to decide what to focus on. The ability to focus on the *good* is a decision. The ability to focus on what you can *control* is a decision. So is focusing on the negative, on the uncontrollable, and letting fear paralyze your decision into indecision. It's hard to admit, but the decision to choose one way of thinking over the other is ultimately all yours.

Now ask yourself, *What am I focusing on?* How does what you focus on help or hurt you? Where and how do you focus your attention? What is important? Why? Do you focus on the negative of difficult events or the opportunities they provide? If you could shift your focus to improve your life, would you?

Social Media Overload

Every day, thousands of stimuli compete for our attention. And it's getting worse. Facebook, Instagram, Twitter, Pinterest, LinkedIn, Reddit—social media bombards us, distracts us, and, according to some studies[15], actually harms our ability to focus on anything at all. Instead of focusing on what's important, we allow our environments to control our focus.

Internet stimuli leave us with little ability "to engage in the kind of deep thinking that requires you to concentrate on one thing," according to Nicholas Carr, the author of *The Shallows: What The Internet Is Doing to Our Brains*.[16]

With the growing extent of stimuli overload, we also become less able to figure out what's important to focus on. "Your mind gets attracted just to what's new rather than what's important,"

Carr explains. In a time when you are trying to figure out how to create a better life for yourself, training your Emotional Fitness to focus on what's important is crucial if you want to accelerate success and avoid getting lost in "weekend warrior" mode and wake up in your late thirties or forties wondering what happened to your life.

You might be thinking it's hard to change your focus. In Chapter 9, we will go over specific exercises and tools you can use that quickly and effectively shift your focus. The big key takeaway for now is to **focus on what you can control and not on what you can't control.**

You might think that shifting your focus is simply a distraction from what's really important in your life. That not worrying about a big project deadline and shifting your focus to happy hour is going to make you feel better. It won't. The point of shifting your focus is not to distract from what's important, but to remove negative feelings that disempower you. The idea is to shift your focus *away* from worrying about that big project and instead put your energy and focus *toward* what actions you can take to prepare for that big project. The goal is to shift your focus from a disempowering perspective to an empowering one that helps you achieve the life you want. Don't lie and tell yourself that you need to worry about something that is truly out of your control, as that is disempowering. Instead focus on what actions you can take to make it better.

With Emotional Fitness, we can train ourselves to focus with intention, to focus on what we can control, and to not worry about others or what we cannot control. We can train our minds to focus on the opportunities instead of the losses. Ask yourself these questions and write down your answers.

Is social media winding you up, making you jealous or keeping you too hooked up and addicted so that you cannot properly focus on what's important?

_____

_____

_____

When something bad happens what do you focus on?

_____

_____

_____

Are you focusing on what you can control, or what you cannot control?

_____

_____

_____

Decision Two: Meaning Is Emotion

In Victor Frankl's seminal work, *Man's Search for Meaning*, he writes about finding purpose even in the most horrific times. Frankl was an Austrian psychiatrist and an Auschwitz prisoner in the Holocaust. He describes his pivotal moment in the camp when he developed *logotherapy*, or "meaning therapy." He was on his way to work in the camp as he contemplated whether he should trade his last cigarette for a bowl of soup. He wondered how he would survive the new foreman who was particularly cruel.

Suddenly, he became so disgusted with how belittled his life had become and how meaningless everything felt. In that moment, he realized that in order to survive, he had to find some purpose. He did so by imagining giving a lecture after the war about the psychology of the concentration camp. Not knowing if he would ever be set free or even survive, he set goals for himself and gave his life purpose. Thus began *Man's Search for Meaning*. He was able to find meaning even in the cruelest and most dire of circumstances. "We must never forget that we may also find meaning in life even when confronted with a hopeless situation, when facing a fate that cannot be changed," he is quoted as saying. A man can find meaning after losing his job, his home, his family, all of his belongings, after being starved, worked to death, beaten like a dog, dehumanized, and left with nothing, even with no knowledge of when the prison sentence would end or if it would ever end.[17]

Jewish people in concentration camps were humiliated and beaten. One in twenty of the men around Frankl died. Frankl saw how even death was linked to a person's mindset. He'd watch the other men let go and give up. According to Frankl, the only difference between those who survived and those who didn't were those who found meaning in their suffering. Frankl observed normal people using Emotional Fitness to find meaning in their suffering in the most dire of circumstances, being Jewish in a Nazi concentration camp in WWII. If they found meaning, they were more likely to survive.

For Frankl, the meaning he gave his imprisonment was that he knew he had to share what had happened in the camps with the world. He'd write down notes for his book, and they would be thrown away, but he'd just keep writing on tiny pieces of paper. He knew that anyone who focused on something that gave them purpose remained alive.

The first decision in our Decisions of Destiny is where we put our *focus*. Frankl focused on what he could control which was the freedom his thoughts provided him. The second decision is what our experiences *mean* to us. For Frankl, this second decision was critical to survival. If the meaning he attached to his experience in those camps was not empowering, he was likely to die. If his meaning gave him purpose, he was more likely to be able to endure the suffering of the camps. This brings to light an incredible point: *the only meaning in life is the meaning you give it.*

For example, if the external event of *I lost my job* happens to you, it might mean *I'm worthless. I'm a failure. I'm not good enough.* Or you could have an experience like Jocko where your mission failed but the meaning you give it is good. You might think, *Let's figure out what went wrong. I'm glad it happened in training. I needed that experience to learn.*

Interestingly, the meaning we give something only occurs once we put words to it. Words give our experience meaning and in turn help shape our experience. This goes for both positive and negative words.

Have you ever met someone who gets angry easily? Maybe someone accidentally bumps into them in line at a restaurant and they lean over to you and say, "Wow, what was that idiot doing? It just *infuriates* me that they are so careless. It *pisses me off that* they didn't see me standing here."

Infuriates is the word they choose to describe their feeling of being accidentally bumped in line? This is such a strong word, emotionally. It is this word they chose to attach to the meaning of the experience, which in turn escalates the severity or meaning of the experience in their mind. They focus on that person being an "idiot" as opposed to seeing the action as simply an accident in which the person simply didn't see them. *Infuriates* is much stronger than a word like *annoys* or *inconveniences.* In fact, when people retell a story where they became angry and they use vivid language like *infuriates,* you can almost see the steam coming out of their ears as if they are angry again, in the moment! This is because language affects the meaning we give to the experience *and* the feeling we get, even in the retelling.

47

The language we use to describe our emotions about an experience creates the very meaning we give to the experience. This meaning we decide on affects the way we react and act. In later chapters, we will go more deeply into how to consciously use words and language to shift the meaning of our experience, and ultimately our perception of life. But let's take a quick example of how a popular acronym creates real negative feelings.

FOMO, the Fear Of Missing Out, is the fear and anxiety that happens when you see images of peers allegedly doing much better than you on social media. You see all your friends traveling, winning awards, and going out with friends. Nearly 24 percent of teenagers are now online almost constantly. Kids see others doing well online and they fear they don't measure up and that something is being taken away from them.[18] They focus on missing out, and the meaning they give to their experience is that they have no life, they don't measure up, and they aren't good enough. Instead, they should focus on the fact that social media is often a highlight reel of someone else's life and only showcases the best of the best. There are even people out there who hate their lives but smile to take pictures for "the gram" to show how great their fake life is.

"The problem with FOMO is the individuals it impacts are looking outward instead of inward," says Darlene McLaughlin, an assistant professor at Texas A&M University. "FOMO is an emotion—driven by thoughts—that can create fear and anxiety." That negative outlook means that young people are so busy focusing on other people's lives that they're missing out on their own.

Do not become so worried about the life you do not have that you forget to live the life you do have. Remember, the only meaning in life is the meaning you give it.

Decision Three: To React or Take Action?

We focus in a certain way on events. We give them meaning, and from there, we either react involuntarily or we take an action.

48

You lost your job. You think, *I have nothing. I'm not good enough. Nobody loves me. I'll veg on the couch watching reruns and eating chocolate. I'll drink and spiral into the hell of my depressed mind.* None of these actions change the fact that you do not have a job.

Even non-action is an action. If all you do is get angry, ignore the problem, and distract yourself, your action is choosing distraction.

What if you re-frame it to mean something different? Would that affect your reaction and subsequent actions? *I lost my job. That's great. I'm free to do what I really want. Thank goodness this happened.* What if you landed a better job, with better hours and more pay? All of this can and does happen when you're Emotionally Fit and can make a decision to take actions that empower you to your destiny.

Pat Flynn is one of my favorite podcasters and a man who turned adversity into success, which not only benefits him, but helps thousands of others.

Flynn graduated with a degree in architecture and went to work for an architectural firm. "I was thriving in my career and had no plans to leave it." But the downturn in the economy hit his industry hard. In 2008, a few months before he was supposed to get married, Flynn was laid off.

In a difficult economy, Flynn had to figure out a way to support himself and his family. After much hard work, he established the Smart Passive Income podcast, which is consistently ranked in the top ten podcasts in iTunes' Business category. In 2017, according to Forbes, Flynn was one of the Top 25 Marketing Influencers.[19] Flynn creates his own work schedule, makes a great deal more money than he did at his previous job, runs his own show, and is in control of his destiny.

What is truly interesting about Flynn is that he didn't just take action; he tied that action to meaning in his life: his family. He built his business around spending more time with his wife and two children. Flynn could have focused on how unfair it was that he lost his job; he could have given it a meaning that he wasn't good enough to be successful, and instead of taking action he could have chosen not to act, to distract himself, as people in hard times often do. Instead, Flynn focused on what he could control. With some money he was making from an online business helping students pass the architect exam, he started to find something: passive income. He took massive action to create a company that provided tons of value. I'm sure now Flynn looks back and attaches a meaning to him getting fired from horrible to the best thing that ever happened to him.

Flynn's podcast was one of the first I listened to on a regular basis. I learned so much from him that it inspired me to create my own podcast, *Unleash Success*. I've interviewed founders of incredible companies like Tom Bilyeu, co-founder of Billion Dollar Quest Nutrition; Thom McElroy, co-founder and designer of Volcom Logo; Alex Brown from The Dollar Beard Club; Jeremy Buendia, four-time men's physique fitness champion; Chris Voss, former FBI lead hostage negotiator; and Ingrid Macher, the number one most influential Latina for health and fitness in North America, with over 15 million followers. I took action to create a podcast because I loved learning from successful people, which in turn allowed me to learn better strategies and become more successful myself.

If you take action, you can change your circumstances and thus the experiences you have in life. Action was the cure for me. After years of feeling like a victim to my emotions, experiencing anger and depression, I finally woke up and realized that I could take back control. Instead of reacting to emotions, I could take action to create a better life for myself.

Once you decide to focus on something, you then give it a meaning in your life and decide what you want to do. You may choose in-action (AKA distraction), or you may decide to *act*. All choices are a decision. Whether conscious or unconscious, the choice is now yours. Action is the best way to get the results you want in life. Taking the right actions can get you that much closer to your goals and dream life. But distraction comes in many forms and often paralyzes our actions, sometimes for years.

Is now the moment that you are going to take action to start your business? Is now the time when you've finally had enough with being out of shape, and you'll commit to going to the gym five days a week? Is now the time to say *yes* to your dreams and *no* to your fears? Will you take action?

In the upcoming chapters, we learn how to control our reactions, how our physical bodies influence the actions we take, and how to take more empowering actions to accomplish goals faster than ever before. First, let's look at how we get and stay motivated to take all this action.

CHAPTER 5

THE SEEDS OF MOTIVATION: PAIN AND PLEASURE

> *The difference between a successful person and others is not a lack of strength, not a lack of knowledge, but rather in a lack of will.*
>
> —VINCE LOMBARDI

Emotional Fitness is about helping you train your mind and emotions to create the success you want in your life. After understanding the emotional experience, you might be thinking, with each decision, what motivates me to make that decision? Why do some people focus on the problems instead of the solution? Why do some people seem to always find a positive meaning no matter how dire the circumstances? And, finally, how do some people not react with paralyzing fear or worry but instead take action that leads themselves and others to success? What motivates us to make one decision over another? The answer to all of these questions lies in our biologic programming for survival.

Where Does Motivation Come From?

Most people think that staying motivated is difficult, and that motivation is elusive—hard to find and even harder to keep. And maybe they are right when they are looking for motivation to do something they really don't want to do. Motivation by definition is the reason you take an action. And every day you are choosing actions. You might choose to take action toward your goals, or you might merely choose *not* to take action.

So many people often ask the question, "Why am I not motivated?" Your brain quickly says, "It's because you're lazy! You're a loser! That's why you don't go after your goals!" But alas, we need to ask better questions like: "Why am I *more* motivated to *not* take action than to take action towards my goals? *How* do I get motivated to achieve the goals I want? And how do I stay motivated? How do I feel the inspiration and the energy that comes along with being inspired every morning and every night on my journey to achieve my goals?"

To understand how to *get* motivated, let's first understand where motivation comes from. Motivation at its core is your desire to do something. Where does desire come from? What are the hidden driving forces of desire that motivate us? Let's look at three influential people— Abraham Maslow, Tony Robbins, and Viktor Frankl—and their theories on human desire and motivation. According to Abraham Maslow, the American psychologist famous for developing Maslow's hierarchy of needs, desire comes from the need that most dominates the human mind at a given time. The hierarchy of needs is portrayed in the shape of a pyramid with the largest, most fundamental needs at the bottom and the need for self-actualization at the top.

Maslow's needs include physiological needs, safety, belonging and love, esteem, and self-actualization. The goal is to attain the fifth level or stage: self-actualization.

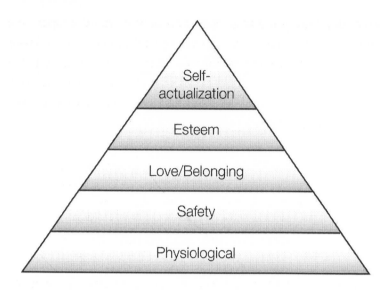

Maslow's Hierarchy of Needs

The base of the pyramid contains what Maslow called "deficiency needs" or "d-needs": esteem, friendship and love, security, and physical needs. If these are not met, the individual will feel anxious and tense. The most basic level of needs must be met before the individual will strongly desire (or focus motivation upon) the higher needs. He coined the term "metamotivation" to describe the motivation of people who go beyond the scope of the basic needs and strive for constant betterment.[20] This is one philosophy on where motivation comes from.

While there have been others striving to understand what drives human behavior, one person who I have personally found to be helpful is Tony Robbins. In order to define human motivation and desire, Robbins created the six human needs: certainty, uncertainty/variety, love/connection, significance, growth, and contribution. Certainty is the need to feel secure, safe, and in control. Uncertainty/variety is the need for something different, exciting, or uncertain in life. After all, if you knew exactly when everything was going to happen and how it would happen, life would feel extremely boring. Love/connection—as it sounds—is the need to feel love and human connection. Significance is the need to feel important. Growth is the need to learn more, expand, do more, and grow. Contribution is the need to give back to others, society, and the world.

Certainty	Uncertainty/Variety
Love/Connection	Significance
Growth	Contribution

All of us meet the first four needs—certainty, uncertainty/variety, love/connection, and significance—somehow, even if at low levels. But the order of our needs varies from person to person. Someone whose top need is certainty would, for example, need to make sure they are always safe and secure. Someone whose top need is variety would need constant variation in life and hate having a daily schedule. Robbins claims that each person is driven to meet each of these first four needs. However, the last two—contribution and growth—are the needs of the spirit. While they are vital to living a fulfilling life, not everyone meets these last two needs. The needs of the spirit are much like self-actualization in Maslow's hierarchy of needs.

Finally, we have Viktor Frankl, the psychiatrist who survived the Holocaust, wrote *Man's Search for Meaning*, and coined the word *logotherapy*. There were three main aspects of logotherapy. First, Frankl argued that life has meaning in all circumstances, even ones as gruesome and horrifying as the Holocaust. Second, the primary motivational force of human beings is to find meaning in life. Third, we have the freedom to find meaning in what we do and what we experience. This does not mean Frankl could escape the Nazi concentration camps, but that he had the freedom to choose what being there meant to him.

Jewish people were held captive in the most inhumane conditions. They were forced to sleep on the freezing cold ground covered in feces, while the Germans worked them literally to death. Their suffering, their pain, and their imprisonment knew no end. As captives, they did not know the war would end in 1945. They did not know whether they would be there for six months, six years, or sixty years. If they weren't beaten to death or killed in the gas chamber, they often died from lack of food and water, and disease. And still Frankl found meaning in this suffering. He realized he had the freedom to choose the meaning of his life. And to him, the ability to find an empowering meaning to life, to find meaning even in suffering, was the only way to survive.[21]

I see varying levels of motivation. The first and foremost is just as Maslow states: we need to find a way to survive. If we are always looking for food or avoiding death, there is not much time to worry about existential feelings or the meaning of life. In the caveman days, such deep thought would have left us vulnerable to attack and death. Unfortunately, this survival mode has found its way into modern society.

Once we ascend out of survival mode, then we have many different driving forces in life. We want to enjoy life and try new experiences; we want to feel needed and important; we want our life to mean something; we want to have good relationships and feel loved; and, of course, we want to be happy.

What motivates you? Why you do what you do? Where did this motivation come from? We are always driven to do something. What motivates you to choose to go to the gym or stay home and watch Netflix? What motivates you to stay at a job you hate, and what motivates you to want to find a new job or start your own business? What drives you and what stops you? The answer lies in our biology.

Pain vs. Pleasure: The Seed of Motivation

Every decision you make comes from a driving force inside you. Ultimately these driving forces stem from what you believe about life and whether you believe saying yes to one action will bring you pain or pleasure versus saying no. Pain and pleasure are the two fundamental stimuli in life. They evolved to help us survive. **Pain and pleasure are the ultimate motivators.**

To understand the pain and pleasure principle and motivation, we must start with the human nervous system, which has not changed much over thousands of years. Once you understand this principle, then you can begin to use biology to your advantage.

Your body is made up of millions of nerves. These nerves sense external stimuli and relay the information to the brain for processing. The brain processes stimuli in one of two ways: either as pain or as pleasure. Very simply, the brain relays if something is good for you or bad for you and acts accordingly.

For example, when you touch a hot stove, your nerves relay this stimulus to your brain, which then interprets it as "Hot! Move now before you burn us, you idiot!" and you respond by moving your hand toward cooler air, or maybe cold water if needed. This is a classic example of how our bodies are conditioned to move us *away from pain and toward pleasure.*

The Pain and Pleasure Principle is designed to keep humans alive. When humans were cavemen, survival was the only thing on their minds. Food was what allowed them to survive—it gave them pleasure. Lack of food made them feel bad. Extreme lack of food meant feeling pain—quite literally the pain of dying from hunger. The pleasure of getting food would not always drive them to hunt, as hunting could result in pain or death, too. However, eventually the pain of dying from hunger would force them to hunt. Why else would they risk their lives? Because if they didn't risk their lives hunting, they would have died from hunger. This illustrates a key point: **humans will do more to avoid pain than to**

gain pleasure. The pleasure of getting food would not drive early humans to hunt as much as the pain of dying a slow death would.

Pain is often more immediate than pleasure. This causes us to pay more attention to avoiding pain than gaining pleasure. This again stems from the fact that early on, pain often meant death, while pleasure meant life. But lack of pleasure didn't always mean immediate death. Therefore, pain signifies to our brain that we *might* be dying and yells, "Avoid!" This natural direction of our focus helps us survive. But in today's ever-increasing technological world, imminent pain and death do not lurk around every corner. Our brains, though, still respond to what we believe to be painful in the same way . . . unless we *rewire* our brains with Emotional Fitness.

Anticipation of Pain or Pleasure Drives Us

It's not just the experience of actual pain we fear. What is interesting is that we will often go through great difficulty to avoid even the *anticipation* of pain. Anticipated pain and anticipated pleasure can influence us significantly. Ever had a problem that gets blown way out of proportion in your mind, only to be solved simply? Say you had a work issue, but really it was a small miscommunication. The anticipation of that pain from the potential consequences of that problem may have caused significant stress or fear. But once it was solved, you never actually suffered the negative consequences, even though the stress or fear you felt was very real.

Even if your perception is incorrect, the anticipation of pain can motivate you to take action. If you believe that a tall man with a mask walking down an alley in the dark is a threat to you, and then you see him carrying a shiny object that looks like a knife, you might be motivated to run away while screaming bloody murder. However, if it was raining out, and this man had a hood on, and the shiny object was an umbrella, you might believe he is not a threat, just a man trying to stay dry. Perception and anticipation can motivate us, *even when we're wrong*, to take strong action.

If you believe that playing sports makes you popular, you might work really hard to be good at sports. Often, it is the denial of the pleasure you seek—the pain of *not* having something you want—that is a stronger motivational force. How many people have you heard say, "I'm going to do it to prove them wrong?" Michael Jordan was cut from his high school basketball team. This motivated him to work harder than anyone to become the best basketball player in the world. Had he not been cut, maybe his motivation would not have been strong enough to work that hard. The pain of not getting the pleasure we want drives us more than getting what we wanted in the first place. Motivation is an interesting emotion. But the more we understand it, the better we get at staying motivated for what we say we want.

Our Biological Barrier to Success

The fact that human beings will do more to avoid pain than gain pleasure is ultimately our greatest barrier. This is because most things that give you success, happiness, love, fulfillment, and purpose often require you to go against the survival programming of your mind and emotions. You don't earn success by staying in your comfort zone. You don't find true love by never getting rejected. You don't experience continuous happiness if you never challenge yourself to try new things. But in the end, these positive emotions require you to go against your survival mind and emotional programming. This programming is the single greatest obstacle that any human will ever have to overcome. And the only way to consistently overcome this simple fact of life is to have Emotional Fitness. Emotional Fitness not only gives you the tools to win the game as it is, but once you become Emotionally Fit, you can now change the game of life to set yourself up for massive, unlimited success.

As we have evolved, our nervous systems have remained the same. They are highly functioning systems designed for one thing: **survival**. This worked extremely well for thousands of years. Then, we evolved. Towns and cities grew. We created automobiles. Now we have the internet. Most of us no longer have to struggle to find or hunt for food. Shelter is a guarantee for many of us; we go to cozy homes without fear that wolves or bears will attack us at night. Life is *good*.

Our nervous system has not updated yet. It still thinks pain = potential death. Therefore, when you associate going to the gym as painful, your nervous system says "Nooo, we will die." And when you eat chocolate cake, it gives you pleasure. Three hundred pieces of cake later, you might be overweight and dying slowly of diabetes and congestive heart failure all because your body was just trying to survive.

The key distinction that human beings possess above all other animals is the ability to change their perception, to decide what to focus on. **You have the ability to change *how* you perceive pain and pleasure.** If you *recondition* yourself to view the gym as pleasure by imagining how great you will feel after it, or even during it, and by knowing you are improving your body and releasing endorphins, then suddenly your nervous system will want to move toward the gym. If you associate chocolate cake with slow death by diabetes and imagine yourself overweight, alone, sad, and depressed, suddenly you associate immense pain with chocolate cake and your nervous system says, "Nooo."

What you view as pain or pleasure underlies every decision you make in life. If you think not going to work will give you the pain of no money and no place to live, it will be a strong motivator for you to go to work, even if you hate your job. We will do more to avoid pain in the short term than we will to gain pleasure. However, pain will not drive us forever. **In the end, only long-term pleasure will keep us motivated.** We need positive feelings or rewards to keep us going. That's why after two or three years, people who work jobs they hate often say enough is enough, quit, and go find new jobs. They are willing to live with the uncertainty of not getting a paycheck because the pain of going to work was now much greater, and the pleasure of getting a new job was a strong motivator.

Double the Motivation

One of the strongest methods I have found to create motivation and to stay motivated is to use both pain and pleasure to drive me. Essentially, I use our pain and pleasure biological wiring to double my motivation. Pain is extremely helpful in the short term to get us going, and pleasure keeps us motivated in the long term. By focusing on the pain of NOT achieving my goals, I am motivated by pain. I visualize 10 to 20 years from now where I have not achieved my goals. I use the anticipation of this perceived negative future pain to motivate me in the present. Once I'm working toward a goal and seeing progress, the pleasure of achieving the goal keeps driving me. I do this exercise so often now that it has become a habit that keeps me constantly motivated toward my goals.

Your motivation to do or not do something comes from your beliefs about whether the thing you want will give you pain or pleasure. What you think will make you happy could motivate you to focus on your relationships but not your finances or motivate you to go to the gym but not focus on your relationships. You might be motivated by money, so you work so hard to get it but end up sacrificing your health, your family, and your friends. Whether you are deciding to take a risk on a business venture, asking someone on a date, responding to your kids, or being with your friends, it all revolves around this simple pain and pleasure principle. If you do not like how you avoid pain in certain situations, re-associate and recondition the situation with immense pleasure. Alternatively, if you do not like the results you are getting from a negative habit you have, you can recondition and re-associate the behavior with intense pain. As a human be-ing, you and you alone have the unique ability to *choose.* Choose wisely. Take back control of your decisions and your life.

In the next chapter, we take a deeper look at our driving forces and discover how beliefs shape our decisions and our lives.

CHAPTER 6

THE INVISIBLE FORCE THAT DRIVES US: BELIEFS

Whether you think you can, or you think you can't, you're right.

—HENRY FORD

There is a powerful invisible force inside each one of us. It is the force that determines whether you feel pain, pleasure, or any other emotion, and it ultimately directs your decisions in any given moment. This force determines whether you react with laughter or fear, whether you cry or hold it in, whether you dedicate your life to medicine or art, and every other decision you make. This invisible force is so strong it has the power to move mountains, to travel the world, to make humans fly, to even go to the moon. This invisible force that I'm talking about is also known as your beliefs.

Beliefs shape us. Our beliefs create and form the reality of our lives.

- Some extremists believe their war of faith against non-believers makes them saviors, and that on the other side, they will be held in glory.

- Mahatma Gandhi believed in praying for his enemies, even those trying to kill him. He believed that killing was wrong and didn't even wish it upon his enemies.

- Amelia Earhart believed she could advance women in aviation and became the first woman to fly solo across the Atlantic.

- Elon Musk believed he could create an electric car to rival hundred-year-old car companies, a solar company that could redefine solar energy, a space company that could build reusable rockets and eventually send them to Mars.

- A husband may believe it is his job to make the lion share of the money that supports his family.

- A parent may believe the only way for their child to succeed in life is to go to college, so they hire tutors for them, and make sure they do their homework every day.

What Are Beliefs?

Let's look at how our beliefs affect our decisions and actions. Every decision in your mind is predicated on a belief you have. We talked about the *road* to your reaction or action is built on decisions you make about what to focus on and what this means to you. If that is the *road* to your actions, then the *map* that road is on is your beliefs. These beliefs guide you through each decision you make.

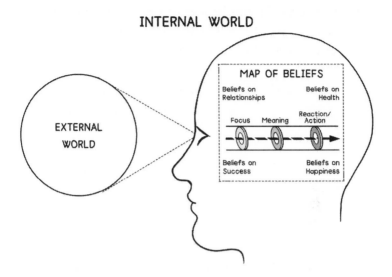

You then manifest your beliefs in the world through your actions every day. We are all driven by our beliefs, whether we're aware of what they are or not. Some beliefs are empowering:

The world is a safe place.

A person can accomplish anything they put their mind to.

Humankind is fundamentally good.

Some are disempowering:

The world is a dangerous place.

All the good men/women are taken.

Life is a battle, and every day you have to fight to survive.

Some beliefs are contradictory. We think we can only believe one side of an issue, but that's not always true. Opposing beliefs do not have to be mutually exclusive:

I hate my job. I love many of the people I work with.

I am an honest person. I only tell white lies to avoid hurting someone's feelings. Everything is my fault. I shouldn't be so hard on myself.

We may struggle with the fact that two conflicting beliefs can co-exist because both feel true to us. This is because beliefs are a construct *built* by our minds to help us navigate the world. They are important because they help us build off past experiences to make decisions about life. **Beliefs are built by our culture, families, how we are raised, what others teach us, and especially by our life experiences.** Beliefs are not "right" or "wrong;" they are simply what we believe to be true. Beliefs either empower you to your goals or limit you from achieving them. There are beliefs that make your life better or beliefs that make your life worse. These beliefs form the road map for all of your decisions, for the meaning you give events, and for the actions you take.

What you believe about life, work, relationships, family, time, and about yourself is built by your experiences. Some beliefs are built in a single moment from an extremely strong emotional experience. For example, one painful incident from childhood can create a massive pillar that supports a belief that lasts for the rest of your life. Maybe your parents forgot to pick you up after the first day of school. For some, this might not be a big deal, but if you already had a difficult relationship with your parents, it may have felt like abandonment. And maybe since that day you felt like you couldn't depend on your parents to help you.

Or maybe you got rejected by a school crush. For some, rejection can be so painful that they never try to date again to avoid that pain. The fear of rejection can affect not only relationships, but also our work life, and this fear can be a struggle to overcome.

Some people let one experience define their entire lives and every subsequent decision related to that experience. But if you want to live a great and successful life, you are going to fail and get rejected. Oprah Winfrey's first boss reportedly told her she was too emotional and not right for television. If she had let this first rejection stop her from even trying, she wouldn't have had one of the highest-ranking shows in history: *The Oprah Winfrey Show*. She is now one of the richest self-made women in the world.

Maybe you failed a test, flunked out of a class, didn't make the team, got reprimanded, didn't get a promotion, lost a job, or lost a girlfriend/boyfriend or wife/husband. You failed at one area of life one time. Does that mean you *are* a failure? What do you believe?

Your beliefs collectively make up your belief system. Not all experiences yield negative belief systems. Maybe you worked hard to get an A on a test or in a class and you felt confident. You believed you were capable. Maybe you spent six months working out and eating a healthy diet and you lost twenty pounds. You believed you deserved to look and feel amazing. You believed you were beautiful. Maybe you received a promotion, or a new job and you reinforced your belief that you are good at what you do, that you deserve to be rewarded, and that life is good.

How Are Beliefs Created?

Beliefs are built on our experiences, positive or negative, through either a significant emotional event or through multiple events that build upon one another. Think of building a belief like building a table. Imagine that each of the four legs of the table represents different experiences. The more emotionally significant the experience, the stronger the legs that support the belief. If you experience one significant emotional event, that single pillar can become so big and strong that it can support a belief for life. Or weaker experiences, like minor rejections, over the years can build up until they create a strong enough leg to support the belief that you are not good enough.

HOW BELIEFS ARE BUILT

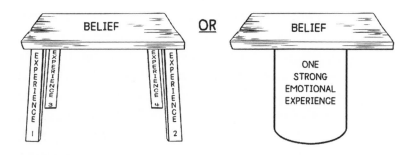

All beliefs are built to serve a purpose with a positive intent. Even a negative belief was built originally to protect or serve you in some way. Doubting yourself can at first help ensure you adequately prepare to achieve your goals. Too much doubt and it paralyzes you, stopping you from accomplishing anything. For some, a belief that they are not good enough helps motivate them to work harder. For others, this same belief helps protect them from putting themselves out there, where they might experience the pain of rejection or failure. If you believe you are not good enough, you might not even try, and therefore you would avoid pain. But if you never put yourself outside your comfort zone, you can never grow and experience life.

We often choose our beliefs unconsciously and at a young age. Beliefs can empower us for a time but then hold us back in the future. Perfectionism as a child, for example, may have brought you praise from parents, family, teachers, and peers. This reinforces the belief that being a perfectionist is good. If you want to be an entrepreneur, perfectionism can be a big drawback because it's an unattainable goal. You may have a perfection issue with finding a partner because you have an unrealistic vision of your perfect partner. You might find amazing person but can't accept their flaws, so you are never happy with the relationship because it can never be "perfect." This perfectionism belief that helped you is now stopping you from living your best life.

I came up against my own perfectionist beliefs as an entrepreneur. Everything had to be perfect to even start. The problem? In business, you just have to get going. There will be many problems that arise, and it will never be perfect! Letting go of that need to feel perfect allowed me to accomplish so much more. Once I let go of perfectionism, I was able to release my podcast in three months. I did ten motivational talks in six months, to community groups, personal development groups, and to the marines, from groups of fifteen people to seven hundred. Perfectionism prevented me from taking action, and therefore I never got a result. The minute I stopped trying to be so perfect, I accomplished significantly more, faster than ever before. At the end of the day, if I make a mistake, I see it as a learning experience. I've been able to do ten times as much letting go of perfectionism.

Now that you see how beliefs are built, you can *become* the builder and consciously choose your beliefs. This is a much better solution than allowing your five-, eight-, or twelve-year-old self to unconsciously choose beliefs that govern your life as an adult. You wouldn't let your five-year-old self make a decision for you now, so why would you let the belief you chose as a child control you today?

Global Beliefs and Situation-Specific Beliefs

What is so interesting about beliefs is that at times we can believe two conflicting things. This is because we have different kinds of beliefs. **Global beliefs** are more general beliefs. They can include a range of things:

I believe I'm an honest person.

All men are pigs.

I believe I'm a strong and healthy person.

All doctors are ethical.

All successful people had money to start with.

You might believe you're an honest person, and you probably are. But you might also believe that telling your friend or wife or husband the truth might hurt their feelings. You don't want to hurt their feelings, so you tell them a little harmless white lie. They might ask, "Do I look fat in these pants?" Even if you think the answer is yes, you answer no. We do this all the time, even when being completely honest is one of our core values. This is a **situational-specific belief**: depending on the situation, our beliefs change. There's nothing wrong with this, per sé. The only real question is, does it limit you or does it empower you?

Different Levels of Belief Strength

There are varying levels of beliefs. The lowest level of belief is an **opinion**. You might have the opinion that a local restaurant has the best Italian food in the world. Of course, this might change if you go to Italy. These beliefs can be fairly easily changed.

In the middle, there are **general beliefs**. These beliefs are stronger and built on more experiences throughout life. You might believe that love at first sight is something you only see in movies, until you fall madly in love with the man or woman of your dreams. General beliefs are harder to change, but it can happen—especially when you see someone defy your belief through their actions.

Finally, there are **core beliefs**. Core beliefs really are the main drivers of your life. What do you believe about happiness and success? What do you believe about who you are? Are you a fun, outgoing person or more of a homebody? Are you the best salesperson or just trying to survive in your job? Are you smart? These beliefs are usually very difficult to change because they tie into your identity. These core beliefs are usually so strong that even if you are shown something different, you usually do not change your belief. If these core beliefs empower you, awesome! Keep them. If they limit you, would you want to know how to change them? If our beliefs are built through our past experiences, then we can have new experiences to create new beliefs.

Core Beliefs

We all have different beliefs from our individual experiences. These beliefs can be empowering or disempowering. Many of our core beliefs are built during childhood. These core beliefs are often ones that define who we are, for better or for worse. Maybe a parent lies to you and you have trust issues. Maybe a parent rewards you for good behavior and you believe being a good person is important. Some of these core beliefs are shaped by many experiences over time, while others are so strong that they develop after even a single event.

I moved around a lot as a kid. I went to three different schools in third grade and four different schools across three states in ninth grade. To date, I've lived in over fifty different "homes." As a kid with so much instability in life, my family became the one constant. Over time, my belief became that home was where we were together. It didn't matter how much we moved because as long as we had one another, life was good. This taught me the importance of family and that no matter what happened in life, I would do anything for my family. Over time, I built a core belief that **family comes first.**

Most of my life, I have envisioned having my family all live in the same neighborhood, always around one another, because when we are together, it feels like home. We may all live in different cities, or even states, currently, but one of my dreams from childhood—and still a financial goal of mine—is to build a couple of houses next to each other where everyone in my family can have a place to stay. As you can see, this core belief still drives so many of my actions to this day.

Another belief I have came from a single day when I was twelve years old. I'll always remember it, as it was a strong emotional experience. I am half-Jewish from my mother's side, and half-Catholic from my dad's side. As part of being raised Jewish, I was Bar Mitzvah'd at thirteen years old. My dad was going to have to spend $3,000 on a party for all of our friends and family. It was a lot of money. My dad came to me and said half-joking that he would rather just give me the money. I didn't want the party. I wanted to take the money. But my mom found out and was actually hurt by even the idea. To her, it was a time for me to grow up, a tradition, a coming-of-age ritual. It was important for the family. Here, my belief that family comes first kicked in. My mom taught me a very valuable lesson. She said that I had already started studying for the Bar Mitzvah, and when you start something, you finish it. For my mom—for my family—I would do anything, and so I followed through with my commitment. I was glad I did—the party was a memorable highlight in my life. And in a single day, another important belief came from my experience: **when you commit to something, you finish it.**

Most of us think that our beliefs are part of our nature; often they are not. They're taught to us by family, friends, teachers, mentors, the media, our cultures, our religions, and our life experiences. As beliefs are built through our experiences, it is important to understand that they can be *rebuilt*. **We only want to change**

beliefs if they limit us. Otherwise, we want to strengthen the beliefs that empower us. It's not easy to create this shift in beliefs, but it is *possible*. First, we start by being aware of them.

Let's start to look at our beliefs. What are your beliefs about the following? What experiences have you had that reinforce these beliefs?

- Family _____

- Love _____

- Money _____

- Happiness _____

- Work _____

- Success _____

- Health _____

- Death _____

- Time _____

Empowering or Disempowering Beliefs

We have defined different kinds of beliefs to create awareness and to help you identify your beliefs. Emotional Fitness is all about helping you get real results, accomplish your goals, and create the life you dream of. For that reason, every belief you have falls into two categories: you have either empowering beliefs or disempowering beliefs. **Empowering beliefs** are beliefs that help you accomplish your goals and desires.

Here are some examples of empowering beliefs:

I'm a confident, intelligent person.

I'm a hard worker.

I don't give up.

I'm a happy, caring, and loving person.

Life is beautiful.

Disempowering beliefs are beliefs that limit you or stop you from accomplishing your goals. Disempowering beliefs are also called **limiting beliefs** because they limit your ability to realize your potential. We will go into limiting beliefs and how to shift them in later chapters.

Here are some examples of disempowering beliefs:

I'm not smart enough to succeed.

No one will ever love me.

All the good men/women are taken.

I don't have the resources to be successful.

I'm just big-boned.

Your beliefs are designed to protect or serve you in some way. Maybe you built a certain belief because it helps you—even a negative belief might have helped you at one time. But now you have to choose whether that belief empowers you or disempowers you. Are beliefs really powerful enough to change our lives that drastically?

A 2014 study led by Kaptchuk and published in *Science Translational Medicine* explored this question by testing how people reacted to migraine pain medication. One group took a migraine drug labeled with the drug's name, another group took a placebo labeled *placebo*, and a third group took nothing. The researchers discovered that the placebo was 50 percent as effective as the real drug to reduce pain after a migraine attack.[22] Fifty percent as effective?! It was a fake pill and yet it worked, powered only by their belief! The placebo response rate for treating depression with fake pills consistently falls between 30 and 40 percent. This means some people have such strong beliefs in the medicine that they actually heal themselves with fake medicine. This is the power our beliefs have to affect our minds and bodies. As you become more aware of your beliefs, you might be thinking, *Can beliefs change?*

> *"I'm trying to free your mind, Neo. But
> I can only show you the door. You're the
> one that has to walk through it."*

—MORPHEUS, THE MATRIX

Can Beliefs Change?

New beliefs can help us reach our goals and create the life we've always wanted. But first, can our beliefs even change? Is that even possible?

Think about how deeply as kids we believed in Santa Claus. We were taught to believe that a jolly fat man in a bright-red suit flew around the world with special reindeer to deliver presents to every good boy and girl. We even worked extra hard to be good in November so we wouldn't be on his naughty list. We believed so much in Santa that we would write him letters, make a Christmas list, and bake him cookies.

Imagine that one day you were at school and some bully came over and said, "Santa isn't real. Your parents lied to you. Your parents are the ones who get the presents. Don't believe me? Ask your mom and dad." In complete disbelief, you went home and asked your parents. They sighed and said, "We are so sorry you had to find out this way, but Santa is not real." In horror, you were faced with reality. Your belief changed overnight.

No matter what you believed in as a kid—Santa Claus, the Tooth Fairy, the Easter Bunny, whatever it was—now that belief has changed. Beliefs can and do change. The key is choosing beliefs that empower us and disregarding beliefs that limit us.

Usually when a belief changes, the change is often *unconscious*. Without consciously choosing our beliefs, they could lead us down a path we don't want to go. Major emotional events often alter our core beliefs about life quickly. For example, the birth of a child often changes a carefree person into a control freak out of fear their child will hurt themselves. The death of a loved one can inspire you to live life to the fullest each and every day or put fear in your heart that maybe you are next. Divorce can shift beliefs about love, from the belief that you will never be loved again, to the belief that no matter your age, you have the opportunity to start anew. Beliefs can and do change. The key is choosing a belief that empowers you. You can consciously choose them or let your life experiences and your unconscious mind choose them for you. When you fail, do you believe it's because you're not good enough and stop trying? Or do you believe that if you work harder you can still reach your goal? You can choose beliefs that empower your life and help you.

People often look to the past to drive their present and dictate their future. It's only natural that you would look to past experiences. The only problem is that memories can be misleading. Also, the perspective you had at seven years old might be different from your perspective at twenty-five or thirty-five years old. So, beliefs that you built as a kid may no longer serve you. I believe that at the fundamental level, beliefs are built by our experiences. While others may encourage you to "find yourself," I instead encourage you to "create yourself." You can choose your beliefs and become the person you want to be. The past doesn't equal the future, unless you live there. My beliefs are different now from what they were when I was depressed in school because I changed my beliefs. I am completely different than who I was during that time, and I am so grateful that I changed. Life is more enjoyable, more fun, and more fulfilling. It's all about aligning with beliefs that empower you.

Beliefs can be the fuel that drives the engine behind our goals, or they can become the very roadblocks that stop us. Without awareness of our beliefs, we either cannot define our goals clearly or our beliefs may hinder us from reaching them. Begin the awareness process now:

What is one empowering belief you have? (If you can't think of any, don't worry. I will show you how to create many empowering beliefs in the following chapters.)

_____

_____

How has that empowering belief helped you in achieving your goals?

_____

_____

Now, write down one disempowering belief.

_____

_____

How has this belief stopped you in the past?

_____

_____

What has this belief cost you?

_____

_____

Start to observe your own beliefs. Look at what your beliefs are, which ones serve your goals, and which ones hinder you. Understanding your beliefs and making them conscious is the first step. Beliefs are the roadmap underlying your decisions. Understanding your beliefs, shifting them, discarding outdated ones, and creating new ones—this is Emotional Fitness. Beliefs are the hidden force that drives every decision you make. Later we will train ourselves to eliminate negative and limiting beliefs and replace them with empowering beliefs.

Next, we'll look at goals. We'll explore how using Emotional Fitness combined with real action in the real world can help you succeed beyond your wildest dreams.

PART II

WHERE EMOTIONAL FITNESS GETS RESULTS

HOW TO CONQUER YOUR GOALS

When it is obvious that the goals cannot be reached, don't adjust the goals, adjust the action steps.

—CONFUCIUS

CHAPTER 7

GOALS:
SETTING THE GPS FOR SUCCESS

*Everyone has a **plan** until they
get punched in the mouth.*

—MIKE TYSON

Goals are where the rubber meets the road, where the training of Emotional Fitness gets you real results. Emotional Fitness is based inside of our minds and emotions. The only thing we can control is our own mind. How then do we transfer Emotional Fitness from our minds to the real world? The answer is *goals*. Goals give us a tool to measure our Emotional Fitness training. The more emotionally fit you are, the easier it becomes to accomplish your goals.

Goals are the ultimate test in your Emotional Fitness training because to accomplish any goal outside of your comfort zone, you are bound to meet some form of failure. What do you do when you fail? Do you give up or do you *step up*? Do you wake up every day with energy, focus, courage, commitment, determination, joy, excitement, passion, and love for your life as you work to accomplish your goals? Or did you hit snooze five times, run late for work, hate sitting in traffic, and spend most of your time wondering what if? "What if I had accomplished my goal? Would I still be here?" Most people don't cultivate and create empowering emotions daily because they don't have Emotional Fitness. The stronger your Emotional Fitness, the better you'll be able to navigate toward your goals, the faster you'll achieve them, and the more you'll enjoy life in the process. In the end, I want you to be able to get *real results* in the *real world* using the information in this book.

When I first started training my Emotional Fitness, I was happier than ever. Life was amazing. I felt purpose-driven, fulfilled, and happy beyond anything for the first time in years. People noticed a change in my attitude and asked what I was doing differently. I explained the basics of Emotional Fitness. Many brushed it off, saying either they'd heard something like it before, tried it once (half-heartedly) and failed, or didn't buy into the "positive thinking" BS. Of course, six months later, when I doubled my income while working less and bought my million-dollar dream beach house, people started to listen *and* take notes.

Emotional Fitness provides you with the mindset to find the best strategy, the mental fortitude to never give up no matter what happens, and the ability to handle failure over and over and over again until you accomplish your goals. Whatever goal you have, whether it's to get straight As, become a doctor, make a million dollars, start a business, lose ten pounds, have a healthy, loving relationship, be a great parent, or just be the best version of yourself, Emotional Fitness is the key.

GPS to Success

We talked a little about the GPS to Success in the first chapter. Here, we are going to go deeper into it. Each step along the way is important for success.

When I was younger, I was told, "Corey, you have to know exactly what you want in life. Set a clear, specific goal." I thought, *That makes sense.* It's similar to a GPS system on your phone or in your car. In order to get where you want to go, you have to type in an exact address. You have to set a destination. A goal is simply a destination for your life.

Before your GPS system can direct you to your destination, however, you have to know where your starting point is. A GPS system is no good if it doesn't show you the exact route from where you are to where you want to be. To identify where you are in life, use the exercise below called the Wheel of Life. Once you know **where you are** in life, you can create a path of success to achieve your goal and get to **where you want to be.**

For the purposes of this exercise, our wheel shown below contains eight sections that together make up your life as a whole. While you may say there are other parts to life, this encompasses most of them. If you need to add a section, feel free to do so; it's your life after all! This wheel is meant to measure how you see yourself in each area of life right now. It is not how you have lived your life in the past or how you hope to live it in the future, but how you are living right now. It's important to be honest with yourself about where you right now, because that is the only way you will be able to get to where you want to go in life.

WHEEL OF LIFE

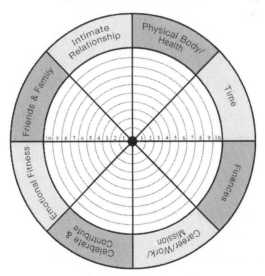

How to Complete the Wheel of Life

The levels for each area of life range from one to ten, with one being least satisfied and ten being completely satisfied. Draw a bold line across the level of the dotted line to determine where you see yourself within each area of the wheel. Then shade in the areas up to the bold line you created to see what shape your wheel comes out as and which areas you want to focus on. Below are a few thought prompters to help you determine your level of satisfaction within each area.

1. **Physical Body** – How physically healthy and energetic are you? Are you satisfied with your diet and your physical fitness level?

2. **Time**— How are you balancing your time and schedule? Do you feel satisfied with your time management skills? Are you able to effectively fit in everything without feeling stressed?

3. **Finances** – Are you generating enough income to meet your current needs? Do you feel financially secure? Are you setting yourself up for financial growth in the future? Do you experience financial freedom?

4. **Career/Work/Mission** – Do you work to just make money? Are you satisfied with your career? Is your career where you want it to be? Is your career in line with your life's mission?

5. **Celebrate & Contribute**—Do you feel like you are truly adding value to the lives of others? How much are you enjoying life? Do you have fun in life? Do you give back?

6. **Emotional Fitness**—Do you feel mentally and emotionally strong? Are you able to successfully handle the little bumps and big bumps life throws at you and still have a strong mindset to keep going forward? Do you feel good about yourself? Loved? Appreciated?

7. **Friends & Family**—Do you support your family, and do they support you? Are you satisfied with your relationships with your friends? Are you socializing enough to meet your needs?

8. **Intimate Relationship**—Are you satisfied with the amount of passion in your relationship? Are you expressing love? Do you feel loved?

Here's an example of a Wheel of Life that has been filled in:

WHEEL OF LIFE

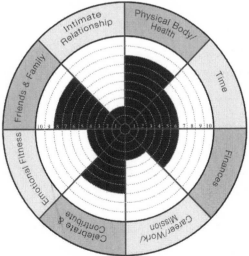

Notice how they filled in physical body, friends, and family with an eight out of ten. This person probably has great friendships, family, and spends a lot of time on their diet and exercise. But they either do not have an intimate relationship, or it is not a good one. They might make money in their career, but it might lack fulfillment or purpose. Knowing where you are now, at the start, allows you to create a road map to your goals. How does your wheel look?

My wheel is filled out, what now?

First, take a minute to appreciate your wheel. For any area you listed above an 8 or 9, congratulate yourself! For any that are not that high, do not get down on yourself. These areas are where you have room to grow, and it's important to check in on your wheel of life periodically, as it will change. There are times when my body feels like a nine and times it feels like a five. **This wheel is an easy tool to check in on your life and reassess what you need to focus on.** Once we know what areas we need to focus on the most, we can begin to take action.

Don't have an intimate relationship? Sign up for a dating website. Don't have a great physical body? Go to the gym. Don't have the finances you want? Work harder, save more, spend less, make a plan!

The Wheel of Life is a lot like the wheels on a car that *drives* you to your goal. The more unbalanced it is, the slower you have to drive, or you might crash and burn. The more balanced your wheel of life becomes, the stronger you become, and the faster you can achieve success in every area of life. But we can't just set any generic goal to achieve success. We have to be **clear** and **specific**.

Through my podcast, I've interviewed countless people who have unleashed success in their lives. Whether it was building a million or even a billion-dollar company, becoming a fitness champion, or cultivating the mindset to overcome anything, there was a formula for success that everyone followed—a recipe to conquer your goals.

THE 3 STEPS TO CONQUER YOUR GOALS

Step 1. Be specific about your goal and know your why.

Step 2. Find the best strategy and take massive action.

Step 3. Exercise Emotional Fitness.

Step 1- Setting Clear and Specific Goals

If you type California *into your GPS*, you could end up in Sacramento or San Diego, and they're eight hours apart! Being crystal **clear and specific** on exactly what you want is just like setting an exact destination. If you set an exact house number, street name, city, state, and zip code, you will eventually end up precisely where you want to be. Just like a GPS, when setting goals, it's important to know exactly what you want (destination) so that you can use the best strategy (route) to get there.

Often when I ask people about their goals, they say something like, "I just want to be happy" or "I want to make a lot of money" or "I want to be in good shape." The problem with these statements is that they are vague, and people define certain words differently. We need to get specific on exactly what has to happen, how many times it needs to happen, and how often you need it.

For the person who says, "I just want to be happy." What specifically does it mean for you to be happy? What exactly needs to happen for you to feel happy? And how often does that have to happen? If you want a lot of money, how much is "a lot" of money? Is it $10,000? $100,000? $1 million? If you want to be in good shape, what is "good" shape? Does that mean six-pack abs? Running a mile in under eight minutes? Having energy? Without specifics, you might end up far from your expectations of this goal. And when your expectations of what the goal *should give you* don't meet *your reality* of what you accomplish, you experience pain and unhappiness.

This happened to me. My expectations did not meet my reality and I experienced extreme unhappiness. When I was a kid, I wanted to be rich, have the freedom to be my own boss, and, of course, I wanted to be happy. I thought being an orthodontist was the best way to do this. But I wasn't happy, I wasn't rich, and I didn't have the freedom I thought I'd have. Happiness to me meant success and freedom, which I didn't have. Success to me was having millions of dollars, not being almost a million dollars in student loan debt. Freedom to me meant being able to make my own schedule, but I felt like a slave to my work, my patients, and my office. I thought my goal to be happy and rich would be accomplished if I just became an orthodontist. I wasn't clear enough when I defined what I wanted. I accomplished my goal of being an orthodontist, but because I did not clearly define what I truly wanted, my expectations of what accomplishing that goal looked like were drastically different than my reality. This led to a lot of heartache and confusion. Had I been clearer, I could have planned better to meet my true goals.

To properly define a goal, be crystal clear about what it is you want, how you want to get it, how much time it will take, and what you are willing to give in order to achieve it. Here are some examples:

Unclear: *I want to make more money.*

Clear: *I want to make $20,000 of passive income every month within the next two years. I am willing to work eighty hours a week, six days a week to build my business up so that I can achieve my goal.*

Unclear: *I want to lose weight.*

Clear: *I want to lose ten pounds in thirty days and have 10 percent body fat.*

There is power in clarity. The clearer you are, the easier it is to create an action plan to reach your goals.

Now, write down your goals. Remember, just by writing down your goals you are forty percent more likely to achieve them![26] Don't just write down goals you know you can achieve. I want you to write down what we call **stretch goals.** These are goals we don't yet know how to achieve, but by using Emotional Fitness, we can find a way to achieve them. I want you to dream big with your goals. Pretend you are like a kid writing to Santa. When you were a kid, you might have asked for a pony and a Ferrari in the same year without thinking about "how" you would get it. Emotional Fitness helps you figure out the "how." Don't limit yourself before you even get started! Be outrageous with your goals. The only limit is your imagination. Dream BIG! What do you want? A boat? A house on the beach? A career in music? To be the best athlete in the world? Cure cancer? Make a million dollars? Travel the world? What are your goals for each area of your Wheel of Life? What are your goals for your body, relationships, business, money, happiness, life? Now, create clear, specific goals. Be as specific as possible.

Goals List

Physical Body and Health Goals

_____

_____

_____

_____

_____

Time Goals

_____

_____

_____

_____

_____

Finance Goals

_____

_____

_____

_____

Career/Work/Mission Goals

_____

_____

_____

_____

_____

Celebrate/Contribute Goals

_____

_____

_____

_____

_____

Emotional Fitness Goals

_____

_____

_____

_____

Friends and Family Goals

_____

_____

_____

_____

_____

Intimate Relationship Goals

_____

_____

_____

_____

_____

All Other Goals

_____

_____

_____

_____

_____

Pick the top three goals you want to accomplish this year.

1. _____

2. _____

3. _____

What has stopped you from accomplishing these goals in the past?

_____

_____

_____

_____

_____

What belief has held you back from accomplishing your dreams?

_____

_____

_____

_____

What has NOT accomplishing these goals COST you in your life?

_____

_____

_____

_____

_____

For each of your top three goals, what is one action you can take TODAY to help you get closer to your goal?

Goal #1 Action) _____

Goal #2 Action) _____

Goal #3 Action) _____

"Why" Is the Fuel to Action

> *If you have a strong enough why, you can survive almost any how to get there.*
>
> —VIKTOR FRANKL

To get to your destination, you need fuel! Fuel comes from knowing y*our why* and being emotionally driven by it. If you are going to accomplish a goal, you have to know *why* you want that goal. **The stronger your *why*, the more willpower you will have.** Knowing your why and attaching strong emotions of pain and/or pleasure to that why becomes the fuel to take action, to keep pushing, and eventually get you to your destination of success.

Ask yourself about your goals. *Why is accomplishing this goal important to me?* For me, my goal began with creating financial freedom, making lots of money, and living the dream life. Later, as my goals changed, so did my *why*. I realized time and time again that money did not bring me happiness and that doing everything for myself when I was capable of helping others left me unfulfilled.

Thus, my *why* shifted. I wanted to:

- help my family live their best lives.

- help others alleviate their mental and emotional pain so they can live their best life.

- impact more people, be an inspiration, and empower others with the tools and knowledge to be successful in every area of life.

- help prevent suicide.

Knowing your *why* is especially important during difficult times. Your *why* can give you the fuel and the willpower to push forward no matter how hard life gets.

So, stop now and define your *why*. Write it down and begin to explore why you want what you want. Do you want that big promotion for financial security? For prestige? To impress your family? **Getting to the *why* provides you with the fuel you need to reach a goal.** Stop now and find your *why* now.

Pick your top three goals and write down your why for each one.

Goal #1 _____

Why _____

_____

Goal #2 _____

Why _____

_____

Goal #3 _____

Why _____

_____

If you are struggling to find your why, one exercise is to take a piece of paper and write down thirty reasons why you want to accomplish a goal. Not all of your reasons have to be huge, important whys—just don't stop writing until you reach thirty reasons. Then circle your favorite. I'm sure you will find a few that motivate you. Sometimes people are motivated by one why when they start working toward a goal, but now that why has changed, or the goal has. It is important to **review your why and *reconnect* with it as needed**, to make sure you stay motivated. If the why doesn't drive you anymore, change it. No one said it had to stay the same.

Not everyone is massively driven by a positive *why*. Remember, the pain-pleasure principle is what directs your motivation. So why not use your biology to your advantage! In tough times, when I'm struggling to get motivated, I focus on why *not* accomplishing my goals will cause me significant pain. I envision what life will be like in one year, five years, and ten years if I don't accomplish my goal. I feel so much pain in that future, so I bring that forward into my current reality. The pain of not accomplishing my goals is so great that it drives me in the here and now. It reminds me that our time is limited, that I only have one life. It gives me fuel because I know that if I don't take action now, then in six months, a year, or five years, that future pain will become my present reality. My dad used to always say, "This is not a dress rehearsal for another life. Make each and every day count."

For me, the *why not* of accomplishing the goal of writing this book would cause me pain because I believe that if people learned this information, suicide would never be an option. Depression would disappear. As someone who has been in tough, dark times, I know life can be difficult. Sadly, I've seen suicide take the lives of many people. Life is such a gift, and I want everyone to enjoy it. It breaks my heart thinking that someone would want to end theirs, and I know that if they read this book, they can have the tools to turn their life around. That pain of not sharing my message to the world, or not helping someone, was sometimes all the reminder I needed to get back on track and take action.

Start writing to find your *why not*. What is a goal, that if you don't accomplish it, will cause you pain in a year or five years? What's a *why not* when it comes to accomplishing your goals that might motivate you? If you didn't accomplish your goals, would it upset you if you looked into the future and saw yourself in five years stuck in a place you don't want to be? Write it out. Use this potential negative future as a *why* to motivate you.

Write down why not accomplishing your goals will cause you pain in the future:

_____

_____

OK, so you have this clear, specific goal. You know your *why* and your *why nots*. You're pumped. You're motivated. Now, what do you do? Having a goal and accomplishing it are two different things. As I grew older, I noticed that some people were more successful than others, even though each had the same goal. What was the difference?

In the next chapter, we'll discuss the next two steps in the formula for accomplishing your goals: **Step 2.** Find your best strategy and take massive action, and **Step 3.** Exercise Emotional Fitness.

CHAPTER 8

GOALS:
HOW EMOTIONAL FITNESS HELPS
YOU ACHIEVE GOALS FASTER

*Take the first step in faith. You don't have to see
the whole staircase, just take the first step.*

—Dr. Martin Luther King Jr.

When you enter your destination into the GPS, what do you see?
Multiple routes! Some are faster than others, and some are better.
You want the best route to success. And to find that best route,
you have to have the best strategy. If only you had an exact recipe
to lose weight, build a business, become an entrepreneur, or make
money. If only you had the best strategy, then how could you *not*
be successful?

In the previous chapter, we discussed Step 1, setting specific
goals and getting to the why. Now let's move on to Step 2 in the
formula for success.

Step 2: Find Your Best Strategy and Take Massive Action

How do you find a great strategy? There are hundreds of thousands of strategies available to all of us. Whatever you're looking
to accomplish, whether in business, relationships, or your health,
so much free information exists on strategies in books, on blogs,

on YouTube, on podcasts, and all over the internet. You can contact someone you know who is already doing what you want to do. Find a mentor or a coach. Every successful person I have ever met or interviewed has always had a mentor. Whether in business or relationships or fitness, they find someone who has dedicated their life to be the best, and then they follow their advice. It's just like when someone hires a trainer at the gym to lose weight or a CEO hires a business coach to accelerate their financial success. Mentorship and modeling work the best. Successful people want to share their information. They're just like you. They've worked their way up. Reach out to them, ask them questions, and follow their advice. If one strategy doesn't work out, be resourceful and reroute to find the best strategy.

What strategy is best for you? Take your goal and begin to research options. Start writing it out. Find books on the subject, Google it, and watch YouTube channels. Find someone doing what you want to do, interview them, and write down their advice. Follow it.

The 80/20 Rule

Create an action plan for your goals. One of the best strategies I use for goal accomplishment is the 80/20 rule. The 80/20 rule is also known as the Pareto principle. Vilfredo Pareto was an Italian economist who noted that 80 percent of the land in Italy was owned by 20 percent of the population. But this rule applies to even more things in life. For example, Microsoft noted that by fixing the top 20 percent of the most-reported bugs, 80 percent of the related errors and crashes would be eliminated. In sports, 20 percent of the exercises would have 80 percent of the desired impact. And when striving to accomplish our goal the 80/20 rule holds true, as well. Remember, **80 percent of our results come from 20 percent of our actions**. An example of this in fitness is simply removing all sugar from your diet and running on the treadmill for 45 minutes first thing in the morning. If you change nothing else but these two things, you are going to lose weight. No fancy meal plan needed, just simple and powerful actions. When creating your action plan, you want to focus on the 20 percent of actions that will give the biggest results. One of the easiest ways to find the right actions to take is to ask someone who has done it before and see what worked for them! These 20 percent actions that get you the most results create your **Power Action Plan**. A Power Action Plan is a plan to get you the biggest results toward your goal. Want to become the lead salesperson? Maybe a power action plan is to go interview the top three salespeople in your company on exactly what they do. Now, follow their advice exactly, and show up to work an hour early and stay an hour later. These are simple daily actions you can take to instantly get bigger results. What is your Power Action Plan for each goal? Write it down.

POWER ACTION PLAN

_____

_____

_____

_____

_____

Still, even with all of the strategies out there, how many of you know someone who wants to lose weight and doesn't do it? Wants to save money, but can never seem to hold onto it? They could find a million strategies online, and still they struggle to succeed. In fact, they often fail. That's because knowing the *best* strategy is not enough. Knowledge alone is not power. Action is. You have to take real action to get real results. And the more action you take, the more likely you are to achieve your goals.

Even when you have a strategy, taking massive action can lead to success, but it doesn't guarantee it.

As human beings, we can survive almost anything. Our brains have evolved and are literally designed to make us survive. Surviving and succeeding, though, are two very different things.

And that leads me to the final step in accomplishing your goals. It's what this entire book is about. It's how to go from merely surviving to succeeding.

Step 3: Exercise Emotional Fitness

Failure is part of the process to success. On your path to success, when your GPS hits an obstacle, what do you do? Do you turn around and go home? Do you sit in your car without moving? No. Your GPS reroutes you. What do you do when you fail in achieving your goals? Do you give up or do you get rerouted?

Emotional Fitness gives you the ability to handle failure and reroute yourself to success.

The aim of every goal is to either give you a feeling of pleasure—happiness, pride, importance, love, or success—or to help you avoid a negative feeling—disappointment, anger, sadness, stress, or fear. Emotions are the fuel that drives us to our goals and the very reasons we stop trying. Emotional Fitness gives you the resourcefulness to always find a way to keep going. It gives you unlimited emotional fuel.

How many obstacles can you hit before you give up? Because on the path to success, you will fail. And it sucks. It hurts. It's downright painful. No matter how far life kicks you down, even if you lose everything, if you have Emotional Fitness, you will not only survive, you will succeed. And that is why this book is dedicated to learning about Emotional Fitness, how it can improve your life, and how training in it will improve your ability to accomplish your goals. The road to achieving your goals is a straight line, right? Wrong! The road to success often looks like this: three steps forward, five back, two forward, six back, and now you wait.

ROAD TO SUCCESS

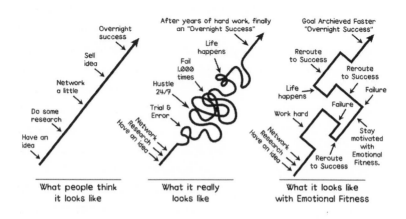

With Emotional Fitness, the road to success is smoother, faster, and better. You quickly reroute to get you back to the path of success. With Emotional Fitness, you not only get back on track quicker, but you also have the ability to redefine how success is even possible. This all starts by shifting your beliefs about what you can achieve.

Raising the BAR

Growing up, my parents would tell me, "Corey, if you work hard enough, you can achieve anything you want." They told me this often enough that I truly believed it. *That single belief has led me to get incredible results.* From this belief, I became the MVP on my football team, graduated high school as valedictorian, and went to dental school. It is a belief that, to this day, empowers me to accomplish my goals. **If you want to get better results, you have to raise the BAR.**

BAR is an acronym for Beliefs, Actions, and Results. The results we achieve are a direct correlation to the amount of action we take. If you want to get better results, you have to take more action. However, the amount of action, the quality of action, the variation of that action, and the intensity of that action is directly influenced by your beliefs about *what you think is possible.* Let's examine these in reverse order to truly see the power of beliefs.

The results we get are usually based on the amount of action we take. And yet, most people struggle to get the results they want in life even when they *feel* like they are doing everything they can. They *think* they are taking all the action they *believe* is possible. But what happens if your belief about what you can do changes? Is that possible? How does that affect your actions?

In 1952, Australian runner John Landy tried to break the four-minute mile. He tried and tried. Over the course of two years, Landy ran the following times: 4:02.1, 4:02.6, 4:02.8, 4:02.5, 4:02.7, and 4:02.3. He just couldn't break it no matter how hard he tried.

Landy was interviewed and said, "Frankly, I think the four-minute mile is beyond my capabilities. Two seconds may not sound much, but to me, it's like trying to break through a brick wall. Someone may achieve the four-minute mile the world is wanting so desperately, but I don't think I can."[23] Those were key words to describe his *belief* at the time. His beliefs weren't wrong. In fact, they were backed up by science! Doctors and scientists at the time said it was physically impossible to run a mile in less than four minutes. They thought it was even physically dangerous and that someone attempting to do it might even *die.* Any logical person would *believe* that this feat was impossible.

Enter Roger Bannister, a British medical student and long-time runner who was in medical school at Oxford studying neurology. Every day, he visualized himself running and breaking the four-minute mile. He knew his goal intensely and had a strong why. He used visualization of his goal to build his belief that he could run a four-minute mile.

On May 6, 1954, Bannister was set to run for the Amateur Athletic Association in Oxford against other runners from the university in their annual match. The conditions were less than ideal; it was wet, and the wind was against him. But Bannister decided this was it. If he didn't break the four-minute mile now, he *believed* Landy would beat him to it. As he came around the last corner, he gave everything he had to finish the race. He ran a record time of 3:59.4. He set a new world record.[24] He defied science. He defied what others believed was even possible.

Still don't think beliefs matter? Later that month, Landy—who swore he could not break the four-minute mile—did so, beating Bannister's record by less than a second. After seeing Roger Bannister break the four-minute mile, the man who thought he couldn't do it suddenly *believed it was possible.*

Within three years after Bannister broke the first four-minute mile, seventeen other people around the world broke it too, all because they now believed it was possible. That is the power of *belief* and how it can help you accomplish your goals. If you believe you can achieve something, you will take every possible action to get the result you want. If you believe you will achieve it no matter what, you will do whatever it takes, for however long it takes, to get the result you want. That is the power of raising the BAR and how Emotional Fitness can change the results you achieve in life.

Action vs. Distraction

When we're setting a goal or when we're on the path to achieving it, we either choose to take action toward our goals or distraction away from them. Distraction can be dinner with friends, partying, email, social media, or Netflix. I'm not saying to give all of this up, but if you are not achieving what you want in life, you need to **choose action over distraction.**

When working toward our goals, there are two main emotions that drive us to action or distraction: fear and faith. I know there are a lot of high achievers out there who say, "I'm not afraid of anything." But fear can come in many different forms and be used under many different names. You might use words like *nervous, worried, uncomfortable,* or *stressed* instead. Faith, too, can also be confidence, belief, or even simply, *I think I can.*

Fear Versus Faith Loop

When we're thinking about our goals, many of us get caught in what I call the fear versus faith loop. Imagine you're on a racetrack contemplating whether you can accomplish your goals or not. Your mind spins from one extreme to the other. First, you've got faith you can do it, but then fear kicks in saying you can't do it. *I'm afraid I might not be good enough. But if I work hard maybe I can do it. No, I can't, I don't know where to start. Maybe I can find someone to help.*

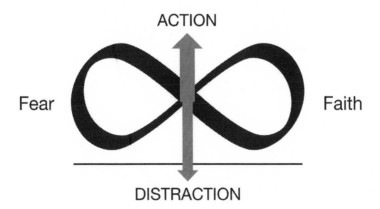

Fear vs. Faith Loop

ACTION

Fear   Faith

DISTRACTION

There are two ways out of this crazy back and forth loop: One is to go down into the world of inaction and distraction and let fear override faith. The other is to **have faith and take action**. When in the fear versus faith loop and it's driving you nuts, take action and the loop will disappear. You could fail, but it's not a failure, it's a result. You can improve on it and get better. Even the smallest action will break the loop.

We don't always use the word fear. We may use softer words such as:

- Discomfort

- Stress

- Worry

- Frustration

- Doubt

You might say "I don't think that will work." Or, "I'm just not good enough to that." Do any of these words sound familiar? What words do you use when you doubt yourself or your ability to accomplish your goals?

Faith, too, can come in many forms:

- Faith in self

- Faith in God

- Confidence

- "I believe I can."

- "I think I can do that."

- "It's possible."

Do any of these words sound familiar? What do you use when you pump yourself up and take action toward your goals?

Let's say your goal is to earn a million dollars in sales next year. On the track, you'll ride from faith to fear until you choose action or distraction to get out of the loop. At first, you might say, "I can do this. Other people have done it before. It's possible!" And then fear comes in and says, "You have no idea what you are doing. You will fail in front of everyone!" And then you start freaking out and look for someone who has done it before to ask them what their strategy is. Except then your fear comes back and goes, "Wait, they might not give me their strategy. They might think I'm not smart enough or good enough!" Eventually, you may turn on the TV, call a friend, scroll through social media, or crack a beer—anything to forget about your goal in the *delusion of distraction*.

This is why being Emotionally Fit is so important in accomplishing your goals. Do your emotions control you, or do you control them? Does fear paralyze you, or does it drive you? Do you use your emotions to your advantage?

Know that you can use fear to your advantage. Fear can be the fuel that drives you. By focusing on the fear of *not* accomplishing our goals, you can often get a quick boost of motivation. Why? Because your desire to avoid pain is often greater than your desire for pleasure. Of course, in the long term, you have to be working towards pleasure or else why would you do it in the first place?

We are all Emotionally Fit at something in our lives. You get in an argument and bite your tongue instead of lashing out in anger. You lose a sale but focus on what you did right instead of what you did wrong.

What we need for success is consistent Emotional Fitness because life won't stop throwing punches. Stress, fear, worry, frustration, regret, guilt, rejection—these are all emotions that can stop us from achieving our goals. We let these emotions occupy our minds, attention, energy, and focus. While these emotions can empower you to take action, most people get "stuck" in them and quickly reach for any distraction they can find just to feel better in the moment. If you are struggling to achieve your goals in life, you need Emotional Fitness. If you want to feel more confident, more focused, happier, healthier, and more fulfilled along the way, you need Emotional Fitness. Having a bad day? A bad month? Emotional Fitness gives you the ability to control how you feel at any moment so you can be your best self all the time.

We have to train our Emotional Fitness. We must train our emotions like we train for our jobs and like we train in the gym. **The mind, like any muscle when trained, gets stronger, and when ignored, becomes weak.** In the coming chapters, we give the mental and emotional exercises to strengthen your Emotional Fitness. Each day you do the mental "reps," you get stronger. By looking at what we focus on, what things mean, and the actions we take, we can train our minds. And it goes deeper by going into how to shift our habits, behaviors, and beliefs, so that we can ultimately live our dreams.

Remember, we have to take real action to get real results. **Because in life, what you give you get to keep, and what you fail to give, you lose forever.**

Now it's time to train yourself and use Emotional Fitness to conquer your goals, no matter what obstacles appear. It's time to strengthen your Emotional Fitness to become stronger every day, and when life punches you in the mouth, when you hit a roadblock on the path to success, you don't give up. Instead, you *step up*, take action, and unleash success. It's time to train your Emotional Fitness.

PART III

EMOTIONAL FITNESS MASTERY

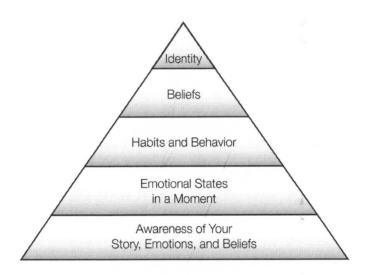

The Emotional Fitness Pyramid of Mastery

In the first part of this book, we focused on awareness of our emotions. In the second part, we set some real goals to achieve. Now it's time to train our Emotional Fitness and become our best to reach our goals.

Just like anything in life, there are stages of mastery. Each stage is represented in the Emotional Fitness Pyramid of Mastery. In order to move up the pyramid, you must first build a foundation at each level. The stronger your foundation is, the faster and easier it is to master Emotional Fitness. Each stage builds upon the next to give you true mastery.

In order to master Emotional Fitness, we first had to learn what we didn't know we didn't know—that's *awareness*. Throughout the first half of this book, we spent a significant amount of time building our awareness, understanding emotions, exploring our stories, discovering the basic principles of why we do what we do, and understanding how all of this affects our goals, dreams, and, ultimately, our lives.

Now we learn *how* to train our emotions step by step. We start with how to manage yourself in a single moment. Once you master Emotional Fitness in a single moment, you have built the foundation for managing many moments, which are also known as habits and behaviors.

Underlying every action, habit, and behavior is your belief system. You can resolve conflicting beliefs and get rid of disempowering ones, leaving you with strong empowering beliefs that help you live the life of your dreams. Yes, this can be trained.

Finally, the top of the Emotional Fitness Pyramid of Mastery is identity: who you are at your core. Most people never take the time to learn what they value in life, or they say they value one thing, but their actions say different. For example, someone might say they value family, but then they spend most of their time focused on work. In this section, we break down the core components of what makes up your character, and we align your beliefs and values, so that you can design your life instead of reacting to it. This is the hardest and most powerful aspect of Emotional Fitness, but it's also the most profound and fulfilling. Once you master this pyramid, you master the world.

Instead of trying to figure out every aspect of your life—relationships, health, career, money, etc.—why not master the fundamental skill that will take care of everything: Emotional Fitness. After Emotional Fitness, everything else just becomes easier.

CHAPTER 9

SHIFTING EMOTIONAL
STATES IN THE MOMENT:
THE POWER OF FOCUS

*I have looked in the mirror every morning and asked
myself: "If today were the last day of my life, would
I want to do what I am about to do today?" And
whenever the answer has been "No" for too many
days in a row, I know I need to change something.*

—STEVE JOBS

In business, it's not only appropriate but expected that managers supervise the people under them to ensure they succeed. Business managers oversee their employees and check in on whether they're late for work, taking too long of a break, or making their sales goals. Just like business managers, we need to check in on our emotions, and then devise actions to correct situations. We, too, need to be the manager of our emotions.

In order to manage anything, you must measure it. Once you measure something, you can create a baseline to make adjustments. It is important to check in with your emotions regularly. What is the state of your emotions right now? Are you in a focused state? Motivated? Sad? Happy? Afraid? Wanting more out of life? In limbo? Numb? Uncertain? Do you want more but feel like you don't have it?

Are you managing what you're feeling right now? We call this ability to manage whatever emotional state you're in **emotional-state management**. This is the ability to switch between emotions like sadness and happiness, fear and relief, anger and excitement, and stress and motivation.

If something feels off with me, or with any situation going on in my life, I used to go no more than three days without stopping and checking in with my feelings. I picked this up from Steve Jobs. I picked three days at first but then decided, *Why wait three days? Why spend days in a negative state until I check in?* When I started checking in daily, even hourly, to manage my state, my Emotional Fitness really elevated my life. Now, at any single moment when I am in a negative state, I use Emotional Fitness to get out of it. The key here is to train your Emotional Fitness *before* you get into that state so that you are better equipped to get out of it.

How do you check in with your emotions? First, bring awareness to your emotional state. What emotion are you feeling right now? Then, take whatever emotion you're feeling and rank it on a scale of 1 to 10. What are you feeling? Anger? Focus? Lazy or uninspired? Motivated? Give it a number from 1 to 10.

These measurements are subjective, but by doing this on a daily basis, you can establish a baseline and begin to see patterns. You can begin to *manage* your emotions. Will some days be different than others? Of course. You might have happiness at a 10 one day and 1 the next. We want to figure out *how* we can shift these emotions to get you to feel what you want when you want it.

Emotional state management is especially important because emotions can often override rational thinking. As we mentioned previously, *emotional hijacking* is when our emotions hijack our brain in a moment and can take over all rational thinking. Fear and anger are strong emotional hijackers. Fear has caused people to lose all wits about them in a panic. People who have rehearsed for hundreds of hours for a play suffer from stage fright and freeze despite knowing exactly what to do next. Rage, too, is all too common. Think of people who suffer from road rage. If someone cuts them off, they curse every third word.

When we don't stop emotions from hijacking the brain, it leads to an *emotional blackout*. This occurs when you have completely lost control of your emotions in the moment. By the time you regain control, you're left asking, "How did that happen? I have no idea why I got so upset. I just saw red." The circuitry of your brain was hijacked, and your emotions blacked out any logical thinking until you calmed down. You see this all the time with rage, fear, and even stress, worry, and anxiety. People get themselves so worked up that they go around and around, worrying and stressing about what they have to do, what's expected of them, what they should do, what might go wrong, and what will go wrong. Before they know what's happened, they're having a meltdown. Some people meltdown by crying, while others yell at the top of their lungs.

How do you stop an emotional hijack or an emotional blackout? How do you change your emotional state in a single moment? Remember focus, meaning, action: what you focus on, the meaning you give it, and your reaction or action in response to it. This process is not a one-way street. Each filter can and does affect the way the other filters function.

There are two main ways to change the emotions you feel and the meaning of an experience. **You can change what you're focusing on, or you can change what actions you're taking**. In order to master Emotional Fitness, you must first master your emotions in a single moment. Then you can build upon that foundation.

State Management in a Moment

We all manage our state in a moment at times and can change our emotional state. Let me give you an example of how fast you can change your emotions in an instant. I have two sisters: Shaina, who is eighteen months younger than me, and Carli, who is eleven years younger. I am very lucky to have an amazing relationship with both of them. It was not always like this for Shaina and me. During our teenage years, we fought—as siblings often do— over the most ridiculous stuff, like who was supposed to do the dishes or take out the trash. Over time, we grew so annoyed with each other that any little comment was perceived negatively and triggered a fight. It was like having a sunburn. When your skin is normal, you can slap it hard and it barely stings. With a sunburn, a simple slap on the back can bring agonizing, instant pain. We were experiencing an *emotional sunburn* in our relationship. Have you ever had an emotional sunburn with a family member, friend, or significant other, where anything they say instantly annoys the hell out of you?! This is why training our Emotional Fitness daily is so important, to prevent and even heal an emotional sunburn.

One time, Shaina, my mom, and I were at the mall. We were maybe ten and eight years old. We were having fun, but one smart-ass comment later, we were at each other's throats. My mom was talking on the phone and noticed us arguing. *Instantly, her state changed*. My mom is an amazingly optimistic and positive woman, but we'd pushed her to her limits. Her state changed quickly from happily shopping to deep frustration as she angrily asked us what our fight was about. Instantly, my sister and I changed our states from arguing to obedient silence. We said nothing but "Sorry, Mom." We knew that saying anything else would get us grounded. We shifted our states to calm, behaved, and focused on not getting into trouble. Then my mom also quickly changed her state. She turned back around and quickly went back to being happy and optimistic.

When my mother turned away, expecting us to stop, I wanted one last stab at my sister. Behind my mom's back, I made a disgusted face and stuck out my tongue at my sister. My sister's state changed from controlling her emotions to outright rage and fury. My sister is one badass. Even at eight years old, you didn't want to mess with her. She yelled at me. My mom turned around and *again* her state shifted unpleasantly as she went from happily shopping to fury. "What happened?!" My sister and I both shifted into fear of what might happen next. My sister pointed at me. My mom looked at her and yelled, "What did Corey do?" Instead of saying what I'd done, Shaina showed her by making a disgusted face and sticking her tongue out. My mom incorrectly perceived this as complete disrespect to her and slapped my sister in the face.

Shaina's state shifted from anger to fear to pain to sadness to tears. My state went from fear to amusement to guilt to regret. My mom's state went from happy to infuriated to shock to fear to horror to guilt to regret to sadness. Our mother had never in her life slapped us, even on the bottom. We had pushed her past her edge like we had never seen before. *I* had pushed her past her edge. I never meant for it to happen, but it was my fault. Due to errors in judgment, what we focused on, and our emotions, we took actions that weren't the best. We laugh about this story now. And it's a great example of how *fast* we can change our emotions in an instant, even as kids, from happy to sad, angry to happy, scared to amused, and angry to sad.

We have all been able to change our emotional states suddenly at some point in our lives. We do it all the time without even thinking about it. Maybe you're having an argument with your spouse and the phone rings. You change your state from anger to calmness as you pick up the phone. Let's say it's your boss. You want your boss to view you as happy, a good worker, and dependable. You change your mood even more. You change your voice, your behavior, your language. Everything. In a moment. "Hey John!" you happily answer.

We all have the ability to control our emotional states. This ability is learnable, trainable, and grows with effort and experience. Let's talk about managing your emotional state in that one moment. Managing your emotional state in a moment is a lot less overwhelming than trying to do it every day for the rest of your life. If you can manage it in one moment, you can manage it in another moment, and another. And you can build on that.

Understanding that you can shift your emotional state in a moment will help you realize that you're not stuck, and your emotions are not set in concrete. You can and do shift them all the time. In these moments, you don't overcomplicate things with labels and analytics, you just do.

Even with long-term ruts, you're still shifting all the time. You say you're always depressed. You tell everyone you're depressed all the time. You use the word daily, hourly. But sometimes you laugh, right? What about when you laugh? Are you depressed then?

"OK," you might respond, "when I laugh, I'm not depressed." So, you're not *always* depressed then, right? You've defined yourself as *always* depressed. But now you see that sometimes you're not. Knowing this means you *do* shift your emotions, you *can* shift them, and you *can* manage them.

Now that you know it is possible to change your emotional state immediately. I want to show you it's easy and that you can see instant results.

How do you change your state in a moment? You've got to interrupt it, then shift it. This is where the fun begins. These are your exercises to become Emotionally Fit in a moment. In the gym, we do "reps," or repetitions, to train our muscles. In life, we use repetition to learn in school or at our jobs. Each time you do an Emotional Fitness exercise, think of it as one repetition or rep. The more reps you do, the stronger you get. The more consistent you are, the better you become.

Shift Focus in a Moment

Imagine you come home after a long day of work and you just want to relax. The house, however, is a mess. No one has taken out the trash, and there are dishes in the sink. Every time you come home, you feel like you have to clean up after other people. You're so angry. You say to yourself, "Why don't they clean up after themselves? Why can't they just put their own clothes away, wash their own dishes, and pick up their own stuff? If everyone took care of themselves, we would never have this problem!"

The first step toward change is to ask yourself, "What am I feeling?" You're upset. Next step. How can you shift your focus? What else can you focus on? How can you change your perception of this external experience? Is there a way to shift your perspective? If you always end up cleaning the house anyway, why not make it a positive experience? If you don't, each week resentment and anger will build until you explode at your friends or family instead of dealing with it.

The Power of Questions

One of the most powerful ways to shift your focus in a moment is through questions. This happens all the time: someone interrupts a conversation with "Do you know what time it is?" or "What are you guys doing this weekend?" You answer them and then say, "What were we talking about again?" Your focus was completely taken away by this question and you couldn't even remember what you were thinking about before the question.

Our minds are constantly filled with thoughts. Most of these thoughts consist of a series of questions and answers:

Q: "What am I going to do today?"

A: "I think I'll go to the gym, then hit the beach."

Q: "What should I eat for dinner?"

A: "Pizza."

Q: "I wonder if I should start a diet?"

A: "Maybe tomorrow."

Q: "Am I really smart enough to start my own business?"

A: "I don't know. I don't have any experience."

Q: "Is there a way to learn how to start a business?"

A: "Google and courses."

Q: "Will my idea even work?"

A: "I have no clue, and I don't have the money to start it."

You might be asking yourself, *Is this really how my brain works?* Did you just ask yourself that question? And what's the answer? Yes. It is. Thinking is a series of questions and answers.

The important thing to understand here is that **the quality of our questions determines the quality of our answers.** When you change your questions to more empowering questions, you begin to allow yourself the opportunity to answer with better, more empowering, thoughts and actions, and this will improve your life. Shifting your focus starts with asking yourself better questions. Instead of asking, "Why do I always screw things up?" you can shift your focus. Immediately, your brain responds, "Because you don't want what you're doing!" Instead, ask, "What can I do to make sure things go as planned?" Now your brain searches and responds with an empowering answer such as, "I can write down everything I need to do in a checklist to make sure I don't forget anything important." Or if something did not go according to plan, you can ask, "What can I learn from this so that I don't make the same mistake next time?" And your brain says, "Don't forget to make a checklist!"

How can you change your focus? Ask yourself what you want to feel. Calm? Focused? Peaceful? Courageous? What can you do to shift something that angers or frightens you? Ask yourself better questions. First ask yourself, **"What *else* can I focus on?"** What you focus on becomes your reality. When you change your perspective in life by shifting your focus, you begin to change everything.

Focus is one of the most powerful tools that we have at our disposal. The ability to direct our attention and energy toward something we *choose* creates a profound shift. If you choose to focus on what's wrong with every situation, you will find negativity in everything. If you choose to focus on what's right in every situation, you will find positivity in everything. We all have a friend who always finds something to complain about: the coffee is cold, this place would be better if it had music, it's too hot and sunny, it's too cold, the grass is too tall. And then we know someone who focuses on the good, no matter what. They are always a ray of sunshine—grateful for life, and enjoying every moment. In life, you can choose a perspective that disempowers you and focus on the problems, the obstacles, and the reasons why you can't achieve your goals. Or you can choose to focus on a perspective that empowers you and one that provides solutions, opportunities, and ways to succeed.

Below is a list of disempowering questions that you should eliminate from your mind (their empowering counterparts appear later in this chapter):

1. Why do I always fail at everything?
2. Why can't I ever catch a break?
3. Why do I always miss out on the fun stuff?
4. Why can't I afford to buy a nice car?
5. Why don't I have what I want in life?
6. Why don't those people like me?
7. Why can't I make more money?
8. Why can't I find true love?
9. Why can't I ever lose weight?

Common answers include:

1. You're not good enough.
2. You're not smart enough.
3. You're lazy.
4. No one loves you.
5. You don't have the experience, tools, resources or money.
6. You're a failure.

Instead of focusing on what you can't control, focus on what you can control. What's wrong will always be there, but what's right is always there too. You might as well look for the good in the situation. You're not ignoring the bad; you're just not wasting your time, energy, and attention on things you have no control over. Instead of focusing on everything that's wrong, focus on what's right.

In fact, shifting focus to be more optimistic has shown to improve people's abilities to accomplish their goals and get the results they want. In an article for the *New York Times* in 1987, Daniel Goleman wrote about the work of Dr. Martin Seligman, a psychologist at the University of Pennsylvania, who conducted research studies on pessimism. "Seligman found that new salesmen who were by nature optimists sold 37 percent more insurance in their first two years on the job than did pessimists. And during the first year, the pessimists quit at twice the rate of the optimists."[25]

That is 37 percent more sales, meaning more money was earned in the real world, all because people shifted their focus to be more optimistic.

Here is a list of questions that can help shift your focus to empower you:

1. What can I learn from this failure so that I can improve and get a better result next time?
2. What can I do so that I'm fully prepared when opportunities arise?
3. How can I create more fun in my life today?
4. How can I find a way to afford the car I love?
5. How can I be resourceful to achieve what I want in life?
6. Where can I meet people who are like-minded to spend time with?
7. How can I become a more valued professional to earn more money?
8. How can I become a person worthy of finding true love?
9. What actions can I take today to start my weight-loss plan?

The disempowering questions in the first list often keep us stuck, spinning our wheels, and distracted, and can cause us emotional discomfort or even pain. Instead, we can ask better questions from the second list, which will empower us to take action.

Questions help *re*direct your focus. You can ask, "What *else* can I focus on that empowers me?" Then ask yourself another empowering question to take action.

When I was driving back and forth to San Diego for work, it would take me three hours a day. I hated that commute. I focused on the bad traffic, hating going to work, and being upset at people cutting me off or driving too slowly. Then I asked myself, "What else can I focus my energy and attention on to make this commute better?" It was a much more empowering question that allowed me to shift my focus, and instead of listening to music, I listened to audiobooks. I love learning, so those three-hour drives became my time to absorb knowledge and better myself. I started to learn so much. I even started to look forward to driving to work. Today, I no longer have that commute, but by shifting my focus, I changed my entire experience from miserable to enjoyable.

Do you focus on being grateful? Or do you focus on what's wrong? **Do you focus on what you can control or what you cannot control?** Do you focus on what's right and good or only on what's wrong? Remember, our brains are designed by nature to focus on what's wrong to help us survive in the wild. While always focusing on what's wrong used to keep us alive, it doesn't help us live happy and successful lives. What's wrong in any situation will always be there for you to find, and if you focus on that, that's all you'll see. And what's right or good in any situation will be there too, if only you choose to focus on it.

How to Find the Good Even in the Worst Pain

My aunt died from cancer when I was a teenager. I had an uncle who died from cirrhosis of the liver, and another uncle who died from failed heart surgery after a life of obesity. My grandmother passed away from a massive stroke. One of my grandfathers died on the operating table after his aorta burst during heart surgery. Another grandfather died after ten years in a wheelchair, heart surgeries, and a pacemaker—eventually, his body couldn't survive any longer. The pain is real. The anger, the sadness, the loss is all real.

We all have suffered a loss. We've all seen how two people can react completely differently to the death of a loved one. One person is triggered, hopeless, and frightened, and the other believes that life is precious and from that day forward they must live life to the fullest.

I once interviewed Johnathon E. Stone, a Navy Chief Petty Officer, whose wife, Sara, died at the tender age of twenty-nine from a rare form of appendix cancer. They had four kids. Throughout their lives together, they'd fought adversity by focusing on the good. When she was diagnosed with cancer, they made a promise to each other to focus on the good, and to find something to smile about morning and night. No matter how bad the chemotherapy, they found the good.

They even turned Sara's treatment into something to celebrate. During the chemotherapy sessions, the kids couldn't be around. It was the only time Sara and Johnny had alone time together. The sessions were tiring, painful, and scary, but they didn't focus on that. Instead, they chose to re-label and reframe the experience. Instead of it just being chemotherapy, they decided to turn it into a special date for the two of them. They called the sessions their "chemo dates." It became something that they could look forward to instead of something they dreaded.

Johnny also told me about the day they found out the cancer had spread to her entire body. Devastated, they decided to focus on something else. The scan of her brain had come back negative, which meant that the cancer was not in her brain. To them, that was good news, and they chose to focus on that instead. Toward the end, when they knew she didn't have long, they still found the good. They found something special each and every day by asking one simple but powerful question: "What is good about this?"

Sara Stone died in Jonny's arms at the young age of twenty-nine, but her spirit lives on as he tells her story to spread positivity and inspiration.

We must all live life to the fullest because we never know when it will end. We must focus on what we can control, not on what we can't. We must ask better questions to shift our focus in a moment. Ask better questions and get better answers.

Start to become aware of, and write down how often, you ask disempowering questions: *Why did this happen to me? Why do I always fail? What's wrong with me?* Watch how often we answer these questions is with disempowering statements: *Because I'm not good enough. Because I'm not smart enough. Because life is against me.*

Make a conscious effort to change your questions. This is the primary tool for shifting your focus in a moment. *What's good about this situation? What can I learn? What did I do well?*

It takes practice to shift from disempowering to empowering questions. And every time you go out of your comfort zone, fear of the unknown will kick in, and you might regress. So, you have to train every day to ask an empowering question.

I always ask, "What can I learn from this situation?" This stems from a belief that as long as I'm learning, I can grow, become a better human being, live a better life, and help others to live a better life. It's easy to get down on yourself when you fail. Maybe you just started working out, but over the weekend you have beer, pizza, and cookies. You tell yourself, "I've failed. I just cannot do it." Instead of continuing, you stop. You fail, so you stop. You fail at relationships, so you stop dating. You fail at starting a new business, so you stop innovating. Failure is never an end point; it's a lesson.

When you fail, what if you shift your focus? Instead of thinking you're a failure and you're not good enough, focus on what you learned from this failure and how you can improve to be better next time you try. Ask yourself empowering questions as you ponder the situation. *What can I change about this? What else can I focus on? What is the good in this? What is the opportunity here? What can I control? How can I make this external experience positive? How can I make this experience empowering? How can I shift my perspective, my viewpoint, to see this situation as something helpful for me? What can I do to make this experience more enjoyable? What can I focus on to make my life better?*

CHAPTER 10

SHIFTING EMOTIONAL STATES IN A MOMENT: TAKING ACTION AND SHIFTING YOUR PHYSIOLOGY

*If you are distressed by anything external, the pain is
not due to the thing itself, but to your estimate of it;
and this you have the power to revoke at any moment.*

—MARCUS AURELIUS, *MEDITATIONS*

300 Pounds of Ice and the Power of Breathing

It was a sunny but cool 62°F in California as I stood in a parking lot wearing just a bathing suit and pouring several twenty-pound bags of ice into a giant metal tin can of water. Three hundred pounds of ice later, the surface temp read just above 32°F. I could feel the cold air coming off the ice, as my adrenaline skyrocketed with fear and excitement. This was a Wim Hof workshop, and I was about to spend two full minutes submerged in this ice. Let me tell you, *nothing* compares to this level of cold.

Wim Hof, AKA the Iceman, holds twenty-six Guinness World Records, many for his impressive feats in extreme cold conditions. In 2007, he climbed 22,000 feet up Mount Everest in only shorts and shoes. Through breathing and mental focus, Hof can control his body temperature. He first caught the attention of scientists when he proved he was able to use meditation, focus, and breathing to stay submerged in ice for 1 hour and 53 minutes without his core body temperature changing or negatively affecting him. Most people would have died from hypothermia after around 40-60 minutes. Since then, he's climbed Mount Everest in his shorts, resisted altitude sickness, completed a marathon in the Namib Desert with no water, and proven under a laboratory setting that he's able to influence his autonomic nervous system and immune system at will. Almost everything Hof has done was previously thought to be impossible, but he's not a freak of nature. To demonstrate that any human can learn his methods, he has taught hundreds of people to climb a freezing cold mountain in their shorts without getting cold. Studies show that his breathing technique calms the nerves and actually helps warm his body.

After a short class on how to control my breathing, I jumped into the steel tub with three hundred pounds of ice and water. The cold rushed over my body with pins and needles, causing me to feel shock and fear. My mind was racing, screaming "Get out!!" I was fully submerged to my head, with cubes of ice all around me. I started to hyperventilate.

My instructor, Dr. Trisha Smith, wanted this to happen. The magic of the method is not just about being able to withstand the cold; it's about creating the physiological shift from panic and fear to calm, control, and focus. And it happened quickly. I almost lost control of my breathing, but I remembered the technique. Focused breathing, with a normal inhale and a long, controlled exhale.

The "magic" of the technique comes from lengthening the exhale in comparison to the inhale. With each breath you want to continuously lengthen the exhale. No need to force the breath out, just slow and controlled exhale. The longer the exhale, the more you are able to calm your nerves and shift your biology, even in a 32°F ice bath. Using the breathing technique, I was able to shift my mind and focus away from the shocking pain of the cold and shift the fear that overtook me when I was submerged. Two minutes in three hundred pounds of ice was terrifying, but I overcame it mentally and physically. When my instructor finally told me the time was up, I couldn't believe it. I stood up, ice falling off my chest, with intent. I knew I had to keep breathing with the technique until my body temperature returned to normal. Using this technique, I created a powerful shift in my mind and body, resisting the cold and melting the fear away.

In fact, now *any* time I feel a negative emotion that causes my breathing to escalate, like jumping into an ice bath, I enjoy using this method the most. It is simple and *highly* effective. Whether I feel cold, fear, or any other negative emotion, this technique has helped me move away from it. I focus on making my exhale *longer* than my inhale and continuously try to lengthen the exhale. It is not about how fast you force the air out; it is about how long you take to exhale. The shift happens quickly. You could see it on my face, from panic to control, and from fear to focused.

I used the power of breath to shift my emotional state in a moment in some of the most intense conditions.

In the previous chapter, we discussed shifting your emotional state by shifting focus. In this chapter, we discuss shifting your emotional state by taking action. Changing your breathing patterns is just one of many actions you can use to shift your physiology and change your emotional state. To change the meaning of anything in life, we can either change what we focus on, or we can change what we *do*.

Action is the Cure

If you don't like the way you feel in life, take action to change it! If you don't like the way your body looks, take action to work out or diet. If you don't want to be alone, take action to meet friends or sign up for online dating. If you've spent years hating your career, take action to get a new career! If you regret not traveling, learning to play an instrument, or anything, take action to change it. Buy a plane ticket, sign up for a class, or any action you need to take. These are all *actions* you can take that will result in a shift in your emotional state. All of these actions are much more productive than staying angry, frustrated, resentful, or afraid. It's easy for our minds to wallow in our emotions. If an emotion doesn't empower you in your life, take *action* to change it. **If negative emotions are a disease that disempowers your life, then action is the cure.**

Let's look at fear, worry, and anxiety. These emotions are all based on the anticipation of what we think *might* happen if we do or do not do something. Instead of just taking action and evaluating our results, we get overpowered by negative feelings. They can often debilitate us, cause stress and increased blood pressure, and overall dampen the joy of life. What if every time you felt fear, for example, you simply took action? How dramatic of a change would you experience in life? What if every time you wanted to ask someone out, you just did it? Or every time you wanted to suggest an idea to your friends or co-workers, you just said it? How invigorated could you feel if you became an *action-taker*?

The difference between those who are successful and those who fail is execution. Are you willing to take action to achieve your goals? Fear, failure, anxiety, and worry stop many people from action. Don't let your emotions control you. Take more action and change your life to *live* it. Instead of merely reacting to our environment and being a *victim* of circumstance, we can choose to take action with purpose. We can become the *victor*. We can rise up to the challenge and take action to better our lives. What actions can you take to shift your emotional state?

The Mind-Body Connection is a Two-Way Street

Choosing to take action with purpose, as opposed to just reacting unconsciously, can and will create a shift in your emotional state and in your life. On the "road," from focus to meaning to action, our reactions manifest themselves in our physiology. When you get angry, your blood pressure literally increases, your heartbeat increases, and your face turns red. People can visually see your reaction. What's interesting is how your physiology actually influences your focus and the meaning you attach to experiences. If you are upset, you tend to focus on—and thus find—more things to be upset about. Being physically upset *changes your perception of the world.*

Your physiology and how you hold yourself, how you stand, how you move, and how you breathe impacts how you feel and what you focus on. Those who just react might unknowingly let their physiology negatively affect their lives. With Emotional Fitness, you can use your physiology to empower you to live a better life. Changing your physiology causes a physical change inside your body at a biochemical and hormonal level that dramatically impacts how your experience is perceived and the meaning you give it. Thus, the diagram of the internal world shifts. Our physiology and our actions actually influence the meaning we give life and what we focus on. It's a two-way street. Instead of just reacting, we can learn how to use our physiology to help us control our emotional states in a moment.

INTERNAL WORLD

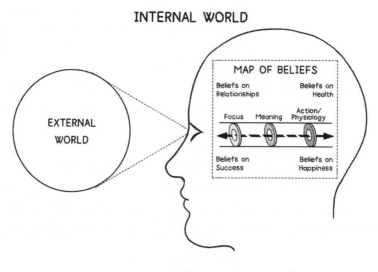

When you engage your physiology, your body sends different signals to the brain, and the mind begins to shift. For example, when people are stressed or upset, they tend to have very restrictive, tight breathing. Often people will say, "Take a deep breath to relax." That's because it's hard to be upset when you're breathing, and your body isn't tense. Changing your breathing is a quick way to change your emotional state. Another one is exercise. When your body is in motion, your breathing changes to take in oxygen. This breath work causes a cascade of changes. Runners get an endorphin high; weightlifters get a pump; and, in general, people report that they feel good after exercise.

Breathing and Physiology

Breathing is a simple and fundamental way you can use physiology to shift your emotional state. What if you are stressed, angry, anxious, frustrated, or nervous? Think about how you hold your body in these states. Often these emotions create a physiological response that can be visually seen in people. Their bodies are tight, and their breathing is short and shallow. They might even show redness in their faces due to a spike of adrenaline. They tend to clench their bodies and squeeze the air in and out.

Now, imagine you get this stressed person to breathe in deeply. You ask them to take deep breaths in to oxygenate the body, and then steadily exhale. You get them to relax their hands and feet and shoulders. What happens? They often start to calm down. When they changed their physiology, it sent a signal to their brain to relax their body, thereby changing the feeling they were experiencing at that moment. Once they calmed down, they could then refocus and shift into a better state.

We've all been there with friends or family who've had a bad day or week and are experiencing several emotions at once. We come over to their house and we find a way to interrupt their state by forcing them to change their physiology. We ask them to come out with us to keep their minds off their troubles. Eventually, they say something like, "I overreacted" or "It really wasn't as bad as I thought it was."

Some people struggle to relieve negative emotions and fall into the trap of emotional eating. They say food makes them feel better. This is often because of the way eating changes our physiology, and it has everything to do with our breath. Our breathing slows as the diaphragm is pushed up from a full belly. This change in our physiology actually causes us to calm down. Unfortunately, emotional eating can lead to negative consequences, like weight gain and health issues. Let's look at different breathing techniques that you can use to change your emotional state in a moment and call on empowering emotions quickly.

Breathing Techniques to Change Your Emotional State

Oxygen is the ultimate life source. We can last roughly three weeks without food and three days without water, but after three minutes without oxygen, our brain starts to die. Every day, we inhale and exhale on average 20,000 times to make sure we absorb sufficient oxygen. Luckily, breathing is controlled by our autonomic nervous system, so you don't have to think about it all the time. **However, breathing is one of the things that you can easily alter and control to change your body's physiology and emotional state.**

How powerful are breathing techniques really? Can they change your state that dramatically? I don't want you to take my word for it. I want you to *do it*. You don't have to jump into an ice bath to feel the power of breathing from the Wim Hof Method. Remember, lengthening your exhale is the key. Below are several different breathing exercises I personally have tried with amazing results. They are backed by thousands of testimonials and scientific studies, but until you try them for yourself, you'll never understand the true power breathing has over your mind. These are just a few exercises to enhance your Emotional Fitness in a moment.

Breathing to Relieve Stress and Relax

When we get stressed out, anxious, or worried, we often fall into shallow breathing patterns. The best way to breathe during these times is to use your diaphragm, or breathing muscle, to help you inhale and exhale.

Proper technique is to relax your shoulders and sit back or lie down. Place one hand on your stomach just under your ribs and the other on your chest. Inhale through your nose until you feel your stomach push your hand out as the air fills your abdomen. You should not feel your hand on your chest move at all. Then slowly exhale from your stomach through your mouth and feel your hand go down on your stomach. Inhale back to the starting point and do it again as air is removed from your stomach. Do this for five to ten minutes and see the power of conscious breathing. Simply by changing your breathing pattern can relax you.

Breathing for Anxiety

People often struggle with anxiety before an exam, a presentation, or a high-stakes situation. Breathing exercises have been shown to lead to decreased anxiety. Being nervous causes shallow breathing, which leads to less oxygen flow. When you take controlled, deep breaths, you increase oxygen flow to the brain for better concentration and energy, and less anxiety. Try this. Sit comfortably. First, note how you breathe naturally. Now, take a breath in slowly, deep into your lungs for the count of four. Hold it for a count of four. Now exhale slowly for a count of four. Do this several times in a row.

Studies show that mindful breathing is a great way to reduce test anxiety.[26] Whenever you need to calm down, try this exercise.

The more you do it, the better you get at proper breathing, which makes it easier and faster for you to relax in the long run.

Breathing for Focus

We've all heard about how people work on breathing to relax, but can it help you focus? Try this exercise. Start by breathing in through your nose and counting to four as you inhale. Pause for two seconds and then exhale for four through your mouth. As you inhale, focus on how it feels for the air to fill and invigorate your lungs with oxygen. As you exhale, focus on the breath leaving your body. Do these five to ten times.

There are many different breathing methods out there. Try them when you're in an overexcited or upset state to see which one works best for you. Anytime you control your breathing consciously, your physiological state shifts and changes how you feel. Breathing is a powerful tool that has been used for thousands of years. Use it daily and watch how much you easily shift your emotional state.

Prime Yourself For Success

The best way to interrupt any emotional pattern is to change your physical state. Think about how athletes act before a big game, or meet, or fight. They get rowdy, thump their chests, and jump around. They're energizing themselves and shifting their emotional states to get focused on winning the game. They think of themselves as warriors going into battle, and they move like it. These physical actions shift their bodies and their minds to prime themselves for success. Do you want to prime your *life* for success?

Power Posing

Let's pull a move from athletes. There is a term called *power posing*. Power posing when you stand in a strong, confident, open, and powerful stance with your chest out, shoulders back, head up, chin up, eyes up, and hands on your waist. Think of how Superman or Wonder Woman stands. A now-famous study done by Amy Cuddy at Harvard University shows that when someone does the power pose for just two minutes, there is a 25 percent decrease in cortisol (the stress hormone) and a 20 percent increase in testosterone. That person is also more likely to take a risk to achieve their goal. This increase in positive signals in the brain has been shown to boost confidence and the ability to handle stress, and it allows people to stay focused on their goals.[27] Do a power pose and watch how it changes your emotional state almost instantly.

Power Posing

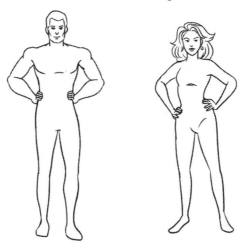

In order to fully understand the "power" of power posing, I want you to try this exercise. Sit down in a chair. I want you to think about a sad person or a sad kid who just got put into time out. How do they look? Their head is down; they are looking at their feet. What do they look like? Just for a moment, I want you to act like them. Act like you're in a sad state.

What if you were to take this negative state and intensify it? Think of someone who is in a depressed state. Pretend just for a moment that you are in a depressed state. Really feel it. With your arms crossed, shoulders down, head down, eyes down, and with shallow breathing, think sad, depressing thoughts (don't worry, we are about to get out of this state). Do this for 30 seconds. As you approach 30, I want you to count to 3 and stand up in a power pose.

1 . . . 2 . . . 3. *Stand up*! Head up, chin up, eyes forward, shoulders back, chest out, hands on your waist! Stand like you are Superman or Wonder Woman. Stand strong and embrace this power pose for two minutes.

If you did this right, you can *feel* the shift in your body, in your mind, and—as studies have shown—in your biochemistry. I have done this for hundreds and thousands of people while speaking at seminars, and every time I do it, everyone feels the difference. They know that their bodies and their minds have created a massive shift. If you want to increase your courage, decrease stress, and be more focused on the goal, power posing works. This is just one simple exercise that can drastically shift your emotions in a moment. Doing this daily in the morning primes your mind and body to be more Emotionally Fit.

In the beginning, we said to change the meaning of life you can either change your focus and perception, or you can change what you do. Taking action can quickly help overcome our negative emotions. Go do something to change your circumstances and emotional state. In addition to taking direct action, you can also shift your physiology through conscious breathing and power posing. These are all great tools to create instant shifts in our emotional state.

Now, what if we could change the meaning an experience has just by shifting the words we use to describe that experience? In the next chapter, we show just how powerful our words truly are.

CHAPTER 11

SHIFTING EMOTIONAL STATES IN A MOMENT: THE POWER OF WORDS

Words can inspire. And words can destroy. Choose yours well.

—ROBIN SHARMA, AUTHOR OF *THE MONK WHO SOLD HIS FERRARI* SERIES

"Take *can't* out of your vocabulary, Corey," my dad used to tell me. I never realized how truly powerful this lesson was until later in life. By never using the word *can't*, I rewired my brain to always look for *how*. Instead of "I *can't* do something," I always looked for "*How* can I do something?"

When I was in high school, I wanted to graduate early. My counselor said, "No." I went to my parents and asked how I could do it. I graduated at the age of 16 years old. When I wanted to get into orthodontic residency, everyone told me how hard it was to get accepted. Nearly impossible, they said. I was one of four in my class of 400 to get accepted into a program. When I wanted to win a fitness competition, people couldn't believe I was doing it. I was supposed to be an orthodontist. In my first competition, I won first place. There is no *can't*.

If you say you "can't" do something in life, then you'll never be able to. Take "I can't" out of your vocabulary and replace it with "I can." If you believe it's possible, everything changes. I would have never accomplished anything if I kept saying "I can't." The words you use, or don't use, create the reality of your life.

The Meaning of Life- Powered through Words

The only meaning in life is the meaning you give it. While you can quickly change how you feel by shifting your focus and perspective, by taking action, or by changing your physiology, what if you could simply change the *meaning* you attached to an experience? Change the meaning you give, and you change the meaning of life.

Meaning is by definition the thing that one intends to convey through language. Thus, the only way to create meaning is by using language to convey it. So, while shifting your focus and your actions can change the meaning you give, simply changing the language you use to convey a meaning can, in turn, alter the meaning itself.

The words you use can help you shift your emotional state in a moment. Language, in fact, alters experience. There are more than 500,000 words in the English language, and more than 3,000 of these words describe emotions. More than two-thirds of these emotion words—or 2,000 plus—describe *negative* emotions. Because language empowers the feeling into communication, and because negative communication, like *complaining*, has been shown in studies to rewire the brain for even more negativity, it's no wonder so many people suffer.[28]

Our words have more power than we previously gave them credit for. I used to say the word *depressed* all the time. All the time. How are you feeling? *Depressed.* Are you OK? *Depressed.* How's your day going? *Depressed.* I used that one word for every negative feeling—mildly upset, sad, a little disappointed, let down, uninspired, irritated, lonely, merely existing, unfocused —they all became *depression.* To me, depression was a deep, dark, lonely, and miserable place to be. I used the word so often that I felt even more depressed. This generalization enhanced the negative effect it had on me. Language has the power to affect our emotions, negatively and positively.

Using a negative word over and over again empowers that word to be stronger, to tie all the experiences of that word into one, to anchor it all into an avalanche of negative emotional flooding that overwhelms us. In my case, depression crushed the very life out of me. And it almost won had I not learned the simple but powerful truth that we all can transform the meaning of our lives through our words. And I'm not just talking about the words we say out loud. I am especially concerned with the words we say inside our own heads. I rarely used the word *depressed* out loud for fear of rejection from friends and family. But they all knew how I felt and what I thought. I wore it on my body, through my actions, and reinforced it with my language. The word *depressed* ran through my mind every minute of every day.

> *How many therapists does it take*
> *to change a light bulb?*
> *Just one, but the light bulb really*
> *has to want to change.*

I noticed I'd written the word *depressed* here more times than I've said it in years, and my body was rejecting the feeling that word used to bring up in me. I needed a joke to shift the emotional state that was building in this chapter! But the joke has a valid point. I was depressed for years because even though I said I wanted to change, I really did not do everything in my power to change. Thankfully, I came to a point where change was no longer a want, but an absolute need to live my life. I never say that I feel depressed anymore, and in fact, that word is no longer in my vocabulary for describing how I feel. I have not experienced depression since I made this shift.

I never used *anxiety* as a word to describe the risk that goes along with starting my own business. Because I don't use the word, I never feel it. Sometimes, though, when describing how I feel, other people have said that it sounded a little like anxiety, and some people would go as far as to say I needed to stop, take a break, and slow down. But my goals were too important. Since I didn't use the word *anxiety*, I didn't let it enter my physiology, didn't feel it, and didn't let it slow me down. Interestingly enough, once people told me it was anxiety, I unconsciously started to label those experiences with anxiety and suddenly felt anxiety for the first time in my life. It was debilitating! Once I realized it, I changed the feeling from "I feel anxiety" to "I feel pressure." In my head, pressure is a good thing, as it empowers me to take action toward my goals. Pressure turns coal into diamonds, and the minute I made this vocabulary switch, my anxiety disappeared.

Take Negative Words out of Your Vocabulary

Let's learn how shifting language changes meaning. What happens if you alter the words you use? "How are you doing today?" What do people usually say? "Stressed"? "OK"? They say these words with sloping shoulders. Or maybe they just say, "Good," with little to no enthusiasm. We don't believe them. *Good* becomes a *go away* word. Good feels so solemn. What if you used a different word like "great" or "fantastic"? Using this vibrant type of language can change your very body into feeling something different. Our hands go in the air. *Fantastic* equates to fireworks, ecstasy, and joy, and you begin to *feel* that emotion.

Notice the difference between "I'm infuriated," "I'm boiling," "I'm pissed," vs. "I'm OK," "I'm fine," "I'm good," vs. "I'm great," "I'm awesome," vs. "I'm fantastical!" You can see how each word represents a slight decrease in the level of anger. Then, when you go from "I'm good" to "I'm awesome," something shifts. Your entire body changes. You're not just saying "I'm awesome," you're *feeling* awesome. Choosing in advance to use better words can dramatically affect how you feel in a moment. For the next week, when someone asks how you are doing, respond with a more exciting emotion like "I'm awesome!" and see how it changes how you feel, and even how they respond to you.

The words you use can also affect an experience. If you say, "I'm outraged, infuriated, irate!" it's much different than if you say, "I'm a little upset." And if you say, "I'm completely miserable and depressed," it's much different than if you say, "I'm feeling a little overwhelmed." Because we define these words with different strengths of emotion attached to them, we give them different meanings. We may use these words to describe how we feel, but the words we use can also continuously affect how we feel.

There are people who think nothing is a big deal, even if their car is totaled. My mother is like this, always optimistic and positive about even the worst situations. Then there are those who are always stressed, always worried. They constantly describe life in a hugely negative way and thus their subsequent experience is altered. Emotional and verbal shifts create massive emotional differences. You can't say "I'm depressed" over and over again without feeling depressed. But saying "I'm just a tiny bit disappointed" softens it to something bearable. These verbal shifts are a way of reframing, a technique we will address in the next section. For now, let's look at some typical emotional and verbal ways we have of communicating.

Emotional generalizations

An emotional generalization is when you use one word to describe many different emotional experiences. When toned down, this can help you get over difficult problems. But when words and phrases like *outraged, depressed, racing anxiety,* and *immobilizing fear* are used for *every* experience, we create a blanket word for all experiences. If you use *outraged* or *irate* to describe how angry you are when you lose your house/job/boyfriend/girlfriend/money, you feel that. But if you use that same word to describe your anger when you get cut off in traffic, that leads to irrational road rage. Or if you use it when you accidentally break a glass, or if someone doesn't take off their shoes, or pick up their stuff, now you become an angry asshole. You experience true anger and outrage with each experience, no matter how big or how small the experiences actually are.

Emotional Intensifiers

Emotional intensifiers include the use of phrases like "I'm *very* depressed," "I'm *extremely* outraged," "I'm *out of my mind* livid," and "I'm *outside myself with* worry." These intensifiers create severity in a situation. Used to portray how upset we are to other people, they, in turn, create even bigger emotions within ourselves. When used with negative emotions, these intensifiers can be debilitating and disempower us. However, when used with positive emotions, these intensifiers can empower us. For example, "I'm *very* excited." If these intensifiers disempower us, get in the way of good judgment, and paralyze our ability to make decisions or take action, then they do not serve us, and we should get rid of them. By shifting the adjectives we use to describe our emotions, we can either increase, an *emotional intensifier*, or decrease, an *emotional softener*, the very experience of the emotion.

Emotional Softeners

The opposite of emotional intensifiers are emotional softeners. Examples include, "I'm only a *little* upset," "I'm just a *tad* disappointed," "I'm *slightly* sad," and "I'm *mildly* worried." These softeners help to mitigate negative emotions both outwardly and inwardly. They control your emotion so that it doesn't blow up.

Once you are using your rational brain to think and do not get overwhelmed by emotion, you can make the best logical decisions. Softeners are an important part in training yourself and your emotions. They reduce the intensity so that you can create a real *shift* in the meaning you attach to an experience, which ultimately allows you to take better action.

Transforming Emotions

Let's pick common negative and positive words and transform them into more empowering phrases or words by using emotional softeners for negative experiences and emotional intensifiers for positive experiences.

- I'm pissed. = I'm a little annoyed.
- I'm depressed. = I'm just a bit disappointed.
- I'm a nervous wreck. = I'm a little unsure.
- I'm OK. = I'm *great!*
- I'm happy. = I'm *awesome!*
- I'm excited. = I'm *bursting with joy!*

Do you see how these words change the meaning? Also, did you notice how, for the negative words, we added "a little" or "a bit" to each one? Why? These help to *soften* the negative feelings. In our minds, when we say, "a little," we picture something physically small and, in turn, this makes it feel smaller. It's a simple but important point to help train your mind to think differently.

You must carefully choose the words you use to describe your life. At first, these words might seem innocent, but if you use them often enough, they will become an emotional label and start to define your life. If left unchecked, you can fall into the trap of generalizing emotions to every experience, big or small. Some people say, "I'm enraged," whether they're getting fired or getting cut off in traffic. Their words hold the power to define their experiences and their meanings. *Choose wisely.*

We've discussed many of the ways to change your state in a moment. Shift your focus by asking better questions. Take action. Change your physiology by doing a power pose or breathing. Change your language by changing the words you use, replacing them with empowering ones, using emotional softeners and intensifiers appropriately.

Before we move on, let's do an exercise about shifting your state in a moment. Consider something that upset you recently. Name it. Write it down. Maybe traffic was horrible, and you were late for work. Your boss yelled at you. You didn't get that client. You got shot down by a someone. Now, write out three strategies you could've used for shifting your emotional state in the moment. How could you have shifted your thinking around it? How could you have changed your perception or what you focused on? What physical action could you have taken? How could you have reframed it? Try a power pose or a power move to shift your focus.

_____

_____

_____

_____

_____

_____

_____

Let's now look at using special tools that engage every part of your mind to help train yourself even further. These are tools that help build on the basics, but they do not replace the basics. Consider the basics a mandatory exercise every day. In the next chapter, we look at strategies to accelerate your Emotional Fitness training.

CHAPTER 12

THE POWER OF PEERS, REFRAMING, AND SCRATCHING THE RECORD

You are the five people you spend the most time with.

—JIM ROHN, ENTREPRENEUR, AUTHOR,
AND MOTIVATIONAL SPEAKER

Power of Peers: People Who Surround You Can Change Your State in a Moment

When we spend time with people, we mirror and match their body language, their mannerisms, and their verbal language as a natural way of building rapport. It's nature's way of building connections and relationships with people. It goes all the way down into our neurons, where there are mirror neurons, which fire to mirror the actions of others. One of the best-known researchers today of mirror neurons is V.S. Ramachandra, a professor of neuroscience at the University of California, San Diego.

A mirror neuron is a <u>neuron</u> that *fires* both when we act and *when we observe the same action performed by another person.* Thus, the neuron "mirrors" the behavior of the other, as though the observer themselves were acting it out. Mirroring the behavior of those around us, then, actually occurs at a neurological level. "There are neurons which fire when I reach out and grab a peanut, another set of neurons which fire when I reach out and pull a lever, other neurons when I'm pushing something, other neurons when I'm hitting something. These are regular motor command neurons, orchestrating a sequence of muscle twitches that allow me to reach out and grab something or do some other action. A subset of these neurons also fires when I simply watch another person—watch you reach out and do exactly the same action. These neurons are performing a virtual reality simulation in your mind, your brain. Therefore, they're constructing a theory in your mind—of your intention—which is important for all kinds of social interaction," Ramachandran told Berkeley's Greater Good magazine.[29] Neuron mirroring made sense to help us survive. In fact, Ramachandran explains that neuron mirroring was one of the things that propelled human development forward at a rapid rate.

Mirror neurons build relationships and trust unconsciously. When you surround yourself with people in a negative state, you're going to mirror those people unconsciously. When I suffered depression, my mother used to say I was so depressed that I'd walk into a room and suck the energy right out of it. I was able to make everyone else in the room uncomfortable. They were mirroring me without even being conscious of it.

If we're around people who complain all the time, we'll feed off their complaining nature on a deep physical level beyond our consciousness. As I did self-development work, as I grew and healed, unfortunately I had to let go of friends because they only focused on problems—often problems that they could control. I call them **safe problems**. Someone with a safe problem could go on and on about always wanting to lose ten pounds, but keep failing, and that's all they'll talk about. They start a new diet every week. They might even lose the ten pounds . . . only to gain it back in three months and have to deal with the same *safe* problem again. They never move past their safe problems, and I believe this helps them avoid the bigger issues in life or the bigger goals they want to achieve.

These safe problems come in all different forms but typically follow a cyclical path that allows people to have the problem, improve, get worse, and have the problem again. People use these safe problems to complain, whine, talk trash, and vent. Overall, it's a negative thought cycle. These safe problems occupy people's time, energy, and focus, distracting them from the real problems that they don't want to face, like what they really want to do with their life, if their relationship is healthy, if their career is going in the right direction, if they are happy with who they are, and if their life means something.

My focus was—and is—to grow. I believe that if you're not growing, you're dying. I wanted to become the best version of myself physically, mentally, emotionally, and financially. I wanted to live life to the fullest, love to the fullest, and contribute to the world. I just couldn't hang out with people with safe problems anymore because that's *all* they talked about. If you're at the same job for five years and you're still complaining about it, well why don't you change it? People get caught up in the minutia of life and let that occupy their time instead of focusing on the big picture and what's truly important to them. Time is so precious, and we only have a limited amount of it. It is the only resource we can never get back. We all have the same twenty-four hours in a day, but it's what you do with that time that determines the destiny of your life. I love all of my friends, but unfortunately some didn't want to grow with me. I wanted more out of life in every area, and negativity has no room in my life.

People ask me, "What if it's your family that you spend the most time with and they are negative?" Maybe your parents are older and ingrained in their negative thought patterns. Maybe your sibling or cousin doesn't care to change their negative ways. My answer? You have to accept them. You can spend time with them because you love them, but you don't have to surround yourself with them *all the time*. Be conscious of that. One trick that I do is this: I pay attention. I listen. I hear the disempowerment in what they're saying. In my head, I say, "That's a disempowering question." I note it, but I don't say it out loud. That way I know I'm remaining conscious. I know I'm being aware, and I know I'm not being pulled into their reality. **Everyone in life is either a warning of what not to do or an example of what to do.** When it comes to negative family members, accept them, love them, and learn from them what *not* to do.

Who surrounds you? People who are negative become contagious and suck you down. Their negative habits, mannerisms, and language may become yours over time. And over time, without even being aware of it, you can find yourself having the same problems they do. Ever notice how groups of friends always connect on the same problems? On the flip side, how many times have you been in a bad mood and had the pattern of your negativity interrupted in a good way? Maybe a friend or family member has this great energy and pulls you out of your funk. A class clown makes a joke and the entire room bursts into laughter. For me, growing up, one of my uncles and my dad would crack jokes that jolted me out of a funk. These people are the ones we need in our lives to promote positivity and empowering habits.

Do you struggle to find a positive influence from the people in your life? It has to start within. Make a decision to fill your mind with positivity.

Who are the five people who influence you? Who do you want to be your mentors? Before I had great real-life mentors, the people I surrounded myself with were the authors of the books I read. I read book after book after book by inspirational people. I filled my mind with the stories of their lives, with the beliefs and habits they had. I wanted to be like them, so I modeled them until I started to see a change in me. Start to be aware of the people around you. I promise you, their energy is affecting you.

The Power of Reframing

Each experience we have we give a *frame of reference.* A frame of reference helps to provide context for an experience and focus our thoughts around it. This frame comes from our past experiences, our surroundings, what we believe is going on, what we think we heard, and what we believe will happen. Frames give us context for how to handle an experience. Think of it as a picture. A picture has a frame to put a border or boundary around it. It defines the edges of the picture. We put frames on every experience in life to give them context.

Once we frame an experience, we give that experience a meaning. Frames can limit us and create boundaries around our thoughts and actions. In order to master Emotional Fitness, it is important to identify these limiting frames and then change them. There is a way to shift the frame and that is through the process called **reframing**. Reframing is the ability to take a frame of reference and shift either the context or the content of the frame to give a new empowering and more resourceful meaning. Reframing is something that we do all the time, unconsciously. For example, someone says, "I have the worst life ever." And people respond with, "There are starving children in Ethiopia that would kill to have your life." That simple reframe can help you suddenly realize your life isn't that bad. That's the power of reframing. The classic saying of "a blessing in disguise" is a reframe. Instead of it being a curse or a problem, it is a "blessing." Suddenly, the saying triggered us to mentally shift the problem into an opportunity. We see things in a different way that makes it better.

Reframing helps us shift how we ultimately react to a situation by combining the power of questions with verbal shifts to change the experience we have. It changes the frame of reference for the experience from bad to good. Reframing is the ability to shift the *meaning* of any situation.

There are two main types of reframing: **context reframing** and **content reframing**. Context reframing is giving another meaning to a statement by changing the context. Ever heard someone say that something was "taken out of context"? What they are referring to is a **context reframe**, which occurs when a behavior or action in one scenario is totally acceptable, but in another, it is completely unacceptable or detrimental. You see this with kids a lot. Parents often complain about their kids talking back to them, or disrespecting them, or going against their wishes. These same parents also tell their children to stand up for what they believe in and to speak their minds. Of course, these parents are talking about every *context* except when it comes to them telling their kids what to do, in which they just want their kids to listen without "speaking their mind." Now in this context, when their kid speaks up for themselves and follows what their parents taught them, they are seen as disrespectful by the parent.

Let's look at another example. Say you worry too much. You worry about whether you're going to make it home in time for your favorite show, or if your friends are going to like your social media post, or if you don't look good in that picture. Now worrying becomes a detriment. *Do a reframe.* Worrying might drive you to work really hard to become the best student or employee you can, and so it helps you. Worrying is your motivator to take action. Worrying is just a signal that says you need to take action, which helps you be more productive. Now worrying can be a *good thing.*

Context is everything. As emotions all serve a purpose, in the right context, they are useful. However, in the wrong context, they are debilitating. The easiest way to do a context reframe is by asking questions: where is this emotional behavior useful in my life? Is the emotion I'm using appropriate for this situation?

Content reframing is changing the meaning you give by uncovering more content which now alters your perception. For example, you're at work and the company has just landed a big client, so your boss gives you double the amount of your normal work to help out. Does your boss hate you? Are they punishing you? A content reframe would be finding out that your boss gave you more work because they felt you were the only person who they could trust to do a good job. Now instead of feeling like your boss is punishing you, you feel important. You realize you are the best at what you do and trusted with big client accounts.

Reframing Failure and Rejection

Reframing is critical when it comes to failure and rejection. One of the biggest lessons I ever learned on the road to success is that you will fail and fail often. All the successful people I've interviewed, from founders of billion-dollar companies to pro athletes **view failure as a learning experience**. Failure is not an end; it is a beginning. That is the power of *reframing*. You could see so many failures as an end, but that does not empower you. What if every failure no longer means failure to you? Instead, you *reframe* it to mean a learning experience, an opportunity for you to improve, and get a better result for next time. Now failure can become a good thing.

What about rejection? What if rejection wasn't the end of the world? Instead of thinking, "I'm a loser. No one wants me. I'll never be loved. I'll never be successful," what if every rejection was reframed to be just one step closer to your success? What if you saw rejection as an opportunity to evaluate why you didn't get what you wanted and learned to try something new?

At the age of sixty-five, Colonel Sanders went to 1,009 people before he finally got *one* yes to create Kentucky Fried Chicken. If you do anything in life that takes you out of your comfort zone, you will fail, and you will be rejected often. **Reframing** allows you to take an experience and shift what it means to you. All of the pain and depression and debt I had was once a bitter regret and resentment, but now I am grateful for it. It molded me into who I am today, prepared me for what I would do next, and brought me to a point where change was the only option. I would never be who I am today without it. Use reframing to empower you instead of letting your emotions disempower you. The only meaning in life is the meaning you give it. Now, let's look at some powerful techniques to deal with emotions.

Swish Pattern, Change the Movie

Swish Pattern is an NLP technique used to create an immediate shift in a deeply rooted emotional pattern. It is a *visualization* technique used to replace a negative emotional state with a strong empowering state.

First, imagine yourself as if you are feeling a negative emotion. Let's use fear as an example. Maybe you're afraid of giving a big presentation, of standing in front of so many people and talking. You're so afraid that it's crippling you. Take that image of fear and put it in your mind. Describe that image. Is it bright? Dim? Fuzzy? Clear? Black and white or in color? Moving or still? Big or small? Close or far away?

For most people who are afraid of giving a presentation or talk in front of people, it can be more debilitating than even the fear of death. They imagine in their heads something that sounds like, "I see myself in front of everyone, scared and frightened. I mess up and I'm so embarrassed. I'm stuck to the stage and can't leave. People are laughing at me, and the pain is unbearable. I would rather die than experience that level of embarrassment and rejection." Because of such overwhelming fear, they *never* step onstage.

This isn't just an image; it's a movie in their mind, a movie on a giant projector screen in full color, like virtual reality. It is so bright and colorful that it feels real. They aren't just watching; they are actually *in* this movie. The pain feels so close that it feels real. They hold this movie in their mind and play it over and over again until the fear of failure, embarrassment, and worry cripples them from taking action.

Maybe your fear is also speaking in front of people. Maybe it's something else. Maybe it's talking to someone you're interested in. Maybe it's asking for help. Asking for a raise. Singing. Dancing. Working out. Whatever you feel that is stopping you, I want you to take that fear and bring it close. We're going to start to **change your fear**.

First, imagine your fear as you normally do, feel it, hear it, see it like a big movie, full of movement. Now, pause the movie to a single image. Next, make it black and white, dim the brightness, make it dark. As it darkens, it's no longer clear but blurry. Slowly, start to push this image of your fear away to a far-off corner. See it get smaller and smaller and smaller, and watch it go farther and farther and farther away from you. It goes so far away that you can barely make out what the image was until it's just a tiny, dark dot far off in the corner of the universe.

Now, replace your newly blank canvas with an image of yourself as courageous, confident, and powerful. Imagine it as real as possible. Imagine you are conquering your fear! You are doing it easily, effortlessly, and with absolute confidence. What are you wearing? What do you look like? What does it feel like? What are you saying? How are you saying it? What do you hear from the people around you? How does it feel? Bring that image of you closer, in color. Make it move; make it really bright and then even brighter. Are you in the movie or just watching it? *Jump in it. Feel it!* Feel how great it is to be up there being successful. Take the positive image and make it bigger. Double it in size. Double it again, until it is huge in your mind and completely fills your vision. This is the positive image we want to use to replace your negative image. This is how we start the swish pattern.

To do what is known as the swish pattern, hold out one hand in front of your face with your eyes closed. Start by holding that negative image in your hand with it "toned down:" dim, dark, black and white, small, still, muted, like a distant memory. Begin by mentally pushing the negative image away. As you push it away mentally, begin to physically move your hand away. In your other hand, you hold the big, bright, colorful image of you being massively successful. As you mentally push away the negative image and your hand moves away, physically pull your other hand with this positive image toward your face and into the front of your mind. As the two hands get closer, allow your hands to clap into each other. When your hands hit, yell, "Swish," and then switch the image. With that clap, the negative image breaks apart into a million pieces that fade away into the distant darkness, lost forever, while the new image continues to grow and fill the front of your mind. It becomes a movie you watch and then act in. You feel your positivity empowering you as if it is real.

Do the swish pattern again and again and again. At first, start slow. Really feel the shift inside you when you replace the old, negative feeling with the new. Then begin to do it faster and faster: ten to fifteen times. Put the positive image in your face, making it brighter and bigger, and really feel that this is you. Do it every day and you'll start feeling differently when you encounter situations that caused those negative emotions to stir up. By retraining our minds to consciously replace a negative emotional pattern with a positive one, we respond with Emotional Fitness. Use the swish pattern for whatever negative state or fear you have.

Let's do a swish exercise right now. Pick something going on in your life at present that has a lot of emotion attached to it. Write it down. Maybe you're having trouble at work, fights with your partner, difficulties with your parents. What emotions are attached to it? Bring all of your senses to bear on feeling this negative situation acutely. Hear it. See it. Feel it. Turn it into a moving picture. Make it real. Now, envision the same situation in a positive light—you're getting a promotion, having a loving relationship with your partner, finding harmony with your parents. Make it vivid. Use all of your senses. See the image of your loving relationship as a bright movie—like real life. See it. Hear it. Feel it.

Now, push away the negative image. Reach out and pull the positive image toward you. Have the positive image crash into the negative one and shatter it into a million pieces. Write down the emotions you experience after this process. Follow the description above to bring the positive image closer to you, in vivid color. Bring it closer and closer.

Note when you see a shift in your situation. Watch for signs of change. How do you feel after this exercise? How does the situation shift?

Single Dissociation and Scratching the Record

Emotional tagging is the process where emotional information attaches itself to the thoughts and experiences we store in our memories. These emotions tell us whether to pay attention to something and whether to take action. Like pattern recognition, emotional tagging helps us make decisions, but it can also mislead us. Emotionally tagged memories can and do affect how we act and how we make decisions in our lives.

In his book *Emotional Intelligence*, Goleman discusses J. Toobey and L. Cosmides and their seminal work, "The Past Explains the Present: Emotional Adaptations and the Structure of Ancestral Environments." "When some feature of an event seems similar to an emotionally charged memory from the past, the emotional mind responds by triggering the feelings that went with the remembered event. The emotional mind reacts to the present as though it were the past. The trouble is that, especially when the appraisal is fast and automatic, we may not realize that what was once the case is no longer so. Someone who has learned, through painful childhood beatings, to react to an angry scowl with intense fear and loathing will have that reaction to some degree even as an adult, when the scowl carries no such threat."[30]

To live your life based on traumatic and emotional memories from the past can be debilitating and crippling. In order to move past it, we need to shift these memories. This is powerful because you already have a selective memory. Your mind already selects what you see by focus, and in your memories, you remember only certain things. You might remember exactly what you wore on your first day of school, work, or to prom. But do you remember exactly what you were wearing on the seventeenth day of third grade? That's because you select what you want to remember. But memories can be distorted and forgotten.

We all have these distorted or lost memories. As I'm writing this, I remember a painful rejection by a girl in junior high—something so unimportant in my life, I'd completely forgotten about—and for the life of me, I can't remember her name. Memories *can* be let go of; we do it all the time. But we hold on to certain negative ones as if they are beyond our control. Instead of telling you to simply forget a painful memory, I'm going to show you how. By using your biology and the way your brain makes memories, you *can* choose to *alter* your negative memories into ones that no longer control you.

If being afraid and upset are your daily norm, let's work with that. Pick a memory that's very strong. Let's say your parents forgot to pick you up from school. You're seven years old, so your parents' forgetting you is extremely frightening and emotionally painful. Because of it, you feel as if no one loves you. Or maybe you got rejected in ninth grade by your year-long crush. Maybe you got reprimanded by your boss in front of your whole office. Whatever it is, pick the strongest experience you can remember. Take that memory and put it out there. Most people tend to relive these memories as if they are happening again, and in that habit, they reinforce the negative experience. By watching this same negative memory all the time, they strengthen the memory and their fear. We do **not** want you to relive it, so change the movie! Close your eyes and put the negative memory on a movie screen and watch yourself have that experience. This is called a **single dissociation**. By watching your memory of yourself on a movie screen, you're dissociating from the memory by placing it outside of you. By having you watch yourself have that experience instead of *feeling* like you are reliving it again, it gives the separation, or dissociation, we need to create change. Simply watch yourself going through the experience.

Now let's **scratch the record**. In doing this, we can change the experience just like we did with the swish pattern. Just as an old vinyl record or CD becomes scratched and can never play the same way again, we too will scratch the memory so it can never play back the same way in our mind and memories again. For this exercise, read through this entirely, then close your eyes and do the exercise. Like the swish pattern, we make the memory black and white, dim, not very clear, and we mute it. Have you ever seen a scary movie and then muted it? It's not so scary without the sound, right? Same thing here: by changing the memory's sound or picture, it no longer has the same effect.

To *scratch* the record of your memory, we are going to make an adjustment to your memory by putting the person who hurt your feelings in big ears and big feet, and giving them a squeaky voice—maybe they are dressed like mickey mouse or in a silly giant banana costume—go ahead, you can laugh at them. Now, as you play back your memory, maybe it was rejection, you watch your younger self in this memory but instead of feeling rejected, you are laughing at this person. Watch your younger self pointing at them, laughing. And you're laughing watching it. You have a remote control to play back the memory on the movie screen. Use the rewind button to watch it again and sure go ahead and laugh again. The "scratch" in the memory is the alterations we did to the person who hurt you, big ears, feet, and funny voice. Each time you re-watch the memory with the scratch in it, it changes the memory. Re-watch it again and again, scratching the record over and over. Have you ever watched a cartoon backwards? Or a boomerang video? Isn't everything funnier in reverse? Try watching your memory backwards, then forwards. Now, use the fast-forward button on your remote and double the speed of watching it. Each time, this person looks funnier.

Keep going, twenty to thirty times, until you scratch the record so much, back and forth, over and over, that it'll never play the same way again. The memory in your mind can never be replayed without associating that same painful memory to the funny image you just created. We all know how scratching records or CDs ruins whatever is on them, and so will scratching your memory ruin the way the memory can be played forever.

I've used this technique with myself and other people, and it is amazing how fast a memory can change, along with the effect of some horrible past experience, sometimes in five to ten minutes. Emotionally tagged memories often dictate how you react in a moment. By going into the past and altering the frame and the memory, you can start to shift how you feel in ANY moment.

Our overall goal here is first to learn how to shift our emotional states in a moment and discover that we can make that state shift again and again in many moments. Then, from that shifted emotional state, we can create a way of acting that becomes part of our new behavior and habits.

CHAPTER 13

HABITS AND BEHAVIORS

We are what we repeatedly do. Excellence,
therefore, is not an act but a habit.

—ARISTOTLE

In the previous chapter, we showed you that you can and do switch your emotional state regularly. You've done it at random times, like when answering the phone, or when someone asks you a question and you get interrupted. But can you do it at will? Can you do it when you want to? Consistently?

Instead of just managing your state in a moment, I want to help you build new behaviors that *become* your new standard emotional state, where shifting to an empowering emotional state becomes a habit.

Why Are Emotional Habits Formed?

All emotions serve a purpose. Emotions are not just the fuel that drives our goals. Every emotion, even a negative one, is designed to serve us in some way. Their original intention was to help us survive. Emotions help us move away from pain and move toward pleasure.

In the beginning, emotions have a positive intention. Anger protects you or helps you get what you need, but it can ultimately destroy the very relationships you really want. Being negative makes other people feel bad for you and want to help you, but if it becomes a habit, it can lead to misery and depression. Fear protects us in the wild, but if you never step outside your comfort zone into that fear, you never grow and accomplish your goals.

It is essential to listen to your emotions. And then it's important to ask, "Why?" "Why am I feeling like this? What caused me to experience this emotion?" You may find that you experience the same emotions over and over again. That's because we have certain triggers that cue our emotions. Such a cue triggers us to go into an emotional routine, and over time, constant repetition leads to an emotional habit. Not all emotional habits are bad, but if you are experiencing repeated toxic emotions that prevent you from living your best life, you will want to know how to change them. It all starts with the habit loop.

What Is the Habit Loop?

The habit loop was first described by Charles Duhigg in his book *The Power of Habit*. MIT researchers discovered a neurological loop at the core of every habit. **The habit loop consists of three parts: a cue, a routine, and a reward.** The *cue* is something that happens or triggers you to enter into your habit, such as feeling tired in the morning. The routine is the thing you actually do, such as drinking coffee. And the reward is what you get from the habit that reinforces the habit loop, such as feeling good because coffee gives you energy and focus. How many people do you know who say, "Don't talk to me until I get my coffee!" or wake up saying, "I need coffee first." And every day, they feel tired, drink coffee, feel good, and the habit loop strengthens.

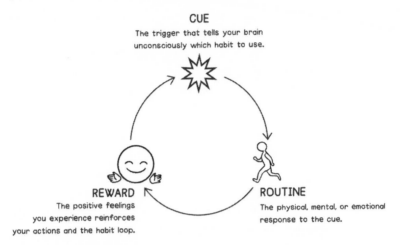

CUE
The trigger that tells your brain unconsciously which habit to use.

ROUTINE
The physical, mental, or emotional response to the cue.

REWARD
The positive feelings you experience reinforces your actions and the habit loop.

These same habits happen with our emotions, and we develop *emotional habits*. We develop habits around how we deal with our emotions, how we react, and how we change our emotional state.

Stress or sadness can also cue the routine of eating, which then causes changes in your physiology to give you the reward of relaxation and satisfaction, and the habit loop grows along with your weight.

These same habits happen with smoking. Stress at work cues a habitual smoke break, which gives the reward of relaxation and reinforces the habit. Why is smoking such a stress reliever? Just like eating changes your breathing pattern, the very act of smoking causes you to change your breathing. Instead of short, shallow breaths common in stress or anxiety, smoking involves a big inhale followed by a slow, controlled exhale. Thus, smoking shifts your breathing to a more relaxed physiological state. So, if the cue is stress, the routine is smoking, and the reward is relaxation, how can we change the habit?

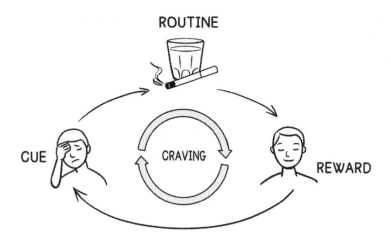

How to Change a Habit

People always try to get rid of bad habits, but *instead* **they should replace bad habits with good habits.** The goal is not *just* to get rid of bad habits because the cue will still be there, and you will still want the reward. Instead *replace* the bad habit with a new, empowering one. We do this by changing the routine. The cue might pop up again, but by changing the routine, we can get the exact same reward, and in the process get rid of an old habit and replace it with a new, better habit.

The next time you get a cue of stress, instead of smoking for ten minutes to change your breathing, try going for a walk and doing deep, controlled breaths: four seconds in, hold for four, four seconds out, hold for four, and repeat. This breathing changes your physiological state in just the same way that smoking does, and it gives you the same reward: relaxation. Thus, the habit can begin to change.

Common Emotional Habits

Anxiety, anger, sadness, and stress are common negative habits that people experience on a weekly basis. Emotional habits can be difficult to identify. Do you experience this just once or several times a week? And while a physical habit may be hard to break, an emotional one can be even more difficult. This is true for several reasons. First, you may not even recognize the emotional habit. Second, many people believe that our emotions control us and that we do not have control over them—we simply just react to what happens around us. Third, we often believe that emotions define us. We say things like, "I'm just an anxious person" or, "I've always been hot-headed." Your very identity is wrapped in your daily emotional responses. The point of mastering Emotional Fitness is that you can identify your emotions, work with them, and use them to help or change yourself.

Let's say your cue is Monday. The routine is, "Oh, I'm bummed. I have to go to work. I'm down. I'm sad the weekend is over. I'm upset I have to go to work." These emotions become a routine. Now you're waiting for next weekend: "I'm tired, stressed, annoyed."

What is your reward for this emotional habit? You get a connection with other people who do not like Mondays. You commiserate and complain together. You bond around your hatred of Mondays.

Someone asks a friend, classmate, or coworker, "Hey, how's it going?"

Their response is, "Ugh, I've got a bad case of the Mondays."

The typical response back? "Oh yeah, I totally know what you mean. So tough. No idea how I'll make through this week, either."

And yet, you do make it through, each and every week. And suddenly, Friday rolls around and you have all of this energy out of nowhere. It's excitement, emotion, passion, and energy. Emotion *is* energy in motion.

Being angry and upset are other big emotional habits in our culture. With anger, a person feels a sense of importance by lashing out. Chemicals like adrenaline and noradrenaline surge through the body, which can give a person moments of feeling empowered, but the moment doesn't last. Their reward is, "I have attention.

I have significance. I have power." Or we can get the reward of actually getting what we want. The power you get from anger is not real power. It is not sustainable. Studies show that people with the highest levels of anger had twice the risk of coronary artery disease and three times the risk of heart attack, as compared to subjects with the lowest levels of anger. Some scientists think that chronic anger may be more dangerous than smoking and obesity as a cause of early death.[31, 32]

In today's fast-paced, success-driven climate, *stress* is a widespread emotional reaction, one that is socially acceptable. Stress is one of the most common emotions that high achievers experience. We're stressed by the onslaught of global information. We're stressed by how much we have to do at work, by traffic, by bills, by failure, by trying to succeed, by succeeding less than we wanted to, by the number of emails we have to answer, by keeping up with the newest technological advances. Stress may even be the daily emotion of choice, as it is expected if you are to be "successful." So, we want stress. Our reward is that we're good, hardworking people. "See how hard I work? See how much stress I carry because I'm a good, motivated worker?"

In any one of the above scenarios, whether it's stress, anger, or sadness, you can change your emotional habit by taking a different action, which gives you a different kind of reward. For Mondays, we can redefine what it means and get excited about it. Maybe you create a goal list that motivates you every Monday, or meditate and call it Meditation Mondays, or go after your financial goals because it's Money Mondays. For anger, you can do something physical (go for a run, go to the gym) when you feel your anger welling up to release all that energy in a positive way. With stress, you can change your breathing pattern, meditate, or workout. *These are all different actions that can give you the same reward to create a positive emotional habit loop.* The fastest and most effective way to change a habit is to change the routine. The cue or trigger can be out of your control, but the emotional routine you enter is in your control. By changing the routine to an empowering action that gives you the same reward, you can create new empowering emotional habits.

To change our emotional habits, we begin again with awareness. Start watching how you feel. Spend the week really watching and acknowledging your emotional reactions and habits to different events. Notice how you feel stressed when you're overloaded with work. What do you do to relieve that stress? Do you complain to friends, or take a break and eat? How might you shift that stress? What if you thought of the extra work as exciting: "I'm going to grow. I'm going to learn. I'm going to make great money. I'll have new opportunities, a promotion." The reward is a positive, reinforcing cycle.

Some habits and behaviors, like drinking alcohol, can make us more social and give us the reward of having more fun. You can be social and have fun, and be calm and relaxed, without substances. You can do something else and still get the same reward.

My goal is to help you choose empowering habits. If you're complaining and not getting what you want in life while you're spending five to six hours a night watching Netflix, then that habit needs to change if you want to accomplish your goals. The average American watches more than five hours of TV a night. Think about it—those five hours every single night add up. That amount of time is almost equal to a full-time job. You could be working on making your dreams come true instead.

Action is the Cure

Candace Lightner is a perfect example of someone who changed her emotional state by taking action. Her daughter, thirteen-year-old Cari, was killed in a hit-and-run by a drunk driver in 1980 as she was walking on the side of the road. Cari was hit from behind, thrown 125 feet, and left on the road to die. The driver didn't stop and didn't render aid. Dealing with intense grief, her mother discovered the driver was a repeat offender of driving under the influence. Instead of sitting in her rage or falling into a pit of despair, just four days after her daughter's death, Candace started Mothers Against Drunk Driving (MADD). *Instead of letting her emotional habits control her, she took action.* A grass-roots activist, she was told it would take more than a decade to shift attitudes about drunk driving and change legislation. It took less than five years, in what was called the most successful grass-roots campaign since the anti-Vietnam War campaign. Today, an estimated 400,000 lives have been saved due to the multiple changes generated by MADD's activism. Cari's identical twin now runs SADD, Students Against Drunk Drivers.[33]

Do all emotional habits need to change? No. Emotions are the juice of life. They're the fuel by which we take action. We're not saying you should get rid of all bad emotions and only feel good emotions. Often the greatest heroes of our time were dedicated their work as a way to avoid the pain of rejection that occurred to them when they were younger. Michael Jordan was cut from his high school basketball team only to become the greatest basketball player in the world. Stephen King's first book was rejected thirty times. Walt Disney was fired by a newspaper for not being creative enough. These rejections often cause the real pain of doubt, fear, frustration, anger, and resentment. Some people find a way to use these emotions to *help* them accomplish their goals. These seemingly negative emotions serve as an intense motivator to work harder and never give up.

If an emotion is working for you, keep it. Courage, love, friendliness, excitement—if these emotions enrich your life, keep them. Only change an emotion if the feeling disempowers you. We're talking simply about emotions that stop you from taking action. Emotions are great; love them, live them, enjoy them. But if they disempower you, why do you want them?

Whatever you consistently do becomes your habits. If you do them long enough, they become your go-to behavior. Unless your behaviors are empowering and getting you what you want, change them.

Become a Person of Action

What if you develop a habit to take action? What would your life look like if you became a person of action? This is one of my favorite habits that I have trained over the years. This is because there is such a thing as decision fatigue, where our lack of energy and focus leads to making poor decisions.

Psychologist Roy Baumeister showed in a 1998 study that people have limited mental resources and that these resources are depleted with use. He put a plate of freshly baked cookies in front of people for a certain amount of time and told them not to eat the cookies because they were for a different experiment. Then Baumeister had the subjects attempt challenging puzzles. The study found that participants who had recently resisted freshly baked cookies were less able to persevere through a puzzle than their peers, who had waited in a room with no cookies. The group with no cookies were more able to complete tasks successfully than the group who had to resist temptation prior to the tests.[34]

If you worry about all the decisions you have to make all the time, you don't make the best decisions. Worrying about what to eat, what to wear, what to do this weekend, etc. weigh on your ability to make decisions and ultimately leaves us with less willpower to make good decisions. When you become a person of action, you make decisions quickly, which gives your brain more energy and gives you the power to focus on bigger, more complicated decisions. If you make a wrong decision, you can quickly make a new decision. This is a much more efficient way to get things done at work, to achieve your goals, to find success and ultimately to live your life. Instead of spending 20 hours a week thinking about decisions, you are already doing it—living life—creating a habit of being a person of action.

How to Change an Emotional Habit Loop

An original habit looks like this: cue-routine-reward. Remember, the reward strengthens and reinforces the habit. Let's look at stress and smoking again: stress (cue), smoking (routine), relax (reward).

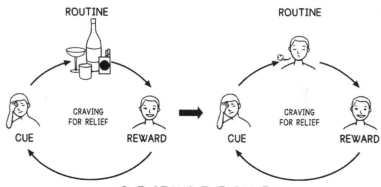

CUE STAYS THE SAME, CHANGE THE ROUTINE TO ONE THAT PROVIDES THE SAME REWARD.

How do you change a habit? **You have to change the routine in a way that it still gives you the same reward.** With smoking, you need to replace the old habit with a new routine to get the same reward. Stress is characterized by short, shallow breathing. Changing your breathing can alter your stress the same way smoking does. For instance, breathing in for four seconds, holding for four, and breathing out for four while walking creates the same changes in breathing patterns as smoking does. Thus, if you get stressed, instead of smoking, you could go for a fifteen-minute walk while focusing on your breathing, and you can experience the same reward as smoking gives you: relaxation. It is more difficult to get rid of a bad habit if you do not replace a bad habit with a habit that is good for you.

What is one emotional loop you want to get rid of?

_____

_____

_____

What is the cue?

_____

_____

_____

What is the routine?

_____

_____

_____

What is the reward?

_____

_____

_____

Now, what is a routine that you can choose to do that will replace your old negative routine and give you the same reward?

_____

_____

_____

Commit to doing this new routine every time you are cued to your negative emotional habit. To reinforce this new routine, visualize what you will do in advance. Imagine you are cued by a negative emotion (stress) and reach for your cigarettes (old routine). Instead of visualizing your old routine, imagine you go for the cigarettes and remember, *No, I have a new routine.* You go for a walk and practice breathing. Visualize this. Visualize how good you will feel after the walk. Do this visualization process over and over in different scenarios (e.g., a friend offers you a cigarette) to plan in advance what you will do in real life when cued. Then, once cued, do the new routine. This is how you replace an old emotional habit with a new empowered one.

New habits take time and energy to form. But once you've created the new habit, it takes little energy to reinforce it daily. Common knowledge says habits take twenty-one days to break or create. But studies show it takes an average of sixty-six days! This is why I recommend training your Emotional Fitness daily. It's not something you learn once and forget. It's a lifestyle. But to start out, commit to thirty days. After thirty days, you'll have the momentum to keep going, and you will find it gets easier the more you build up your empowering emotional habits.

I recommend you start with one area of your life and create one habit. Don't expect yourself to create ten new habits and master every area of your life at once. And don't get down on yourself if it takes a little longer (like sixty-six days instead of twenty-one days) for the habit to stick! Now, pick one habit you want to create. Let's say you want to create a habit to calm you down every time you get anxious or worried. You can say you will focus on your breathing and make sure your exhale is longer than your inhale. Once you calm your breathing, ask yourself, "Is this something in my control? Is there anything I can do to make it better?" If the answer is yes, do it! If the answer is no, continue to breathe and focus on what you can control. This is a simple but effective way to overcome anxiety.

Once you have devoted enough time and energy to create your new behavior, it will become a habit. When it's a habit, you will behave that way automatically without even thinking about it, which requires only a small amount of energy and time to maintain, thereby freeing you up to focus on a different area of your life.

A good sequence of habit development is to start with your morning and night routines. When it comes to Emotional Fitness, training your mind to start the day is critical. We will talk about different morning exercises, but I personally like setting an intentional goal for the day, reciting an empowering belief I have, and getting myself pumped up. At night, I enjoy reflecting back on how the day went. I'm not perfect, so in every mistake, I look for a lesson. As long as I can learn from a mistake, I can improve upon it the next day. Practicing gratitude before doing this helps as well.

These are just two examples of Emotional Fitness exercises you may want to make a habit. There will be more in the coming chapters. Maybe you want to simply start one small habit, like waking up at 6:00 am every day. It may sound simple, but it will build a foundation for you to build other habits upon with confidence. Remember, how you do one thing is how you do everything.

The Words We Habitually Use Have Power

We discussed earlier the power of language in the example of how many people complain about Mondays. Scientists are learning that complaining actually makes the situation worse. According to a study by Dr. Andrew Newberg and Mark Robert Waldmen, authors of *Words Can Change Your Brain*, "A single word has the power to influence the expression of genes that regulate physical and emotional stress." Negative words raise stress levels. Too many stress hormones take over your body when you are negative.

Positive language, on the other hand, affects the parietal lobe, which is in charge of how you view yourself and others. A good view of yourself through the use of positive words can help you see the good in others.[35]

Positive or negative words have tremendous power. It is important to remember that while saying the word aloud is powerful, so too is how many times you say it in your head. You may often say words in your head multiple times without even realizing it. Whether out loud or in your head, the words you choose to say, whether positive or negative, greatly affect your physiology and Emotional Fitness.

Words Don't Just Describe an Experience; They Become Part of You

If I say I'm overwhelmed all the time, I *become* overwhelmed. If I'm in a grocery store and there's a line of people behind me and I've lost my credit card, I feel overwhelmed. If I've missed a deadline and the client's calling, I feel overwhelmed. If people are expecting so much from me in my relationships, I feel so overwhelmed.

We generalize several different experiences into one word until that one word defines us. Now, all of a sudden you wake up five minutes late and you're overwhelmed. Even saying the word to yourself will change the biochemistry in your body. You might stop attaching actual experiences to a word. Now you're attaching the word to everything all the time. Now you *are overwhelmed.*

Period. **The words you use actually change the experiences you have**.

Often, we'll take experiences from our childhoods, when we're young and impressionable, and make a decision very young about what we believe, and this stays with us into adulthood. These early decisions affect how we behave, how we love, and how we grow in life—until we change them. If you've been using certain words to describe yourself all your life, that language can be deeply embedded. I'm asked often if it's even possible to change embedded language quickly. My response? It depends on your belief system. Do you believe change can happen quickly? If you think change takes years and years, then can you shift that belief? Remember, you can and do change your emotional state in a moment all the time. Could you change the embedded language you use to describe yourself quickly, even in a moment? If you *believe* you can, then yes. We will talk more about beliefs in the later chapters.

Consciously choose to upgrade your language. Do a software upgrade for your mind. If you commit to choosing a different language all the time, it'll eventually become your go-to response. Do it enough times and you'll strengthen the connection between neurons.

Words Shape Reality

"Neurons that fire together, wire together."

—Donald O. Hebb, Renowned Canadian Neuropsychologist

The relationship between the words you use and your mind's neuronal connections is profound. The more you say a word out loud, and even the more you think a word in your head, the more your neuronal connections fire. The more these connections fire, the more easily they fire again. Thus, a negative word used habitually becomes easier for your brain to use again. It physically reinforces it in your mind with a neuron pathway. You turn a mental and emotional habit into a physical reality.

This occurs because there is something known as the myelin sheath, which surrounds your central nervous system, wraps around your cells and provides a protective barrier. Myelin is a fatty white substance that surrounds the axon of some nerve cells, forming an electrically insulating layer. It allows your brain to send information faster and more efficiently, which is essential for the optimal functioning of your nervous system. When the myelin that insulates your nerves is destroyed or deteriorates, mental health symptoms and neurodegenerative diseases can occur, from depression to Alzheimer's.

Studies have found that the more you practice something, the stronger this myelin sheath becomes.[36] In essence, your thoughts repeated over and over again manifest themselves in your brain as a physical growth of new dendritic branches of neuron cells. In turn, the neurons can have a growth of the myelin sheath, which strengthens the firing of these cells.

Think of memorizing a telephone number. Say it once and you might remember. Say it ten times and your memory improves significantly. Say it thousands of times and you will never forget it. The same thing goes for your emotions, both good and bad. If you get depressed, anxious, or worried, you think these negative thoughts day in and day out, and the myelin sheath grows to support those thoughts. If you stay focused on the positive and force yourself to look for the good in life, that pathway grows, as well. This is why Emotional Fitness is a training program. These are literally exercises for your brain cells to grow.

Spend this week watching your language. Write down the negative words you use about yourself, about your loved ones, about work, or on social media. Explore which negative words you use over and over again. Note what happens to your body when you express them. What positive words could replace them?

CHAPTER 14

UNCONSCIOUS HABITS AND THE POWER OF ANCHORING

The reason man may become the master of his own destiny is because he has the power to influence his own subconscious mind.

—NAPOLEON HILL

How are unconscious habits triggered? How is it that a cue is so powerful that it can throw you into an unconscious routine that you may or may not be fully aware of? You might get a nervous twitch and start bouncing your knee, biting your nails, pulling out your hair, or scratching your skin. These habits all happen before you are even consciously aware of them. How?

Anchoring

Anchoring is a term that started with classical conditioning. Remember Pavlov's dog? In the 1890s, Pavlov, a Russian psychologist, was researching how dogs salivate when being fed. He rang a bell every time he gave food to his dog. The dog would then see and smell the food and begin to salivate. Pavlov noticed that after enough repetition of this procedure—ring bell, give food, salivate— the dog eventually expected food the moment he heard the bell. Even without food, once the bell rang, the dog would begin to salivate. The bell created a physiological response even without the original trigger present. This became known as classical conditioning, and it still applies today.

The bell is the *anchor* that creates a physical response. Anchoring is the process of associating an internal response with some external or internal trigger so that the response may be quickly, and sometimes covertly, re-accessed. If you're new to the concept of anchors, don't worry, it will become clear as you keep reading. We'll be explaining all of this in much greater detail in the following sections. It's a powerful tool and one worth understanding. So, how does anchoring work for us as humans, and how can we actually use anchoring to help us get what we want?

Human beings, like dogs, are mammals, and due to the biological similarity of our nervous system, we respond to classical conditioning, too. At a basic level, our bodies respond to cues like the bell. We anchor all the time, unconsciously, whether it's a physical bell or something else. When the school bell rings and there is an instant rush to the door, you might feel excitement and freedom. If you get a scolding look from your mother or father and you've anchored that, the look means you did something wrong and they want to talk. You might anchor in the fact that Friday is the last day of the work week and feel excitement build as you look forward to enjoying your time off with family and friends.

Anchors can come in different forms based on our five senses. Anchors can be triggered by a smell, taste, physical touch, visual cue, or auditory stimulus. The bell is an auditory anchor. Seeing a picture of a loved one can trigger an anchor of love. Eating your favorite food can anchor comfort.

Touch can anchor us intensely. A soft touch on the face or a kiss from your partner can elicit an intense feeling of passion and love. In football, guys will start hitting each other, headbutting as hard as they can. *Let's go crush it. We're going to kick some ass.* The anchor is a rough, impactful physical touch, and that's how they get pumped up for the game.

Physical anchors can also trigger a very different response: fear of being attacked. And if you have been attacked, that anchor can leave such a deep emotional imprint that you cannot tell the difference between a friendly touch and an assaulting anchor. So, even when you know you are in a good environment, you respond with fear by assuming every pat on the back is the deeper, more emotionally painful anchor of fear of being attacked. Instead of being triggered unconsciously, we can consciously create our own anchors.

Creating an Anchor

If I'm going to give a talk to a large group of people, I'll do this quick hit to my chest and Say: *Get ready. YES. I got this!*

This triggers an anchor I've created for confidence and courage. You can train an anchor anywhere in your body to instantly activate an empowering emotion. Below is the process to create an anchor and then I will show you an example of an exercise you can try.

In order to create an anchor, you need to:

1) Choose a trigger point on your body or a movement to create the anchor.

    a. This can be clenching one fist, throwing your fist in the air, putting your hand on your heart— any physical trigger you want.

2) Cultivate the empowering emotions you want to feel by using memories or role models to envision what it feels like to embody that emotion.

3) Intensify the emotion to a level 10 out of 10 and activate the anchor from step one.

Repeat this process at least three times or until activating your anchor causes you to instantly feel the empowering emotion you chose. Below is an example of how to create an anchor using a trigger known as a power move.

Anchoring the States You Want with a Power Move

A **power move** is a strongly effective anchor exercise. Similar to a power pose, a power move is a body movement that you do for yourself to fully engage your mind and body and put yourself in an empowering emotional state. One that I personally enjoy is simply saying *yes* proudly and hitting my hand over my heart. To me, it signifies confidence, courage, and purpose. A power move can be any move that you choose. You can squeeze your right fist, stand like Superman or Wonder Woman, or hold both your hands over your heart. The idea is to engage your physiology to anchor the empowering emotion you want, so you can trigger it at any time.

The idea of a power move is to put yourself into an extremely energetic state. It can be one of courage, drive, passion, love, or strength. We will cultivate the emotions to be strong and empowering. Let's pick courage as an example. You have to condition a new stimulus to get the response you want. Start by standing up, closing your eyes, and imagining a time where you experienced an immense amount of courage. Take that memory and put it in your mind. Close your eyes and see what was happening. See what you saw, hear what you heard, and feel what you felt.

If you don't have a memory of your own, then pick someone in your life, real or fictional, whom you would like to model for courage. I used to have a poster of Superman above my desk in college. Whenever I had self-doubt or fear, I imagined being like Superman, how he can do things no ordinary man can do. I imagined myself *as* Superman to give me the courage to face my fears.

While the poster cost less than ten dollars, it gave me a whole world of confidence.

Whoever you imagine, fictional or real, imagine them as your ideal for courage. Really feel what it feels like to be that courageous. See what they saw when they were that courageous, feel what it feels like to be them in you. *Imagine yourself being this courageous person.* Feel it in your body. Feel it in every cell of your body. See yourself as courage and make that image bigger, brighter, more colorful, and more vivid. Bringing up all these feelings of courage often gets us motivated in a moment, but now we can call on them whenever we need them by anchoring them into our bodies. But first, to make the anchor really powerful, we have to increase the feeling.

Now I want you to take that feeling to a level eight or nine out of ten. Intensify it as much as you can. Once you get to level eight or nine, say "Yes." What do you see and feel as you walk around the world feeling so courageous? Once you have done this, take this feeling of courage that vibrates in every cell of your body and double the intensity one more time until the energy is bursting out of your body. At this point, do your power move and yell "Yes!" If it feels good, do it again, and then again—three times.

Now stop! Shake it all off and do the process three more times to really anchor in your power move. Each time you embody this level of courage and use an anchor like a power move, you are training your mind and emotions to be able to activate courage when you need it. You can anchor any feeling, emotion, or state. Use this purposefully so that you no longer are the victim of your emotions but now have the Emotional Fitness to change your state, your behavior, and your life at any given moment. Use these anchors and your cues to create your own emotional habit loops that empower you. Next time fear cues you, you can do a power move to feel empowered. Use these anchors to trigger the emotional habits and behaviors you want in life.

Strengthening and Stacking Anchors

Strengthened anchors come from daily repetition. You train your nervous system to respond to your anchors when you call upon them. The best way to do this is to train your anchors every day for five minutes in the morning until they become completely ingrained into your nervous system.

Stacking anchors is a great way to strengthen them. In the example of courage, you can stack every memory you can think of onto this one anchor to create a super anchor, an anchor that derives its strength from every courageous moment you have ever had in your life. If you are one of those people who has not had many of these moments, you are about to create them! One of the most powerful things I have done to strengthen my anchors is to stack new memories onto them immediately after having an experience.

When I first started speaking, I had a lot of fear when I had to go up to give my speech. Give an hour-long talk? Yikes! I wasn't sure if anyone would like my talk, if I was qualified enough, or if I would do a good job. I had so much self-doubt. I lacked courage, confidence, and strength. Before the seminar, I would build confidence and courage into my mind through visualization. Afterward, people would congratulate me on what an outstanding speaker I was. I was told that my seminar changed peoples' perceptions and lives. The sincere gratitude and appreciation were overwhelming. To know that I helped in such an immense way literally annihilated any memory of fear I'd had. And then it hit me: I did not want to lose this feeling of courage, confidence, and strength. On the spot, I created an anchor to never lose that feeling and to be able to remind my body and my mind that I am a successful motivational speaker.

After every talk I give now, I use this anchor to stack the memories of confidence and success that I already have onto one another. That anchor becomes stronger each and every day. As the memories stack, they begin to synergize to create an even stronger anchor. To this day, I activate that anchor before a big event to eliminate fear and reinforce it afterward to reinforce courage.

What happens when it's not just one trigger that makes us feel bad, but it seems our whole life is one big negative trigger. We always experience a negative emotion. The answer lies in what is called our emotional home.

Emotional Home

When pushed to our limits, we each have one central core emotion we tend to go to. This is your **"emotional home."** This is your safe place, where you feel most comfortable.

We all know someone who is always worried. No matter what happens, all they do is worry. They leave the house: "Did I leave the stove on?" They have a big work project: "Will I have enough time to finish it? Will it even be good?" They get bad news from work: "Will I get fired?" They get good news from work: "How will I be able to sustain such success?" Their emotional home is worry.

Let's say your emotional home is guilt. If you don't get the promotion, you feel guilty you didn't work hard enough. If you have a fight with your spouse, you're guilty you're not doing enough. If you say no to an event, you feel guilty that you'll hurt the other person's feelings. If a natural disaster hits and people lost their homes, you feel survivor's guilt. Guilt is your go-to emotion, your emotional home.

Then there are people who get angry all the time. If they lose a deal, they're pissed off. If they miss the subway, they're angry. If they have bad news from their doctor, they're enraged. Anger is their emotional home.

My emotional home for eight years was depression. Even if something exciting happened, after it wore off, I went back to my most comfortable safe place, depression.

After years of self-development, I worked to create a

different go-to emotion, a different emotional home—resourcefulness. When I feel resourceful, I can accomplish anything. Resourcefulness allows me to choose an emotion that gets the best results. If a deal goes badly, I'm able to easily let it go and refocus. If Option A doesn't work, I'm not outraged. I simply find a way. If I need more work done, I look inside myself and become hyper-focused on the task. Being in a resourceful emotional state allows me to use whatever emotion I need to achieve my goal, whether that's calmness, forgiveness, or confidence. I cultivate resourcefulness daily to help me live the life of my dreams.

What do you feel when something negative happens at work or in your relationships? What is your go-to emotion? You lose a client. You lose your job. You lose a loved one. Someone lies. Someone doesn't invite you. How do you feel?

When pushed down by the severity of an event, what do you feel in the moment? What emotion do you embody? Regardless of the event, there's usually just one emotion we go to as our emotional home. You may think that there are a couple of emotions, but these are usually similar in nature. At times, you might switch between two—such as worry and anxiety or anger and frustration—but at the center, you will find that you say one more often than the other. You might say the word *anger* in your head. You may experience frustration, but when you get frustrated, you get angry. That means anger is truly your emotional home. If you something upsets you and you become frustrated, then frustration is your emotional home. It's usually just one. What's yours?

If you want to shift your emotional home, answer these questions:

1. What is your go-to emotion and emotional home?
2. How does this emotion serve you or make you feel better?
3. How does this emotion empower you or disempower you?
4. What is a new emotion that you want to cultivate to replace your emotional home?

5. Why is this new emotion better for you?
6. Use the habit loop formula to shift your emotional home:
    a. What cues put you in your emotional routine?
    b. What is a new routine you can go through to get the same reward?

Over time, as you replace your emotional habit loop, you will begin to replace your emotional home with the emotion you choose.

Start to locate your go-to emotion, your emotional home. With every major event that happens this week, whether at work, at home, or on social media, note your reaction. Write down the event and the emotions you're having. What is the same emotion that keeps coming up? Does this emotion empower you or disempower you?

Emotional Flooding

Using a powerful anchoring technique called **emotional flooding,** we can begin to shift our emotional home. Imagine if every time you went home, you saw your best and brightest memories all over the house. That's what an emotional flood does: it floods you with emotion. Emotional flooding which was coined by psychologist Thomas Stampfl in 1967. It can be performed unconsciously in a negative way. If you have ever described yourself as "spiraling out of control," this is often the result of letting emotions stack up and build until they explode. Instead of unknowingly being overtaken by an emotional flood, you can consciously choose to flood your mind and emotions with your best memories.

You can create an emotional flood for *any* emotion—courage, happiness, love—whatever you choose. Take your incredible memories and magic moments of life and begin to flood your mind with the emotions from those memories. Would you like to feel happiness at a level one hundred right now?! Let's do an emotional flood for happiness!

Try this. Focus on your favorite memories. They can be big or small, recent or from a long time ago. Close your eyes. Start by thinking of one memory that makes you feel deeply happy, grateful, and loved. Imagine you are back in the past reliving this incredible memory. Really put yourself in that memory. What does it feel like to be back there? What do you see and hear as you relive this incredibly beautiful memory that makes you so happy and grateful? Feel everything you felt inside this memory as if it were happening to you right now. Then I want you to think of another magic moment from your life, when life was just a gift. Life just happened for you, and you were so grateful to be so lucky. Maybe it was the day you met your significant other, maybe it was your graduation, maybe it was a birthday, or maybe it was the day you got a puppy. Whatever it was, really feel the love, gratitude, excitement, and joy this magic moment gave you.

If you are having trouble finding more memories, think about your future and what you are going to do to create new memories. Really visualize the experiences you are going to create. Now we're going to speed this up a little. I want you to think of another memory, something that makes you feel confident, happy, and excited. Really feel what it felt like to be in that incredible moment. And now choose another great memory, maybe from childhood. Choose something that you might have forgotten until now, but it's come back to you just as you needed it most. And faster now. Find another wonderful memory, and another, and another, until after about three to five minutes, you have completely flooded your mind with memories of intensely joyous, grateful, passionate, and happy magic moments.

Now let's anchor that incredible feeling. Create an anchor. Maybe for happiness it's a hand over your heart or both hands over your heart. After doing this intense emotional flood for happiness, put your hands over your heart and anchor in all of the positive emotional experiences of happiness on top of one another. When you've got all of your memories in your heart with your hands there, say, "*Yes.*" This allows you to stack memories of happiness into a single anchor. You can do that with happiness or any emotion. By using the same anchor for multiple experiences, you are essentially stacking the anchor to make it even more powerful. The effect of this emotional flood, if done correctly, usually lasts a few hours and sometimes up to a few days!

When you wake up every morning and fire off an anchor that puts your mind and body into a resourceful and empowering state, when you do power moves, when you anchor a positive emotion physically in your body, when you visualize emotional flooding to envision the best self you can be, when you do all of these things and keep doing them, you have begun to master the second level in the Emotional Fitness Pyramid of Mastery. Now you have the ability to control your behaviors. Being able to take control of your habitual patterns of behavior and conditioning and replace these with empowering ones means you are already ahead of 80 percent of people in the world who merely react to their emotions. Now you have the Emotional Fitness to create the life you want. Are you ready for the next level?

Identity

Beliefs

Habits and Behavior

Emotional States
in a Moment

Awareness of Your
Story, Emotions, and Beliefs

CHAPTER 15

BELIEFS

Man is made by his belief. As he believes, so he is.

—JOHANN WOLFGANG VON GOETHE

Many people believe that in order to be successful you have to go to college, get a good job, and work from eight to five, Monday through Friday, month after month, for the next forty years. Get married, have two or three kids, and move to the suburbs. Save every penny, rarely take vacations, and retire. *Then* you can enjoy life. At sixty-five years old, you can do all the things you want to do, like travel the world. You may find, though, if you follow such a system, that at sixty-five, you're no longer healthy, you're not young and full of energy, and you've made poor investments, so your retirement fund is not as big as you expected. Or maybe the financial system crashed, and you lost your investments, your job, and your pension.

To be educated, to work, to have a family, to retire, and to die: that is the "blueprint" of life. When you don't follow this blueprint, you meet resistance. My hope is that the system was originally designed to help create order and structure in our society. It has led, however, to a waking prison for many people. They work miserably during the week and live for their "free" time on the weekends. Is there another way to live?

On social media, we all have that one crazy, adventurous friend or person we follow who lives like there's no tomorrow. We think, "Oh my god, what are they up to now? Are they getting paid to do this? To travel the world posting pictures?" We look for an explanation. *How is this even possible? They are lucky; that would never work for me.* The truth is that their belief system is not the norm. Do you have to work eight to five, Monday through Friday, saving for that two weeks off every year for forty years? Is that all there is to life? Or is there more?

More and more people are breaking from tradition. The internet revolution has created a movement of freelancers and others who work remotely. I interviewed a young woman who built an entire company of remote workers stationed all over the world. She traveled all the time, all over the world, and still ran her business. In the company's first eighteen months, she made more than $1 million in revenue while traveling the globe. She was twenty-six years old at the time.

Some people believe that they *need* a stable eight-to-five job to survive. They take whatever job they can get and never even think that there are other possibilities. And some people work when they want for as long as they want, doing what they love, embracing every amazing part of life with no boss and no financial worries. How is this possible? It starts with what they believed was possible. Their beliefs empowered them to create the life of their dreams. If you are holding onto old beliefs that stop you, you are a prisoner to your own mind.

How do we not understand that we can choose a different belief system? How is it that even when we see examples of others doing what we want, we *still* limit ourselves and we *still* find reasons why it would never work for us?

The answer is in our beliefs and how and when they were built. Many beliefs are built when we are too young to know the difference, to know that we can choose. These beliefs can be so strong that when we are older, we just think that's the way things are for us. It is the water that surrounds the fish; it becomes so ever-present that we cease to realize its existence.

Take elephants, for example. Have you seen pictures of elephants tied with a rope to a feeble pole? They could easily tear the pole out of the ground and escape, but they don't. Why?

I first saw elephants at a sanctuary in Thailand. They were the size of pickup trucks with thick skin and beautiful eyes that seemed to beam inner peace. These enormous and beautiful animals eat hundreds of pounds of food a day. When they move, it is quite a sight to see. They are surprisingly quick and agile. Walking up or down hills at forty-five-degree angles, they cover ground far faster than any human. If something in the jungle scares them, they can run six miles at speeds of fifteen to twenty-five miles per hour. They will run over trees and anything else in their way. I asked our guide why they stay in the sanctuary. He said it is because the people who run the sanctuary take care of them. But how do people get elephants to stay in one place when they are part of a circus?

In order to train an elephant for the circus, they have to be trained not to escape. When an elephant is young, they tie a strong rope around its neck and attach it to a sturdy pole. The baby elephant tries to escape, but the rope prevents it. It tries again and again. Eventually it gives up, *believing* that this rope will never let it go. When the elephant grows up, it is easily strong enough to rip any pole out of the ground, but it no longer tries. The rope *represents* a belief of entrapment. It is the only truth the elephant knows.

Despite your strength, and despite knowing that *you* have the ability to choose empowering beliefs, your experiences may have taught you limiting beliefs that hold you back. You might not even be aware of these beliefs.

We discussed how your state can be changed in a moment, how your habits and behaviors can shift over time, but what controls how you change? What is the driving force behind these actions? What is your motivation? Remember that your decisions are based on the map of your beliefs. This map guides you through the world to help you make decisions. But sometimes the map is incorrect, old, outdated, and limits you from realizing your full potential.

In this chapter, we're going to annihilate the disempowering beliefs that limit you and explore how to create empowering ones instead. We'll design a map that helps you to achieve the life of your dreams.

What Stops Us?

Why is it that when things get tough, we start to doubt ourselves? Why is it that when there is a problem in life, we stress about it, worry about it, and question our ability to handle it? Why do we spiral out of control and fret about all the ways things *might* go wrong? We live in fear about a future that may never happen. Why do we do this to ourselves?

While these beliefs were originally built to help us, they can sometimes be the very thing that limits our ability to go after our goals and dreams. To some people, these beliefs are as real as the ground you walk on, the car you drive, and the chair you sit in. These beliefs become their reality. Landy believed that he could not run a sub-four-minute mile. That limiting belief became his reality *until* Roger Bannister changed it. These beliefs that stop us are called limiting beliefs.

Limiting Beliefs

"Limits, like fears, are often just an illusion."

—MICHAEL JORDAN

Limiting beliefs are any beliefs that limit you from reaching your potential. Beliefs like *you have to have money to make money. I'm not smart enough. I'm not sexy enough. Life is a struggle. I have to go to college to get a good job. No one wants to buy my product. I always fail. I'm just big-boned.* We all carry our own limiting beliefs and also deal with other people putting their limiting beliefs on us. These limiting beliefs often stop us from achieving greatness, living life fully, loving more, and enjoying more of life.

Limiting beliefs can also stem from old, outdated beliefs that used to serve a positive purpose, like protecting yourself, but now limits you from accomplishing your goals. For example, a belief that being a perfectionist is important might have helped you find success in school at a young age, but it can cripple your ability to execute as an entrepreneur.

When going after goals, people have a lot of limiting beliefs in the form of **excuses** that stop them from being successful: *I don't have the time, the knowledge, the money, the right background, the support, the skill, the ability.* Some people back up excuses with true and rational logic: *I grew up in the ghetto and never had a chance at college. Without money, I couldn't get a good education. Without a good education, I couldn't get a good job. I was screwed from the beginning.* It's a common story but remember that stories are what we tell ourselves. And tons of people have a similar background and turn it into a success story. We have the ability to choose to write a different story.

That's what Daymond John did when he went from waiting tables at Red Lobster to building FUBU, the American hip-hop apparel company worth over $300 million, and now is one of the "sharks" on the popular show "Shark Tank," which is a symbol of entrepreneurship in America. Maybe you don't have the money, or the time, or the education, or the ability, but if you want something badly enough, can you find the resources? We all make time for what's important to us. Ever met someone who could never find time to go to the gym, but then their doctor told them they were going to die if they didn't exercise and all of a sudden, they *found* time? How many people don't have the money to start a business but prepare a presentation and get investors to give them millions of dollars?

Just look at Juicero. Dubbed the "Keurig for juice," Juicero involved a sleek machine and juice packs that created fresh-squeezed juice. The company raised over $125 million and went into production. It wasn't long before the general public realized the sleek $700 internet-connected juicer was barely more effective at producing liquid from the juice packs than a healthy adult just squeezing the packs with their hands. In 2017, Juicero stopped manufacturing. Even though the company failed, think about how the original creators had no money and somehow raised over $100 million.

Every day, people pitch business ideas to friends, family, banks, and investors. And every day, people are getting millions in funding. You might not have the money, but if you are resourceful, you can find a way to get it. Whether it's money, time, or any other resource, it's never a lack of resources, but rather a lack of resourcefulness that stops us.

Excuses come from limiting beliefs. Other people, the economy, your past—these excuses stop you from achieving your goals. You cannot change other people, or the economy, or your past.

These are all things that are out of your control, which is why people love to use them as excuses. If you cannot change them, it's not your fault. In reality, it's up to you to be resourceful, to break through limits and especially limiting beliefs. Knowing that you are in full control of your success is scary because it also means that you are in full control of your failures.

Muggsy Bogues was 5'3" and the shortest player ever to play in the National Basketball Association. He had a 44-inch vertical leap and played 14 seasons in the NBA. **But what if his limiting beliefs told him he was too short?** What if he listened to everyone else who said he couldn't be successful? What if he'd never even *tried* out for basketball? If he had let others limit him, he never would have played in the NBA. How often do we minimize our own dreams by toning down our beliefs in ourselves and our potential?

Another person who is currently defying many of the world's limiting beliefs is the visionary Elon Musk. He's a perfect example of a man driven by a passionate vision to change the world despite the rest of humanity's limiting beliefs. "When something is important enough, you do it even if the odds are not in your favor," he is quoted as saying.

Musk has accomplished things many thought impossible. If he'd listened to his critics, and even many of his friends, he would not have founded SpaceX or SolarCity, envisioned Hyperloop, or Tesla. Most told him he couldn't create a new, successful car company. They said the current companies dominated the market and had been around for one hundred years or more. Doubters would reference all of the facts about how others had tried and failed. If Elon had listened to them, he would never have taken on the automobile industry and created the Tesla electric car.

As of December 2018, Musk has an estimated net worth of $21.1 billion and ranked in the 2017 Forbes 400 as the twenty-first wealthiest person in America. In December 2016, Musk was ranked twenty-first on <u>Forbes'</u> list of The World's Most Powerful People.

Elon Musk clearly strongly believes in himself. His belief system is largely reliant on his internal view of the world. He doesn't let others alter his beliefs with their own limiting beliefs. The guy is arguably a madman workaholic entrepreneur who had a grand vision of transforming the world and taking humankind to space. But his beliefs have turned that *vision* into a reality and in the process made him a billionaire.

Money: The Root of All Evil

Lots of people have disempowering beliefs about money. People may say money is the root of all evil, wanting more money means you're greedy, or to get rich you have to take from the poor. They might say it's selfish to want more money or you can either be rich or you can be happy. These are all beliefs about money.

At one point, I associated making too much money with greed, lack of friendships, and lack of balance. I let other peoples' limits and beliefs about money invade my own. These are just beliefs, and once I changed those beliefs, I was able to make even more money, even though money was not what I truly wanted. What I actually wanted was what I thought money would give me: *love, acceptance, and freedom*. Now I understand money is merely a vehicle to get what I want in the world. I still set financial goals, but I am no longer motivated by inanimate currency. I am motivated by the freedom and impact our currency can provide. What drives me is the lifestyle, the freedom, and the ability to help more people that money brings, not the money itself. Money is a *vehicle* to help accomplish goals. Our society and economy are built around money, and therefore it can make things happen. The key is making sure that money doesn't have power over you, but instead understanding how the power of money can accelerate your ability to get what you want in life.

Money isn't the only way to achieve your goals; it's just a vehicle to get you there. For example, Mother Teresa was able to raise millions of dollars for her charity to help feed and take care of those who could not help themselves. And yet she had humble beginnings and was never a millionaire. She used her passion to make a difference.

Money and limiting beliefs seem to go hand in hand for most people. Many of us tell ourselves we will never make enough money, and certainly not a lot of money. We convince ourselves that our limited income is the only amount we can bring in, so we manifest that as reality.

I was talking to a young guy at one of my seminars who said he'd love to own an Audi R8. You could tell it was the car of his dreams. "I'll never own one," he said.

"Why not?" I asked.

"They're over $100,000. I make minimum wage," he answered.

"Don't you think if you work hard that you could get there?" I asked.

"It'll never happen," he answered.

"Maybe not right away, but maybe in five or ten years? Do you think it's even possible you will be able to own the car of your dreams?"

His limiting beliefs were keeping him from realizing his dream car. This guy is not alone. Many people limit their earning potential by a fundamental belief that they can only earn to a certain level. They don't believe they have the ability to earn more, so they don't even try. Maybe they don't have that ability right now. But five to ten years is a long time to grow. In five to ten years you could become the top salesperson, a realtor, you could save, invest, and become a doctor, lawyer, whatever you want. Most people look at their limited resources right now and make a decision that says *I can't do something* instead of looking at their **unlimited potential** and **resourcefulness** and saying *I can find a way to make it happen.*

What are some limiting beliefs you have about life, business, money, relationships, success, and change? Write yours down. Here are some examples:

1) Life is a struggle and I'm just trying to survive.
2) To make a lot of money, I have to cheat other people out of theirs.
3) To be successful in business, I have to be ruthless and aggressive.
4) All the good people are taken, so I'm single.
5) I'll never find true love, so I'll settle for what I can get.
6) Successful people are lucky they had that opportunity. I'm not successful because I don't have what they have.
7) Real change happens over years and is hard to do.

Instead of letting your beliefs limit you, why don't you change your beliefs? In order to that, we first need to look at what you believe about your ability to change.

What Do You Believe About Change?

Can we change our beliefs? Is that possible? In order to create real change, let's look at what people usually believe about change. So many people think they can't change, or that change is really hard, or that change takes a long, long time, but they are also not reading this book. They don't know that their state in any given moment is controlled by the questions they ask, the language they use, and how they hold themselves. They don't realize that their negative habits have reinforced their behavior. They don't know that they can choose to feel different and they can choose a new belief. So, to them, change is too hard, rarely works, and takes a long time. They back it up with experiences. Maybe their friend quit smoking five times and failed every time. They are still a smoker. Another friend tries a new diet every other week but somehow manages to gain weight instead of losing it. They see that few people around succeed at change, and even when they do, it takes them several years! Who has the energy for that?

The truth about change is that you need to find the right **leverage**. With the right leverage, change can happen in a single moment. In fact, all change happens in a moment: you finally make a decision that enough is enough. *I can't live like this for another year, another day, not even one more second! I am changing now.* This decision comes from finding the right leverage. If a person failing to lose weight is told they have diabetes, high blood pressure, and that they might die twenty years earlier, they finally have the right leverage to lose weight.

It doesn't have to be as severe as death. If someone gets rejected by a person who makes a comment about their weight, the humiliation, the rejection, and the pain might drive them to change. **Change does not take years. What takes years is finding the right leverage for you to change.** Change is not hard. People think change is hard because they don't want to change *more* than they want to stay the same. What if you believed change happens in a moment? What if you believed change was easy? Do you think it's possible that you can change your beliefs about change? How would that change your life for the better?

Let's go back to that list we made earlier. Look at the beliefs you wrote in the first list. Which ones are empowering, and which ones are limiting beliefs? Write an *E* beside the empowering ones and an *L* beside the limiting ones. Do the exercise now.

Beliefs about yourself are neither right nor wrong. There are only beliefs that either empower you to your goals or limit you from achieving them. There are beliefs that make your life better or beliefs that make your life worse. So why not create empowering beliefs? Why not choose beliefs that make your life better? How do you find the right leverage? Where can we get the motivation to change?

My dad was our seventh-grade basketball coach. I was the

starting point guard and objectively was the best guard to start. If I made a mistake, even a minor one, I was severely punished. I was benched, forced to run more, and made to work harder. My dad was tougher on me than anyone else. Why? Because he wanted me to be the best. I could have quit, but what my dad didn't know was that I wanted his acceptance and love, and that worked in his favor. I thought being the best at sports would earn that. I was motivated by one of the strongest emotions in humankind: the need to feel loved. As a kid who looked up to his dad, I would have done anything to earn that love. Of course, my dad loved me no matter what, but these are the beliefs we create in our minds as kids! And they are not always accurate! The key is not letting these beliefs limit you later in life. As a kid, believing I was not good enough caused me to work hard to become better. However, as an adult, that same belief can make living a happy and successful life miserable if you feel that no matter what you do, it is never good enough. The key is keeping beliefs that empower you and upgrading beliefs that don't.

Annihilate Disempowering Beliefs

Limiting beliefs ultimately disempower us. What are some of your limiting beliefs? *I'm just big-boned. I'm not confident. I'm not good enough.* By believing these limits, you continue to live within the confines of them, further fulfilling that limiting belief, which helps create your reality.

These limiting beliefs then create a negative pattern of self-sabotage. These disempowering beliefs could stop you from earning the money you want, losing weight, finding true love, and even enjoying life. If you really want to create a breakthrough in your life, you have to shift your limiting beliefs.

Now we're going to focus on getting rid of our disempowering beliefs. To annihilate your disempowering beliefs, you need to first identify what they are. These beliefs may have helped you in the past but now they no longer serve you. If you really want to change your old beliefs, there is a three-step process. First you must clearly identify the old belief and ask yourself how this belief has limited your potential or disempowered you in some way. Acknowledging the possibility that this belief limits you allows you to create doubt in the belief.

Second, associate a significant amount of pain with your old belief. What has this belief cost you in the past? How has this belief hurt you? What has it cost you in your life financially, physically, mentally, and in your relationships? If you are honest with yourself, you'll realize that most limiting beliefs stop you from taking action toward what you want in life. Third, replace your old disempowering belief with a new empowering belief:

Do the exercise below.

1. Identify your old, disempowering limiting belief.

2. How is this belief limiting you now? Why does having this belief hurt you or stop you from accomplishing your goals? What has this belief cost you?

3. Replace the limiting belief with an empowering belief.

Finding an Empowering Belief

You might be wondering where to find a new empowering belief. Sometimes you don't need to create a new one; you can look inside yourself and use what you already have. Look at your past experiences to see if you can find any empowering beliefs that need to be brought to the forefront and reinforced. This can be hard to do because people tend to focus on what went wrong in the past. We want you to focus on a positive, empowering experience. For example, maybe you studied really hard and got an A on a test. From this, maybe your belief is, "If I work hard, I can accomplish anything I put my mind to." Maybe you gave a presentation at work and people came up to you afterward and said, "Great job!" and you believed that you are a confident presenter. Maybe five years ago you decided finally to get in shape and lost fifteen pounds in three months. Instead of beating yourself up over the fact that you haven't maintained it, you can look at yourself and acknowledge that, when you wanted to, you were *capable* of doing it. Instead of focusing on the failure, build on your success.

What if you don't have a past experience to draw from? The beautiful thing is that at one point, all of us were new to the world and had no experience. This means we had to learn by watching someone else. This is called **modeling.** We did this as kids to learn how to walk. We failed many times, over and over again. One day, it clicked, and we walked. So, it doesn't matter if you have don't have a past positive experience to create a new belief. You can model someone else's behavior and create your own new belief that way. You can model someone's confidence by the way they walk and talk. You can model someone's courage by seeing how they respond to fearful situations. You can pretend to be them until these beliefs become your beliefs.

Find someone who has done what you want to do and use modeling. With over seven billion people in the world, there is somebody out there who has done what you want to do: lose weight, build a billion-dollar business, fall in love, or fall in love again. Find them or find their stories. Now, dissociate from yourself and associate with that person. Feel and pretend what it would be like to be them. Walk, talk, and act like them until you think like them. Model them. This may sound weird to try at first, but this is exactly how we did it as kids to develop the beliefs we have now! For example, my dad was the life of the party with a big personality. Everyone engaged with him. He told great stories. I wanted to be like him. I was so shy as a kid and not very confident in social situations. I had a few friends, but I was far from Mr. Popular. But then I started to watch *how* my dad told stories, how he engaged people's emotions, and how he was able to make friends with everyone instantly. I watched him. Then I modeled him. My dad was my idol. I imagined what he would do. I followed in his footsteps and held myself how he holds himself—chest out, confident, and shoulders back. As I did that physically, I felt more confident. When you mimic and model someone physically, your brain and physiology changes. Over time, I no longer had to pretend to feel confident. I started to believe it until I became it.

How to Create a New Belief

Over the course of my speaking career, I have given tons of training seminars where I get people to create new beliefs. By creating several new beliefs, we are able to shift in an hour their entire belief system, and as a result, shift what they think is even possible.

In my seminars, I walk people through the power posing exercise. I have them start feeling sad and depressed for a minute and then I have them stand up into the power pose just as I instructed you in Chapter 9. This creates a biochemical shift in their bodies. In most of my seminars, I typically see two types of people: people who are at the bottom and need massive change to help get them out of a slump or people who are at the top and are looking for the *edge* to go even higher. Both typically want to create a belief that makes them feel like they can accomplish anything. So, I created an incantation to create a new belief.

Incantations are a lot like affirmations. They are positive statements you say to yourself to solidify positive beliefs. Think of them as "I-CAN-tations." These are not wishful thinking but dynamic and practical statements you say to yourself to train your uncon-scious and conscious minds. They engage your physiology and shift your biochemistry and hormones, so that you not only say how you feel, but you begin to actually feel different. We're going to be using incantations to ingrain new ways of thinking through-out the following chapters.

Remember, if we *believe* we *can* do something, we will take more *action* to make it happen and get better *results*. The key to accomplishing your goals and living your best life starts with your beliefs. After reciting this incantation out loud in the seminars, I always ask the audience, "What do you believe you are able to do now?" and the responses that get yelled back to me are often one of two words: "ANYTHING!" and "EVERYTHING!!" They literally believe in that moment that anything and everything is possible, that they can accomplish any goal and live their best lives all the time. Would you like to feel this way? Then stand UP right now and do this exercise with me!

Incantation Exercise

First, do your power move and get into your power pose! Now, while engaging your body, mind, and voice, I want you to yell with 100 percent conviction the following:

I OWN THIS.

I OWN YOU.

I AM UNSTOPPABLE.

I WILL NOT BE DENIED.

NOW IS MY TIME.

I OWN THIS.

I OWN YOU.

I AM UNLEASHED.

After doing this exercise three times in a power pose, you too will start to believe that anything and everything is possible. Do this daily and your beliefs will shift massively.

Whether you're struggling in life or are massively successful, we all have moments where our beliefs start to limit us. Even with as much success as I've had in life, even with all of my accomplishments, *I still find limiting beliefs every time I step outside my comfort zone.* Sometimes I don't even realize they are there until I reflect back. And that's why awareness is so powerful because once I identify a limiting belief, I immediately have to crush it. I have to remember that I AM UNLEASHED. I will scream it at the top of my lungs for just a few minutes while engaging my body with power posing. After doing this for just a few minutes, you will feel on fire. Every cell of your body will be electrified. You will truly believe that you can do anything, that you are unstoppable, and that you are UNLEASHED. Life is yours. **Now is your time.**

This is how you train beliefs. But you must train them daily. You must train your Emotional Fitness to make sure it is strong every day. And like the people at my seminars, you too will feel that you are capable of anything and everything.

The most effective way to create a new belief is by utilizing everything you have learned with Emotional Fitness. You want to engage your physiology, your voice, your language, and direct your focus. You can use the above incantation to create a new belief or you can create your own incantation. For example, one of my empowering beliefs is that *as long as I work hard enough, I can accomplish anything.* This belief empowers me to keep taking action. Another empowering belief I have is that failure is just a result that tells me where to improve and get better for next time. Therefore, failure is never an end but a beginning. Failure means I am about to learn something. Failure means I am growing and getting better. Another empowering belief I have is that life happens for you, not to you. This empowers me because no matter what happens in my life, even during the worst times, I believe there is something I can learn or use to help people in the future.

Below, write down your own personal empowering incantation. You can use the one above, incorporate it into your own, or create your own. Remember to use words that physically and mentally engage you. Maybe you want to be a world champion. Maybe you want to be filled with love and joy. Maybe you want to be the best model, actress, doctor, lawyer, or entrepreneur. Whatever you want to become, you can become it. Use your incantation to create your new belief.

Steps to create a new belief:

1. What are some beliefs you would like to have? Write down your empowering belief. For example, *I am confident and successful. I am happy and passionate about life. I am open, vulnerable, and in love. I never take no for an answer and always look for solutions. Nothing can stop me from achieving my goals, I always find a way. I am resourceful.*

_____

_____

_____

_____

_____

2. Use I-CAN-tations. Engage your whole body in your empowering belief. Use your voice and your body. Do a power pose. Be very energetic. Stand up and shout out loud your empowering belief with 100 percent conviction. Repeat it five times. When you engage your physiology, you shift your hormones and even the wiring of your brain.

Get out there and try it. Yes, you might fail. Will you recoil and go back into your comfort zone? Or will you try again and again? The only way to reinforce an empowering belief is to put yourself out there. Failure is just a stepping stone to success. The biggest question is: *What do you do when you fail?*

The Key Belief about Failure

How you handle failure is very important. At some point everyone fails. And the truth is you're going to fail too. Does one failure stop you from your goals or help you achieve them? What if you shifted your perception and belief so that you see every failure as a lesson to get better? Then failure won't be debilitating, but instead empowering, as you start to see yourself getting better with every failure. Shift your belief around failure to something that empowers you. Plan in your head ahead of time what you are going to do when you fail. Be prepared to flip failure into a lesson and become a student ready to learn. This is the key to overcoming failure and achieving success.

I used to be an indoor skydiving instructor inside of a 25-foot tunnel with a giant propeller shooting out air at 120 miles per hour. My clients and I simulated skydiving inside this wind tunnel. It's exhilarating. As you do it, you can learn to control your movements using the power of the wind. In the tunnel we were using, there was about 3 feet of dead air, and I taught people how to tuck and roll if they hit this dead air so they land on giant, cushy pads.

As instructors, we learned how to fly out of the wind into the dead air, put our feet on the wall, and backflip back into the wind. It was pretty cool. As I got more advanced, one trick I learned was to backflip while flying to the wall and then backflip back into the wind. I was kind of an adrenaline junkie in college. I kept visualizing doing it and saying to myself *I can do this. I can do this. I can do this.* I nailed it on the first try. I had so much confidence.

I tried it again with some friends a week later, but the results weren't the same. I had too much power going forward, and I didn't get all the way around on the flip. Upside down, I slid fifteen feet down the wall. If you watched, it looked ugly. I knew I had to do it again immediately because I had failed so badly. I did it again, mistimed it, and cracked my neck, head, and shoulders. This time it was really bad, like I didn't know if I should go to the doctor bad. I was out for a couple of weeks, but I knew I had to go back. I couldn't let that one trick hold me back. I couldn't end on a failure. I knew I would never give up until I did it again. I visualized it, and this time I threw the flip too soon. A "miss." Eventually, after five or ten times, I got it. I didn't look at the whole experience as a failure; I saw it as a learning experience, and so each time I failed, I learned what to do better, and I kept going forward. I was not a failure; I was a student learning.

Failure Is a Learning Experience and an Opportunity to Grow and Get Better

If you believe that failure is just the beginning, just a lesson, and just a learning experience to help you get better, then you never have to feel bad about failing. Failing becomes a stepping stone to success.

What beliefs do you want to have? Do you want to never give up? Do you want to feel confident and successful every day? Do you want to feel loved? As you begin to create your new beliefs, you will start to shape the very building blocks that make up your character. The next two chapters break down these core essentials of your identity so you can become who you want to be.

CHAPTER 16

VALUES

*Happiness is when what you think, what you
say, and what you do are in harmony.*

—MAHATMA GANDHI

At this point in this book, you have built awareness, identified your emotions in a moment, changed your state, asked better questions, and begun to annihilate disempowering beliefs and replaced them with empowering beliefs. For most, this is a life-changing process and creates incredible change far beyond expectations.

Still, even with all of the information we have gone over in this book, people still struggle to get what they want in life. They struggle to become fully successful in every area of life. They struggle to do what they say they will do. You may have all the empowering beliefs and goals in the world but still can't seem to accomplish the life you envision. In the pursuit of your goals, you may feel torn between what you want and what you don't want. In the last chapter, we made it easier for you to move towards these goals when we created empowering beliefs and got rid of disempowering ones. These were great exercises, but with each layer of the onion, you will uncover one more layer of depth as you get to the core of what drives you, the building blocks of your character, and your values. This is the most intensive part of Emotional

Fitness, but it is the most rewarding and the final key to unlock the true power of Emotional Fitness and live the life of your dreams.

Values

What do you value most in life? Do you know? We're all driven by core values, whether these are conscious or unconscious. The dictionary defines core values as "the fundamental beliefs of a person, guiding principles that dictate behavior." What you want is based on your values. What you *do* is based on your values.

Everything we do is driven by a desire to either meet a value or avoid a value. Examples of values include things like happiness, family, success, money, love, freedom, honesty, resourcefulness, faith, purpose, creativity, intelligence, and importance. Some of these values are simply a means to an end. These **means values** are basically vehicles to get you to your ultimate end value. An **end value** is an emotion or feeling that you consider important for you to feel or experience. For example, family is something that I value very much and is extremely important to me. However, family is only a means value. Family, ultimately, is a vehicle to meet my end values of love and happiness. When looking at your values, you want to try to get to the root end value. We move *toward* the end values we want to experience in life. Therefore, these are called **toward values**. We each have a distinct order to our values that dictates which value is more important. You might value family, money, and health as your top three values. If money is more important than health, you might sacrifice sleep or even food to get the work done. When faced with an internal conflict, this order determines what we do.

There are also values that we move *away* from called **away values**. Remember, one of the basic principles of human biology and psychology is that we move either toward pleasure or away from pain. This is the same for values. We move toward the value of happiness and away from the value of sadness. Some examples of values we move away from are sadness, loneliness, depression, anger, rage, anxiety, worry, regret, rejection, guilt, disgust, not being loved, not being good enough, lack of importance, and lack of purpose or meaning. There is also an order to these away values.

Some people fear not being good enough over everything else and so take massive action to ensure they are more than good enough, even boasting about their accomplishments to ensure you know how good enough they are. Others fear not being loved so much that they go out of their way to help others, listen to their friends, and give love. **The order of your values determines your actions, consciously or, more often, unconsciously.**

Unwritten Rules

Why is it that some people experience debilitating anxiety, depression, and anger to such a degree that they have to be treated with medication or even hospitalized? And yet others experience blissful joy, happiness, love, and purpose each and every day? We all know someone who is always a ray of sunshine no matter what happens. Maybe you think, "I wish I had whatever drug they are on." Or maybe you think they are crazy and can't deal with reality, so they "drink the Kool-Aid" and live in a false utopia.

What *is* the difference? How do some experience their top toward values (happiness and love) while others are crippled by their top away values (anxiety, anger, and depression)? The answer lies in our rules for our values. These rules determine whether we feel our values are met. **Rules are beliefs we make up to determine whether we meet a value.** Thus, rules are what you believe should happen in order for you to feel that your value is being met. Some rules are easy to meet; others are difficult. The rules we create for ourselves determine how easy or hard it is for us to feel our value of happiness or sadness, love or depression, joy or anger. The biggest issue is that we often create these rules unconsciously through our experiences as kids and young adults. Now it's time to create them consciously. For example, what must happen for you to feel happiness? Some people believe they need to have a good job that pays over six figures, a new luxury sports car, yearly vacations, $100,000 in the bank, a family with two kids (one boy and one girl), a dog, and a house with a white picket fence. It's the American dream. Others feel happy as long as they have a roof over their heads, food, and they wake up six feet above ground. Some peoples' rules are so extremely specific that they are difficult to follow, while other people have rules that are so easy to follow that they always experience their values.

How Our Values and Rules Affect Our Life

I was depressed for eight years. I was miserable, unfulfilled, angry at the world, regretful of my choices, and I had no idea why. Then I ranked my values. My number one value was happiness. I always said I wanted to be happy. Isn't that what everyone wants?

My number two value was success. I wanted to be happy and successful. But then I asked myself an interesting question: if I am not successful, will I be happy? At the time, the answer was no. That's when I realized that I *wanted* my values to be happiness at number one, and success as number two. But the way I *lived* was the opposite. Success was the number one value in my life at that point. Happiness was second. Our values can and do have many rules to be met. The problem is we often unconsciously think we have to meet all of our rules in order to meet our values.

My moving toward value of success was number one, and my rules for that value shocked me when I finally sat down and wrote them out. I couldn't believe the rules I had for myself. And it was only when I got brutally honest with myself that I realized why my rules had led me astray. My rules were as follows:

- I must have $10 million in the bank.
- I must be worth $100 million.

- I must own a nice car.
- I must own a boat.
- I must own a beach house.
- I had to be the best at everything I did, *all the time.*

On paper, I was a board-certified orthodontist and highly achieved in my own right. I had competed on the national stage for men's physique, and I was living in California. It was "the dream." But the problem was that if all of my rules were not met all of the time, I did not *feel* successful. It's no wonder that I never felt successful. My rules were insanely specific, hard to meet, *and* I had to meet them *all*. I had to be the best, not sometimes but all the time.

Remember, I said what I really wanted was to be happy. But the order of the values I lived by were success first and happiness second. In fact, in order to feel happiness, one of my rules was that I had to be successful. With my rules to be successful and happy, it was no wonder I *never* felt happy.

While I was trying to achieve my top toward values, I was also trying to move away from my number one away value of *depression*. I didn't want to feel depressed, but I had old rules and beliefs around depression. These rules made it really easy to feel depressed and even harder for me to experience happiness. My rules to feel depressed were as follows:

- If I'm not successful, I'm depressed.
- If I'm not happy, I'm depressed.
- If I'm alone, I'm depressed.
- If I see someone I know and they don't say hi, I'm depressed.
- If I wake up and don't feel like I'll successful that day, which is impossible to meet based on my rules, then I'm not happy and I'm depressed.

There were many more. Basically, it was incredibly easy for me to feel depressed. And if even one of these rules were met, I would feel depressed.

My rules and beliefs about how to meet my toward values and away values were making it impossible to feel happy and easy to feel depressed.

What Are Your Rules?

First, we have to understand what our rules are. As I've shown with my rules above, we often attach very specific needs to go with each of our values. These are requirements that need to be fulfilled before we feel like we've attained that value. **These rules are our beliefs about what has to happen in order for us to *feel* we met this value.** For example, let's say success is one of the values on your list. What does it take to make you feel successful? What rules have you attached to the concept of wealth? How much money do you need? Millions? Billions? A house? How many houses? Do you need to be the founder of a massively successful business? How many cars must you have? Do you need airplanes? Boats? Staff? Do you need to be featured in prominent business magazines? Do you need to be famous?

As you dig down, you'll see just how detailed your rules are and how often until you say them out loud how unconscious they are. In fact, if you don't know the rules of the game, how can you ever win it? You want to be successful, and you have so many rules for being successful that even if you reached a few of your goals, you still wouldn't be content with your wealth. You wonder why you never feel successful. You might say, "*I need millions of dollars and a second home, and a nice car, and a loving* partner *and family to feel successful, and, and, and . . .*" You compound so many rules into this value of success that if any one of them do not happen, you may *never* feel successful. All it takes is one thing not to happen. Even if ninety-nine other things do happen, you don't feel successful because in your mind you need to meet *all* of your rules. Your expectations for life and for yourself are so restrictive that you make it almost impossible to feel successful. **When our expectations do not meet our reality, we experience pain.** And if you do the same thing for happiness, gratitude, and fulfillment, it's no wonder you are in a rut! But *no more*! You have to ask yourself how you can make your *rules* easier to meet, so you achieve this value you want. My point is that there are more Emotionally Fit ways to look at your *rules*, and, in turn, this helps you fulfill your values.

What Are Your Toward Values?

We're all living out our deepest beliefs and values every day, and we're often not aware of them. Let's start by becoming aware. Look at the values list below. By just using your gut and without thinking too hard, pick five of the following values that are most important to you. The easiest way to do this is to give stars to each one: three stars for very important and one star for not important. If you can't decide which is most important, ask yourself, "If I had to pick one, which is more important to me?" For example, love or freedom?" You can use any two you are struggling with. Look at what your actions are, not what you say you want. I always said I wanted to be happy, but success came first. And where was love on my list? It was further down because when I asked myself which value was more important, success or love, I used to think that I couldn't be loved if I wasn't successful. So, success was number one.

What do your actions say you value most? Look at what you do every day. Self-honesty is vitally important here. The only way you can improve upon yourself is to get completely honest about where you are today. Once you have the starting point, you can make improvements to get you to where you want to be. What are your top moving toward values that you live by right now? Below is a list of examples.

ACCEPTANCE	ACCURACY	ACHIEVEMENT	ADVENTURE	ATTRACTIVENESS
AUTHORITY	AUTONOMY	BEAUTY	CARING	CHALLENGE
CHANGE	COMFORT	COMMITMENT	COMPASSION	CONTRIBUTION
COOPERATION	COURAGE	COURTESY	CREATIVITY	DEPENDABILITY
DUTY	ECOLOGY	EXCITEMENT	FAITHFULNESS	FAME
FAMILY	FITNESS	FLEXIBILITY	FORGIVENESS	FREEDOM
FRIENDSHIP	FUN	GENEROSITY	GENUINENESS	GOD'S WILL
GROWTH	HAPPINESS	HEALTH	HELPFULNESS	HONESTY
HOPE	HUMILITY	HUMOR	INDEPENDENCE	INDUSTRY
INNER PEACE	INTELLIGENCE	INTIMACY	JUSTICE	KNOWLEDGE
LEISURE	LOVE	LOYALTY	MASTERY	MINDFULNESS
MODERATION	MONEY	MONOGAMY	NURTURANCE	OPENNESS
ORDER	PASSION	PLEASURE	POWER	PURPOSE
RATIONALITY	RESPONSIBILITY	RISK	ROMANCE	SAFETY
SECURITY	SELF-ACCEPTANCE	SELF-CONTROL	SELF-ESTEEM	SELF-KNOWLEDGE
SERVICE	SEXUALITY	SIMPLICITY	SOLITUDE	SPIRITUALITY
STABILITY	TEMPERAMENT	TOLERANCE	TRADITION	TRAVEL
VIRTUE	WEALTH	WORLD PEACE		

Write down the values you picked:

1. _____

2. _____

3. _____

4. _____

5. _____

Now look at your top five values. If you were completely honest, they may not be what you'd thought they'd be. Some people might have family as a top value, but they sacrifice all their time to work. Some people say financial success is their top value, but they party every weekend. What values do you truly live by? Once you've figured out the values you are currently living by, it is important to identify your current rules to meet those values. Maybe your values are in the exact order you want but your rules make it impossible to meet these values and so you never experience things like happiness, success, love, certainty, or freedom.

Toward Value #1: _____

Rules: _____

Toward Value #2: _____

Rules: _____

Toward Value #3: _____

Rules: _____

Toward Value #4: _____

Rules: _____

Toward Value #5: _____

Rules: _____

Now that we have identified our current toward values and
their rules, let's look at our away values to fully understand all of
the factors that drive us.

What Are Your Away Values?

Away values are things you don't want to feel. Perhaps you were
rejected once, and it was such a painful experience that you will do
everything in your power to never feel rejection again. While that
might help you from feeling the pain of rejection, it may also stop
you from ever opening up and experiencing one of life's greatest
emotions: love. So, what values do you move away from? Choose
from this list:

ANGER	ANXIETY	BITTERNESS	CONDEMNATION
CRITICISM	CYNICISM	DESPAIR	DEPRESSION
DESPONDENCY	DISCOURAGEMENT	DISAPPOINTMENT	DISINTEREST
EMBARRASSMENT	FAILURE	FEAR OF [SPECIFY]	FRUSTRATION
FUTILITY	GLOOM	GREED	GUILT
HOSTILITY	HUMILIATION	INADEQUACY	INSIGNIFICANCE
JEALOUSY	JUDGMENT	LETHARGY	LONELINESS
MISERY	OSTRACISM	OVERWHELM/OVERLOAD	PESSIMISM
POVERTY	REGRET	REJECTION	RESIGNATION
RIGIDITY	SADNESS	SELF-DOUBT	SORROW
SUSPICION	WITHDRAWAL	WORRY	

Maybe you don't know what your away values are. Most people never consciously think about them, so you're not alone. Stop right now and think about something that you will do almost anything *not* to feel. Here's an example: a boy gets rejected when trying out for varsity, and he associates so much humiliation with that rejection that he will do anything to avoid the feeling of rejection. He may give up sports altogether. Or he may work so hard that he becomes the most athletic person in school, so he never gets rejected again. Or rejection could be so painful it affects his professional life. At work, he may never ask for a raise or promotion as he's more afraid of rejection than anything else. He may do everything he can to avoid putting himself in a position to be rejected because he has associated rejection with so much humiliation. He may also not want to feel anxiety, worry, or anger, but if he gets angry or anxious, it's not that big of a deal. Rejection is associated with so much pain that it overrides every other negative emotion, and thus, his highest *away* value is the fear of rejection.

Most Common Away Values

Many people commonly experience away values that include not feeling good enough, fear of failing, or not feeling like their life has any meaning or significance. The away value of not feeling good enough is very common. It can drive people to work insanely hard so that they are adequately prepared or, more often, it can stop them from ever trying in the first place. Not feeling good enough is a common characteristic of high achievers and workaholics. They never feel like anything is good enough because their biggest fear is that *they* are not enough.

Some people are so afraid of being alone or not being loved that they will do anything to prove they are worthy of love. Unfortunately, many people get confused about what it means to be loved. They might think that in order to be worthy of love, they need to accomplish something great: be the starting quarterback, the Olympic gold medalist, make $100,000, or build a million-dollar business. And when they do accomplish something great, they get admiration and love, although it's brief and only in the moment. Thus, they spend their whole lives trying to one-up themselves and accomplish goal after goal after goal because in their heads, they feel that in order to be loved, they have to be significant in life. But love is not based on merits and accomplishments, so their rules for feeling loved need to be redefined.

Often, these away values are embedded during major events in childhood. Perhaps it would help to think of the top three significant memories that negatively impacted you. What happened? What was your emotional reaction? How did others react? How did that make you feel? What did you avoid afterward? What negative emotion would you now do anything to avoid experiencing?

Yes, it may be difficult at first to pin down your away values, but it's worth it. To change, you must be willing to bring these values to your awareness. Then you can change them. Do you avoid talking to men or women? Do you avoid risk so that you never fail? Do you double- and triple-check every work project to make sure you look good enough? Do you fear not being enough or not having significance or meaning in life? Do you fear being alone and unloved? What is it that you move away from?

Write down the values you're moving away from in order. Which value is the one you try to avoid the most? If you absolutely never want to feel insignificant, put that first. If you never want to feel rejection, put that first. If rejection is worse than failure, then put rejection first and failure second or vice versa.

My top away values are:

1. _____

2._____

3. _____

4. _____

5. _____

Now, in order to fully understand how your away values affect your decisions and actions in life, we need to know what your rules are for these values. What do you believe must happen in order for you to feel rejection, failure, etc.?

Away Value #1 _____

Rules: _____

Away Value #2 _____

Rules: _____

Away Value #3 _____

Rules: _____

Away Value #4 _____

Rules: _____

Away Value #5 _____

Rules: _____

Are you beginning to see what's most important to you? Some people can have fifteen to twenty top values, but most of us focus on about five to ten. Typically, the top three away and toward values are our go-to values, the ones that dictate most of our decisions.

Understanding our values can help us look at the decisions

we make and align more fully with what we truly hold dear. They can also help us to see how sometimes our actions and what we think or say we want are in conflict. This is the infamous internal struggle...

Chapter 17

The Internal Struggle

*What you think, you become. What you feel,
you attract. What you imagine, you create.*

—Buddha

Most of us are familiar with the struggle between finding what
we want in life and what we don't want, but there's another even
more difficult conflict. What if the struggle is between something
you want and something else that you *also* want? What happens
then? What is going on consciously, or more likely unconsciously,
that dictates what you do or do not do?

Do you go out with friends or do you go to the gym? Someone
might say they want to be a millionaire but never wants to work
weekends. Many of us want to be rich, but what are we willing to
sacrifice to get there? Some of us want to be fit to be seen as attrac-
tive, but we want the freedom to eat whatever we want, whenever
we want. We want to be healthy, but we love eating pizza, fries,
and ice cream. We want to be loved, but we don't want to get hurt,
so we rarely put ourselves out there. Maybe you want to end your
intimate relationship but don't because you don't want to be alone.
Maybe you want to quit smoking or break an addiction, but you
don't want to deal with the withdrawal symptoms. You may want
the freedom to work wherever and whenever but also the security
of a salaried job. You may want to quit your job and start your own

business, but you want the money from that very job you want to quit. These are all examples of the internal struggle.

The internal struggle is why you go to the gym and stop. It's why you buy a book but never make it past the first chapter. It's why you build a website but never market it. It's why you sign up for dating apps but never go on a date. **The internal struggle is why you stop taking action toward what you say you want so badly.** This often leaves us somewhat dumbfounded as we question ourselves. *Why didn't I do that sooner? Why wasn't I consistent? Why didn't I follow through? Why didn't I just commit? Why do I always fail?* These questions are not what you should be asking yourself. What you should be concerned with is understanding how these internal conflicts come about because your beliefs, your values, and your goals are not fully aligned. Often, unconscious beliefs from childhood create internal struggles later in life without you ever understanding why.

Until now.

In this chapter, we will break down the internal struggle and how your values play an important role within them. Where does the internal struggle come from? It comes from beliefs that are in conflict with each other. On the inside, you are being torn apart by two beliefs that want different things. Your biggest struggles, and your greatest internal conflicts, arise in one of two ways:

1. **You are trying to meet one *toward value* while avoiding an *away value*.**

   Perhaps you want love but are avoiding rejection. Remember, pain is a stronger motivator than pleasure. And if your rules to feel rejection are easily met, then you will experience more pain. Your *need* to avoid the pain of rejection will overpower the *want* to feel loved, leaving you with quite an internal struggle. This is the classic example of wanting to feel a toward value and not wanting to feel an away value.

2. You are trying to meet two or more values at the same time, but they have conflicting rules or beliefs.

Look at success and love. You might have a rule that says no one will love you if you're not financially successful. You want to spend time with your family, but you work long hours and weekends in order to be financially successful because your beliefs and rules move you to this action. In this case, success is more important than family and you don't know why, so you have an internal conflict every time you leave the house to work. First, you have to order your values correctly. Do you consciously know which is more important to you? Then you have to look at your rules to meet these values and see if they are in conflict. Ultimately, we take action to meet the value we unconsciously feel is most important.

It's easier to consciously identify and resolve internal conflicts when it's between something you want and something you don't want, like in example one of internal conflicts. *I want to feel healthy; I don't want to be overweight.* It's a lot harder to resolve internal conflicts when it's between something you want and something you want *more.*

A classic example people struggle with is hitting the snooze button so they can sleep in instead of getting up early to go work out. Some people might say, "I want to sleep in because sleep feels so good, but I also want to go to the gym before work because it's the only time I have, and I feel good about myself when I exercise. I believe sleep is important and so I want to get as much of it as I can. If I don't get enough sleep, I'm cranky, irritated, and I'll have a bad day until I can get home and rest. I also believe that if I go to the gym, I'll exercise, stay energetic, and be fit and healthy. If

I wanted sleep more than I wanted to go the gym, I might never end up going to the gym. I might become overweight and the problems in my family with diabetes, obesity, and heart attacks would become my problems." The easy way out is to just sleep, as it provides the instant gratification of feeling good in the moment. The harder choice, and it is a choice, is to wake up and go to the gym. The real question is, what do you want in the long run? What do you value?

I once read that if we sleep six hours a day instead of eight for sixty years, we will effectively get five more years of waking life. For me, what's most important is living my life to the fullest, experiencing everything, accomplishing my goals, and impacting the world. For me, an extra five years of waking life in a sixty-year career is a huge difference. I value my dreams over my sleep, so I usually get six hours. Of course, I have days where I get eight, but it's our consistent habits that define who we are.

Easy Choices, Hard Life. Hard Choices, Easy Life

When you choose instant gratification every time, you make easy choices to feel good in a moment. But in the long term, these choices only lead to more pain. Making the harder choice to delay instant gratification may seem painful in the moment, but it ultimately leads to more happiness, success, and fulfillment of your needs in the long term. For example, I may want to eat at In-n-Out Burger, a popular West Coast chain. I may want burgers with animal-style fries (delicious fries with sauce, grilled onion, and cheese piled on top) and a milkshake. As I drive by the restaurant on the way home, it sounds so good. The internal struggle I go through becomes, "Do I eat it now and satisfy my hunger, or do I go grocery shopping for healthy food and cook at home?" The easiest and fastest way to make myself feel better is to eat fast food. I even want fast food. It tastes great, it's fast, and it makes me feel so good. However, if I came home every day and chose the easy way, I would end up getting out of shape very quickly. So instead, I decide to cook something healthy at home. Of course, after doing this for weeks, I can go eat a cheat meal because I know I have stayed the course. Again, I have to ask what's most important to me in the long run. If I go for instant gratification every time, is that really what I want for my life? Often the answer is no.

Many people use food as emotional comfort. We have a stressful day, so we eat. We have a bad day, so we eat. We are upset, sad, or angry, so we eat. This is because eating changes our physiology and our breathing. It calms us down. But then we get upset that we eat bad food and the cycle continues.

Many people want to go to the gym to lose weight, but they also want the freedom, comfort, and enjoyment of being able to eat whatever they want whenever they want. They stack good feelings associated with food ("it makes me happy, comfortable, satisfied, warm, cozy") instead of stacking good feelings and beliefs about the gym ("it makes me healthy, energized, fit, sexy, confident, strong, courageous").

These internal struggles come about because our beliefs, values, and goals are not fully aligned. Often unconscious beliefs we established from childhood can create internal struggles later in life without us ever understanding why.

Many of our beliefs are unconscious, passed to us as children from our parents, our teachers, our friends, and our family. We live these beliefs out without question, letting them dictate our actions and our results in life. To break out of this internal struggle, we have to bring our values, our rules for those values, and our beliefs about how to meet those values into the conscious mind. Once we are aware of them, we can then understand them, and finally shift them to empower us to live the life we want. What rules do you have that are unconscious? What rules are driving you down a path that doesn't feel right to you? Can you look at any area of your life that causes you pain or suffering and explore your rules and your core values around the situation?

What Does It Cost You?

Internal conflict can actually lead to illness. Being out of alignment can be hazardous to your health. There are a vast number of studies that show serious consequences to hating your job and living outside your value system forty-plus hours a week. Researchers recently looked at 485 such studies, with a combined analysis of 267,995 individuals. The survey showed strong "evidence linking self-report measures of job satisfaction to measures of physical and mental well-being." And it's getting worse. "Employees are regularly being required to work well beyond their contracted hours, often unwillingly, as organizations struggle to meet tight deadlines and targets. Work practices are becoming more automated and inflexible, leaving employees with less and less control over their workload."[37]

There are numerous consequences to working at a job you hate: it causes stress eating, a compromised immune system, stress and anxiety, and trouble sleeping, with dimensional consequences.[38] Look at the cost to your life if you continue in a belief system that isn't working for you. The above research speaks to jobs we hate, but we can have belief systems in a variety of areas that aren't working for us, ones that are causing serious mental, emotional, and physical health problems. Do you value raising your children but spend too much time at work? Do you believe in the benefits of being in nature but spend all of your time indoors? Are you passionate about creativity but never create? These internal struggles aren't just frustrating problems; they can be serious health risks.

Start to define your internal struggles. Do you want a relationship but also freedom? Do you want to be right or be in love? Do you want to get fit but don't want to give up donuts and ice cream? Do you want to be an entrepreneur and own your own business but not take any big risks?

Write down your top five internal struggles.

1. _____

2. _____

3. _____

4. _____

5. _____

We often stop ourselves from taking action or we make our lives harder because the belief to accomplish a goal, is conflicted and sabotaged by a belief that says we *need* to feel comfortable. The very goal we want creates an environment where we feel uncomfortable, afraid, or uncertain. It was only when I wrote down my values and looked at my rules behind them that I really overcame my limitations. It was only when I separated out my different beliefs that they became conscious, and I was able to shift and create a *breakthrough* in my life. When we have conflicting beliefs, unless we're consciously aware of the order of those beliefs, we often *self-sabotage.*

You have begun to make your habits, behaviors, beliefs, conflicting beliefs, and internal struggles conscious. With the building blocks of your character unveiled, you can become the builder of your life, create the identity you want, accomplish the goals you want, and live a life that you feel is successful, purposeful, and makes you happy and fulfilled.

Is it possible to create yourself? To shape your identity at your core? Is it possible to change it? We often view our identities as set in stone. We're always trying to *find* ourselves. Maybe instead we should choose to *create* ourselves.

Let's look at a famous example of a man who came to terms

with internal conflict and lived by his values. Benjamin Franklin, one of America's greatest entrepreneurs and inventors, an author, scientist, civil activist, and diplomat, developed his incredible character by design. He didn't fall into the role of America's greatest entrepreneur by chance. He didn't stumble into his passions, purpose, and the man he became by accident. He developed his character. He *chose* his identity. How? By writing down the values he thought were important. He also wrote down how he would meet those values each day. In doing so, he gave himself a system to create his very identity. He reviewed these values, which he called his virtues, on a weekly basis. He was only twenty when he penned his now-famous thirteen virtues in 1726:

1. **Temperance**. Eat not to dullness; drink not to elevation.
2. **Silence**. Speak not but what may benefit others or yourself; avoid trifling conversation.
3. **Order**. Let all your things have their places; let each part of your business have its time.
4. **Resolution**. Resolve to perform what you ought; perform without fail what you resolve.
5. **Frugality**. Make no expense but to do good to others or yourself; i.e., waste nothing.
6. **Industry**. Lose no time; be always employed in something useful; cut off all unnecessary actions.
7. **Sincerity**. Use no hurtful deceit; think innocently and justly, and, if you speak, speak accordingly.
8. **Justice**. Wrong none by doing injuries or omitting the benefits that are your duty.
9. **Moderation**. Avoid extremes; forbear resenting injuries so much as you think they deserve.
10. **Cleanliness**. Tolerate no uncleanliness in body, cloaths, or habitation.
11. **Tranquility**. Be not disturbed at trifles, or at accidents common or unavoidable.

12. Chastity. Rarely use venery but for health or offspring, never to dullness, weakness, or the injury of your own or another's peace or reputation.

13. Humility. Imitate Jesus and Socrates.[39]

To train himself in these new values, Franklin devised a system to focus on developing and strengthening each principle. Here's the methodology he used to master his thirteen virtues:

1. "I made a little book, in which I allotted a page for each of the virtues."

2. "I ruled each page with red ink, so as to have seven columns, one for each day of the week, marking each column with a letter for the day."

3. "I crossed these columns with thirteen red lines, marking the beginning of each line with the first letter of one of the virtues, on which line, and in its proper column, I might mark, by a little black spot, every fault I found upon examination to have been committed respecting that virtue upon that day."

In his autobiography, Franklin includes this chart he used:

TEMPERANCE

Eat not to dulness; drink not to elevation.

	Sun.	M.	T.	W.	Th.	F.	S.
Tem.							
Sil.	*	*		*		*	
Ord.	*	*	*		*	*	*
Res.		*				*	
Fru.		*				*	
Ind.			*				
Sinc.							
Jus.							
Mod.							
Clea.							
Tran.							
Chas.							
Hum.							

Franklin then decided to take action by focusing on the first virtue intensely for one week. "Thus, in the first week, my great guard was to avoid every offense against *Temperance*, leaving the other virtues to their ordinary chance, only marking every evening the faults of the day. . . . Thus, if in the first week I could keep my first line, marked T, clear of spots, I supposed the habit of that virtue so much strengthened, and its opposite weakened, that I might venture extending my attention to include the next, and for the following week keep both lines clear of spots. . . . Proceeding

231

thus to the last, I could go through a course complete in thirteen weeks, and four courses in a year."[40]

During the first week, Franklin focused on temperance. The second week, he focused on temperance and more intensely on silence. He built upon each virtue. However, he monitored the others each day, as well, and if he had any faults, he would take note of them. This type of self-awareness further enhanced his ability to improve upon his other values.

Franklin understood his internal conflicts, defined the values and rules that he wanted to live by, and then trained himself week after week until these honorable virtues became his very character and identity. In the next chapter, we reveal the strategy to reshape and build your very identity brick by brick to become who you want to be and who you were meant to be.

Identity

Beliefs

Habits and Behavior

Emotional States
in a Moment

Awareness of Your
Story, Emotions, and Beliefs

CHAPTER 18

IDENTITY:
DESIGN YOUR DREAM LIFE

Limits, like fear, are often an illusion.

—MICHAEL JORDAN

As I write this chapter, I'm on the deck of my beach house in southern California. I can't believe I have the home of my dreams. It was just a thought, a goal, but I decided I wanted this, and here I am. How did it happen? How did I afford it? This house began as words on a piece of paper. It was just a vision- a vision I designed.

I thought about it. I took action. I never gave up.

As I'm working on this chapter, I find my list of goals from years ago in my journal. I am moved by how many I've accomplished. *Speak in front of 100 people*—done regularly these days. *A one-week vacation abroad with my girlfriend*—done, every year. *A beach house in southern California*—done. *Unleash Success Podcast*—done. *Write a book*—done.

People often think that it was easy for me to accomplish all of my goals because that is who I am—a confident and hardworking person. But I wasn't always like this. I was shy when I was younger. All I wanted to do was play video games and sports instead of do homework. And then, years later, I was depressed for eight long years! When someone says I've always been confident, happy, and successful, I want to say to them, "Yes, that's who I am *now* because I *chose* it."

And you can choose it, too.

What Is Identity?

Psychologists define **identity** as the qualities, beliefs, personality, looks, and/or expressions that make up a person. Erik Erikson (1902–1994) was one of the earliest psychologists to explore identity. He mapped the distinction between the ego identity (the self), the personal idiosyncrasies that separate one person from the next (the personal identity), and the collection of social roles that a person might play (the cultural identity).[41]

More recently, Ghanaian-born, British-American philosopher Kwame Anthony Appiah has written extensively on identity. His multicultural identity is in part the reason for his fascination with the subject. He explores how people misunderstand the five types of identity, which he calls creed, country, color, class, and culture. We think these identities are unchangeable, that they are a given, and therefore we do not question them, he explains.

For example, with creed, Appiah explains that we think of religious identity as "sets of immutable beliefs" instead of as "mutable practices and communities." What we think is a noun is actually a verb. He explains that religion is an activity, and when we can see that, it can be used for great change in the world and not turn into fundamentalism. *All areas of our identity, in Appiah's mind, are active and mutable.* And it's not only essential to our happiness to understand this, but also to our evolution and the planet as a whole.[42]

My goal in writing this book is for you to begin to understand that who you are is based on your decisions and actions. You have a choice. You can choose to become whoever you want to be. You may think your identity is written in stone, but it isn't. It's not only malleable; you can actually decide who you want to become. When you decide your identity, you can set your destiny. It's as simple as that. Most of us just adopt the identity handed to us by our parents, socioeconomic background, religion, race, gender, and culture. We never question it. We never ask if we want to change it, who we want to be. You can and will in this chapter.

We'll look at how to take the habits, beliefs, and values that we've discussed up to this point in this book and go deeper, so that you can form a fully authentic identity that is in alignment with who you want to be. And we'll look at the big questions we ask ourselves. Instead of just adopting the identity handed to you, we want you to forge a genuine idea of yourself.

Remember, this book is not just about being touchy-feely. We're exploring identity here for a purpose: so that you can get real results in the real world. How does exploring identity help you set and achieve your goals? You cannot get what you want if you do not know what you want. If you are not fully aligned in your identity with what you value most, with your rules and beliefs, you will self-sabotage or struggle to accomplish your goals.

Letting go of some of your lifelong limiting beliefs about your identity can be intense. It may feel raw and confusing and leave you feeling a little unhinged or lost. But this is the highest level of mastering Emotional Fitness and the most rewarding. If you allow yourself to choose who you want to be, you can build your character, and re-create yourself. It's OK if you feel resistance at first. The strongest force in the human mind is to protect your identity and who you believe you are. People will lie, cheat, and steal to protect their identities. They will even lie to themselves and violate and break their values to protect their identities. This often happens in times of immense grief or loss.

If someone loses a loved one through death or a breakup, or goes bankrupt, or loses a long-standing job, they experience a massive shock to their identity. They don't know who they are anymore. They have a mid-life crisis or an identity crisis. Their identity was tied to money, a job, or a career. It was tied to other people, a relationship, or a marriage. Such loss can push someone to completely re-evaluate their life. Often these experiences create significant change and sometimes severe depression. Some people turn to the gym or personal development to help them. Others choose alcohol or drugs to distract themselves from the pain of losing their identity. This deep loss of self-identity leads to an identity crisis or a loss of purpose, meaning, or reason to live. Some people are led to contemplate or even commit suicide.

In 2008, during the worst financial times of modern history, we still saw people driving their Mercedes, eating at fancy restaurants, and buying expensive jewelry, right up until the point they declared bankruptcy and lost it all. Under the surface, they were barely making ends meet as the housing bubble burst, the economy tanked, and the job market got squeezed. They did everything they could to hold up their identities of being successful, smart, good with money, and powerful until they couldn't hide the truth any longer and lost it all. People can become so delusional that they rationalize why it's OK to break their values. This is because if you lose your identity, you question who you are. You feel lost because you were never told that you could rebuild your identity at any time. No one taught you not to tie your identity to external factors out of your control. You can rebuild, and you can tie your identity to things that are in your control.

If you really want to create your identity to be empowered so that you can accomplish your goals, you have to look at yourself in the mirror. You have to get honest. You have to pull back the curtain and reveal your true self.

We're going to dive into figuring out your identity by going even deeper into your values here—your toward values and away values—and we're going to utilize certain language to help you get there.

Define the Real End Goals

We often think we have one goal, when behind it sits the real goal. You often hear people say, "I want to be successful!" But what does that mean to you? Define that. Maybe you want to be successful to feel financially safe, which means you'll be comfortable for life because comfort is an important value to you. Or maybe financial success is not what you're really after. Maybe you think that you need money, a big job, a title, and success, but what you really want is to feel that you are important. And maybe feeling important isn't even your end goal. Maybe you want to be important because you think people will love you. What you really want is love. Many great people strive for excellence and success in their chosen fields because their parents want them to do it. If they are good at something, their parents give them love, and that is what they really wanted all along. Or maybe success makes them feel like they've made it and people will finally accept them. They've proven themselves; they are enough. Success equals acceptance.

Remember that your values are really emotions or feelings you want to experience in life. And while you may value money or family, these are just *means* values or vehicles to get you to the true *end* value you want, which may be importance, comfort, freedom, love, happiness, etc. You want to get to the real end value, so you can get to the end goal of what you really want. When you can define what you really want in your life, you have the ability to take massive action toward attaining it.

What Do You Really Want Out of Life?

In Chapter 16, we began the process of looking at our values. That was just the beginning. Get out the values list you made in Chapter 16.

Now, let's go deeper. Let's look at how to design a new *order* for your values according to what's most important to you. What's the first one on your list? For me, when I first looked at how I was *living*, my number one value was success. I had lived my life with success as my number one value and happiness my number two. As such, I had been somewhat successful in my life, becoming an orthodontist, but I was miserable. What I *really* wanted was to be happy. Therefore, when choosing and ordering my **new** values to become who I really wanted to be, I would put happiness above success.

What about love? Well, truthfully, I wanted to feel love. Then I asked myself, "Is love more important than success?" The answer was yes. I moved *love* up the list.

1. Happiness

2. Love

3. Success

Then I asked, "Is love more important than happiness?" I struggled for a minute. In my gut, I knew that if I didn't have love in my life, I wouldn't feel happy. Thus, love moved up the list.

Here's an interesting one: what about health? So many people sacrifice their own health to take care of others. They stay up late, they work long hours, and they eat bad food—all because they spend so much time taking care of other people. Likely these people have a rule that says they need to do something for someone else to feel loved. Love is likely their top value. But the question becomes, "Can I truly help others to the best of my ability if I am not healthy? If I am tired, stressed, or overweight? What if I just don't have the energy to be totally present at work, at home, or in my relationships?" For me, the question was, "Is health more important than love?"

The answer at first was no because I had been living that way for some time. But how did I want to *live* my life in the future, by design? I value health and energy. If I am healthy, I am energetic, passionate, and more alive, which allows me to *give* even more love. In fact, I want to be healthy and energetic because it makes everything in life easier and better when I am. Disease slows us down by literally killing us slowly.

I want to be alive, to experience everything life has to offer, to work hard and achieve, to travel, to love intensely and passionately, and to live without regrets. But if I didn't value my own health, how could I possibly do all of this? In fact, I know people who get sick every few months and lose weeks of their life recovering. In those same weeks, I am getting better, progressing in my goals, and experiencing life, love, and laughter. Simply put, when I'm healthy, I am allowed to live and experience even more of this wonderful journey of life. I can't imagine losing two to four weeks a year to sickness or—even worse—losing five to twenty years at the end of my life. I realized I wanted to live with my top value being first my own health and energy, then love, then happiness. So, my values go in that order:

1. Health and vibrant energy

2. Love

3. Happiness

Where did my value for success go? Well, success was never what I really wanted. What I really wanted was all of the things I thought success would give me: a feeling of happiness, freedom, and love. Those are what I really value, the real end goals. In fact, success is no longer on my towards value list. Oddly enough, I feel more successful than ever before. That is the power of knowing your true values and their rules. Now let's order your toward values.

Ordering Your Toward Values

Look at the list you made. For each toward value, ask yourself, "Is Value A more important to me than Value B?" Then ask, "Is Value A more important than Value C?" Go down the list just like I did in the example above. If any value is more important than Value A, move it up the list. Just like love moved up the list for me, adjust your values to the correct order. Then repeat for each value to create your new ordered towards value list. Let's focus here on five of them.

Value A _____

Value B _____

Value C _____

Value D _____

Value E _____

If Value C is more important than Value A, immediately move it to the top of the list.

Value C

Value A

Value B

Value D

Value E

Then ask yourself if Value C is more important than Values B, D, and E. If it is, keep it at the top. Then go back to Value A and compare it to all the other values below it. If Value E is more important than Value A, move it to second place on your list. Now your list becomes:

Value C

Value E

Value A

Value B

Value D

Keep going until you have compared and ordered *all* of your values, even if you have ten or fifteen toward values. It is crucially important to ask yourself these questions. I recommend you ask them out loud. Why? It's better to engage your entire body. Remember how much your physical state affects you. If you are lying on the couch after a long day of work, you might say comfort is your number one value. If you're in an excited state, with an excited mind, it's easier to get to what is *most* important to you. This is *your* life. It is whatever you choose it to be. And the beautiful thing about learning that we can design our identities by our values is that it gives us the ability to change them.

As we evolve, grow, and experience different phases of life, our values might change, as well. The key is to **consciously** choose them. After a health scare, health might go to number one on your list. After a bad investment or losing a job, security might jump to number one. Be careful that these experiences don't unconsciously dictate your life. That's how so many people wake up after ten years and say, "I used to be an athlete. How did I get this overweight?" Or, "I had so many dreams of success, but the economy ruined them." Or, "How did I end up here? Is this all there is to life?"

The list you've made outlines your moving toward values and what you want to move toward in your life.

Ordering Your Away Values

Let's now look again at the values you want to *move away* from in your life. Get out your move away from value list. Use this exercise to create your new order for your away values. Explore which away value is the strongest for you, which is the weakest, and where the others fall in order of importance. Bringing this to awareness can help you see what is blocking you in getting what you want in life.

My away values were ordered like this:

1) Depression
2) Fear of not being good enough
3) Fear of not being loved
4) Fear of failure
5) Worry

I was so depressed that I never ever want to feel it again. I would rather feel not good enough than depressed, and so depressed became my number one away value. Now, I never wanted to feel "not good enough" either, but this is how you order them.

Go through your away from values. What do you move *away* from the *most*?

Look at the list you made. For each value, ask yourself, "Is Value A more painful for me to feel than Value B?" Then ask, "Is Value A more painful for me to feel than Value C?" Go down the list. If any value is more painful than the one before it, move it up the list. Let's focus here on five of them.

Value A _____

Value B _____

Value C _____

Value D _____

Value E _____

If Value C is more painful than Value A, immediately move it to the top of the list.

Value C

Value A

Value B

Value D

Value E

Then ask if Value C is more painful than values B, D, and E. If it is, keep it at the top. Then go back to Value A and compare it to all your other values below it. If Value E is more painful than Value A, it moves to second place on your list. And your list becomes:

Value C

Value E

Value A

Value B

Value D

List all of your away values in order of most to least painful and hold on to them. We are about to uncover how to create *new* rules for your values that will make it easy to feel your toward values and hard to feel these negative away values!

Play by Your Own Rules

When I was originally looking at my top values, my number one value was success and my number two value was happiness. I wrote everything down I wanted to have in order to succeed. I had a lot of rules that I believed I needed to meet in order to feel the value of success. I wrote that I needed a lot of money: $10 million in cash in the bank, *and* to be worth $100 million, *and* to own a private jet, *and* to be debt-free, *and* to own a home. I also had to have a great, loving relationship, *and* have lots of friends, *and* a good relationship with my family, *and* freedom to travel the world, *and* I needed to be the best at everything I did all the time.

Then I wrote down all my rules I needed to meet in order to feel happiness. I needed to feel loved all the time, *and* I needed to be rich, *and* I needed to be successful. No wonder I wasn't happy. I had to be successful in order to feel happy, and in order to feel successful, I had this near impossible list of rules to meet. It suddenly made sense why I was so miserable and depressed. My rules were way too difficult! It made me realize how I had negatively impacted my life for years. How did I cross my wires so badly? The problem was that I never chose these rules consciously. I never ordered my values consciously.

Look at your list of values again. How do you define your values? What needs to happen in order for you to feel that you have met your needs to fulfill that value? What are your rules for each?

What is the frequency you need to have that value, the duration? If love is one of your values, how do you feel love? Do you need to be with your family all day, every day? For how long? Look at each value and ask yourself, do you need this all the time, some of the time, or just once? For what length of time do you need this value? Rewire your brain by consciously choosing new rules. Let's *rewrite* your rules to empower you.

Your Words Power Your Rules

The use of language is important here. In my success list, I needed $10 million in cash in the bank, **and** to be worth $100 million, **and** to own a home **and** freedom to travel the world, **and** ... I made it almost impossible for myself to feel successful because I needed this **and** that **and** those. I didn't need just one thing to feel successful; I needed **all** of them at the **same time.** This made meeting these rules *very difficult.*

You need to make it easy to feel successful. When I realized that success was just a means to an end for me to feel happiness and love, I took success out of my values list. Instead, I created rules to fulfill my value of happiness that were easy to meet. And each one alone could make me happy. I wrote my rules in such a way that instead of needing to meet *all* of them in order to feel like I had met my value of happiness, I only needed to meet *one* of them, at any time, for any moment of time, to feel complete happiness. It was a simple but powerful strategy that changed my entire life. Now I experience more happiness than ever before. Instead of using **and** in my rules, I replaced that key word with **or** to allow me multiple ways to feel happiness. I also added the word *anytime* to allow me to easily feel happiness anytime any of these rules are met.

Look at the use of the words *or* and *anytime* in the following example:

I feel happy

- **anytime** I remember a happy moment

OR

- **anytime** I remember that I have certain gifts to give to the world

OR

- **anytime** someone smiles at me

OR

- **anytime** I look at the ocean

OR

- **anytime** I look at a photo of a good memory.

By using **or**, all I have to do is fulfill one of these rules to be happy. Now it's easy to feel happiness. And by using the word *anytime*, I make is so incredibly easy to meet these rules and fulfill my value for happiness because literally **anytime** someone smiles at me or **anytime** I remember a happy moment, I know that I can choose to feel happy.

As another example, let's look at one man's rules to feel loved by his wife. In this example, in order for him to feel love, she has to clean the house every day **and** tell him she loves him every time she sees him **and** give him a kiss every time she sees him **and** do nice things for him, like buying him a gift **and** buy him gifts often, at least once a week. This may seem absurd to you, but we all have such rules for one value or the other. Dig down and I promise you have a particular list of rules, too.

To make it easy to feel loved, the man in our example needs to use *anytime*, instead of *every time*: "I can feel loved *anytime* my wife looks at me, or *anytime* she gets me a gift, or *anytime* she cleans the house." It's a game changer.

What if you break up with your significant other? How many times have we seen someone's identity completely destroyed by a break-up? Instead of tying your identity to others, you need to tie it to things you can control. We can't rely on our values being met based on what other people do for us; we have zero control over that. Your feelings of self-love cannot be reliant upon other people. That's a recipe for disaster. Tell yourself, "I feel love anytime I remember the atoms from my body are made from the stars, **or** I feel loved anytime I give love, **or** I feel love anytime I remember feeling loved as a kid, **or** anytime I remember that my heart, which is made from love, beats 100,000 times a day whether I work for it or not."

Make sure you are in control of every value you want to fulfill. If you rely on someone else to do something for you to meet a value, then your ability to meet that value is out of your control. Then you become a victim to the whims of chance and the world. If your happiness or love is dependent on someone else, then the minute they are not in your life, you lose that happiness and love.

Let's take action to design the life you want. Let's rewrite, redefine, and redesign your rules and your life for your toward values. Grab your list and write down your values in order from one to ten. Next to each value, write down your new rules.

Remember, we want to make it easy to meet these rules. The formula is this:

I feel that I have met my value of _____

- **anytime** I _____

- OR **anytime** I _____

- OR **anytime** I _____

- OR **anytime** I _____.

Make these simple and easy to accomplish each and every day, at any moment in time. Remember to design them so that you are in control of them and they are not dependent on anyone else. Do this for all of your values. The clearer you are in your rules, the easier it will be to feel you have met your values and are the person you want to be.

Toward Value #1 _____

I feel that I have met my value of _____

anytime I _____

OR **anytime** I _____

OR **anytime** I _____

OR **anytime** I _____

Do this for every value now.

How to Integrate Your New Values into Your Identity

Remember the story about my parents telling me I could do whatever I wanted as long as I worked hard enough for it? They didn't just tell me this once and I believed it forever. They told me this over and over again until it became my belief. They essentially did incantations to my younger self until I created the belief inside me. Other people told me I couldn't be starting point guard, MVP of my football team, or graduate as valedictorian an entire year early at sixteen years old. But when they said those things, I remembered my parents' incantation and repeated it to myself: "I can accomplish anything as long as I'm willing to work hard enough for it."

Now that you have written down each value and its rules, it is important to do incantations for these new rules and values with emotion and physiology to ingrain your new beliefs. This is training your Emotional Fitness. The more you train your Emotional Fitness, the stronger it will become. You must recite these incantations powerfully by engaging your mind (focus), language (meaning), and body (physiology). Each time you do incantations for a new belief, the incantation reinforces the belief.

At a minimum, incantations should be done once per day for ten days. Ideally, repeat them over and over again every morning and night for ten days and then every day for a month. Once you memorize them, I recommend reciting them in the car or while you're cooking, showering, or cleaning, or when you have any extra time to maximize their effect.

Grab your list of toward values and practice saying them out loud, completely engaging your physiology. You can stand up, move around, use your hands, and yell loudly, proudly, and with absolute conviction. Say these incantations for 10 minutes or more each day as you rewire your brain to become more Emotionally Fit.

Let's use one of your toward values and do an incantation now! Let's say love is your toward value. Say, "I feel love *anytime* I give love **or** *anytime* I remember my parents telling me they love me **or** *anytime* I help someone **or** *anytime* I remember the atoms in my body are made from the stars."

Let's take success and do an incantation now! If you value success, say, "I am a successful *anytime* I make progress towards my goals **or** *anytime* I remember a moment I accomplished my goals **or** *anytime* I fail because failing means I'm learning and one step closer to success."

When you incant your new values and rules intentionally with conviction and repetition, you too, like my younger self, will start to believe the incantation to be true. I wasn't always confident, but I incanted it until it became true. I wasn't always courageous, but I focused on who I wanted to become and incanted the idea of a courageous man into my mind and body until I believed it to be true. Over time, if you tell yourself these incantations, they will become deep-seated beliefs and eventually reflect who you are. All it takes is time and training to become Emotionally Fit.

Make Away Values Hard to Feel

Let's look more deeply now at your away values. You've picked your toward values and ordered them and redefined them. But something *still* seems to stop you from taking action. It's your away values, and you need to redefine them clearly, as well. You need to make it hard to feel a negative value, such as fear, which stops you from becoming the person you want to be and hinders you from accomplishing your goals.

We talked about fear of not being good enough, depression, anxiety, fear of not being loved, and rejection. Let's look at rejection. If you are going to be successful in any area of life, you are bound to get rejected. You will be told no more often than yes. To some people, that's no big deal. To others, a single no can be emotionally destructive. So many of us have too much fear around rejection. Anytime we get a no, every time someone brushes us off, or whenever we don't get what we want, we lose our faith in ourselves and our ideas: "The investor said no to my idea so I must be worthless and the idea's no good." "A major player in the industry wouldn't take my call because I'm a nobody." "The agent rejected my book because I'm just not good at what I do." "The person I like said no when I asked them out, so I'll never find love."

Take it as a given that to be successful, you're going to get rejected, a lot! Let's make it impossible for you to feel rejection. Releasing these feelings and conditioning your Emotional Fitness will take effort because the negative is so ingrained in us, but I did it, and you can, too.

Here's an example of an Away From Value Rule list. Many people who struggle with rejection have rules that say they feel rejected *anytime* a person says no **or** *anytime* someone doesn't respond to their text or email **or** *anytime* someone doesn't call them back **or** *anytime* they don't get picked first **or** *anytime* a friend doesn't invite them over for dinner.

Notice all the ***ors*** and *anytimes* in these rules? Using **or** and *anytime* in your <u>away</u> rules makes it <u>easy</u> to feel these *negative* values. That's not what we want for an away value rule!

There is a formula for creating rules. For *away values,* it is the **opposite** of our *toward value* rule template. We want our rules to make it easy to meet our toward values, and difficult to meet our away values. So, in order to make it hard to feel rejection, you need to change your language and redefine your rules for your away values.

Instead of using **or** and *anytime* in your away rules, we are going to change the formula for away rules to make it very hard to feel these negative away values. Pay close attention to the keywords we're using here: <u>and</u>, **unless**, *consistently, lie to myself,* and *illusion.*

- I refuse to feel rejected **unless** I *consistently lie to myself* and believe I'm not good enough and the *illusion* that no one will ever say yes to me.

<u>AND</u>

- I refuse to feel rejected **unless** I *consistently* forget that everything happens for a reason under God's guidance to lead me to become the person I am meant to be.

<u>AND</u>

- I refuse to feel rejected **unless** I *consistently* choose to stop working to become a better version of myself and believe the *illusion* that one no means that I am not good enough.

Start to ponder your own personalized statements about how to deal with rejection. Use these keywords to make feeling rejection difficult, almost impossible. You might be thinking, *how is it possible to simply just redefine how I feel something on paper to become my reality?* That's what Emotional Fitness is all about, and there are specific techniques to accomplish this. It starts by writing it all out. Then we will condition ourselves to our new rules and values. By using incantations, we wire the neurons in our brains to create change. Let's take action. Write down your away values and rewrite, redefine, and redesign their rules to make them impossible to ever feel again.

On the next few pages we will do a powerful exercise to rewrite your away from values.

The formula to make it hard to feel your away from values is:

I **refuse** to let myself feel the stupid, negative, debilitating feeling of _____

unless I consistently *choose* to *lie to myself* and believe the *illusion* that I _____

and only if I *consistently* choose to *lie to myself* and believe the *illusion* that I _____

and only if I *consistently* choose to *lie to myself* and believe the *illusion* that I _____

instead of remembering the truth that I _____

or remembering that I _____.

The language is incredibly important. I have seen people use different words and not get the same results. You must *refuse* to *let* yourself feel this negative emotion **unless** you *consistently choose to lie* to yourself and believe in the *illusion* **and only if** you consistently do it **instead of** remembering that failure is not an end, only a beginning **or** that every successful person has had failures.

This acknowledges so many aspects. First, that you have to consistently **choose** over and over again to lie to yourself, ignore the truth, and believe a false illusion, all of which you have to do in order to feel this **instead** of remembering any number of things that the minute you remember them pulls you out of this negative feeling.

In the rejection example, we'd write it like this:

I **refuse** to let myself feel the stupid, negative, debilitating, feeling of rejection, **unless** I *consistently* choose to *lie to myself* and believe that I am not good enough **and only if** I *consistently* choose to believe the *illusion* that a "no" means that I am a complete failure **and** only if I *consistently* choose to *lie to myself* and believe the *illusion* that a "no" means I will never be successful, **instead of** *remembering* the truth that I am the only one who can stop myself from achieving my goals **or** *remembering* that Colonel Sanders got rejected 1,009 times at the old age of sixty-eight and still got a "yes" to build the famous KFC and if he can do it, I can too **or** *remembering* that every "no" is one step closer to a "yes" **or** *remembering* that the only person who has control over me is me.

Your turn. Let's rewrite the rules for your move *away from* values.

Move Away Value #1 _____

I **refuse** to let myself feel the stupid, negative, debilitating feeling of _____

unless I consistently *choose* to *lie to myself* and believe the *illusion* that I _____

and only if I *consistently* choose to *lie to myself* and believe the *illusion* that I _____

and only if I *consistently* choose to *lie to myself* and believe the *illusion* that I _____

instead of remembering the truth that I _____

or remembering that I _____.

Do this for every value.

Freedom through Pain

In order to make sure you never experience your negative away values, you must use an intense emotional exercise to free yourself from their power. This exercise is not for the faint of heart. It might even be a little painful, but on the other side, there is the freedom you want. These away values and emotions, when taken to the extreme, are the most debilitating and disempowering emotions we can ever feel. **Immediately** following this exercise, proceed to do a *power move* to shake off the disempowering emotions and override your nervous system with empowering feelings. Then follow that with the *gratitude exercise* below and do your toward value incantation for ten minutes to leave yourself in a positive, empowering state.

For this exercise, take your disempowering away values and visualize everything they cost you in life. Take one away value and visualize all the pain you get from allowing yourself to feel this emotion. Feel it with every ounce of your body and soul, in every part of your being. Visualize what you don't have now and what you won't have in ten years by allowing yourself to be debilitated by this negative emotion. <u>Make the pain feel real.</u> Then *shift* by doing your power move to get into an empowered state.

Then with all of your being, with every truth in your soul, engage your mind and body and in your most convincing tone say out loud, "I will *never* let myself feel the stupid, negative, disempowering emotion of _____ **unless** I *consistently* choose to *lie to myself* and believe_____ **and** only if I *consistently* choose to believe the illusion of _____ **instead of** *remembering* that I am _____[insert empowering statement] **or** *remembering* that I _____[insert empowering statement].

Stay in that empowered state for thirty seconds following each incantation to soak your mind and body in positive empowering emotions.

Do this for as many reps as you need for each away value

until you believe that you will never again choose to feel that emotion. After each rep, do a power move to override your mind and body with empowering emotions. Then move to the next away value in the exercise. Following the away value exercise, proceed to the gratitude exercise below, then repeat your toward value incantations.

Practicing Gratitude

When creating new values, it is important to prime your mind correctly. Gratitude not only helps you look for positive empowering emotions, but when it's combined with your power moves, it quickly helps you eliminate those negative away value feelings.

To prime each day for success, start your day with ten minutes of gratitude and reflection. Get into the mindset that whatever happens in the external world, you have control over the internal world. Be grateful for everything good in your life now and even the pain you experienced in the past. Pain in so many ways forces us to grow, to find new answers. Pain led me to Emotional Fitness, and if you've made it this far, it could have been what led you here.

Here's an example of practicing gratitude: "In the here and now, I am eternally grateful for the opportunity to choose how I feel, what I focus on, and what I do. I am eternally grateful for the smiles I see every day, that you are reading this book, and the opportunity to continue to build the life of my dreams. I am eternally grateful for this journey and this gift we call life."

Practice your own gratitude by thinking of at least three things you are grateful for.

1. _____

2. _____

3. _____

Remember that you can find the good in anything as long as you look for it.

Alignment Creates Unstoppable Power

You hold so much power when you are fully aligned with your values and goals. Your identity becomes tied to deeper truths instead of external factors like jobs and money. If you align what you want (your goals), what you value in life, and your rules and beliefs with your actions and you put in the work, I guarantee that you will accomplish your goals. You will no longer hold back, second guess, or self-sabotage. You hold so much power when you exhibit this level of congruence. You say what you want, and you do what you say. In this state of Emotional Fitness, you will never give up and never stop, and you'll be able to bring a level of resourcefulness that allows you to get whatever you need to accomplish your goals. Then there's nothing that can stop you. Only you can stop you.

We're not talking about aligning and then magically your goals just happen. We're talking about aligning and taking as much action as you need to achieve your goals. Some people believe thinking and wishing for something will make it happen. I agree that when you're fully aligned things can happen. But the truth is that when you're fully aligned, you'll take unstoppable, massive action toward your goals in order to live the life you want.

Remember, it's not a lack of resources but a lack of resourcefulness that stops most people. It is their limiting beliefs that prevent them from their goals. By taking full responsibility and owning the fact that you have control over everything in your life can be too scary for most people. *They might think it's too much responsibility, too much work, and too much effort, so they find a scapegoat.* They blame others, the past, and the environment because that's easier than admitting they are the driver of success and failure. And often their values and conflicting beliefs are unconsciously causing them to self-sabotage.

Once you align, you no longer self-sabotage, and you take massive purposeful action. If there's a will, there's a way. It's not about magic. It's about alignment and hard work. Don't rely on the sudden miracle. Take massive action and opportunities will come.

Luck is When Preparation Meets Opportunity

People often say to me, "You're so lucky." That's bullshit. I worked for this. It's not luck. I worked really hard and somebody took notice. I aligned my values, I kept pushing even when there was no opportunity, and it was only a matter of time before something "eventually fell into my lap," and I took advantage of the opportunity life presented.

Sometimes, though, after we work hard and an opportunity appears, we say no to it. We're too busy. We can't fit it in. Maybe we do this out of fear. Years ago, I was asked to speak to seven hundred people—the largest group of people I had ever been asked to speak to. I said yes with 100 percent confidence. The person asked if I was sure that the dates would work—didn't I want time to check? I told them no, I didn't need to check it. I knew my values, beliefs, and goals were aligned. This was what I wanted. And so—without hesitation—I said yes, I would take the gig. In truth, I didn't know if the dates would work, but I knew *I* would make it work. It wasn't, "Let me think about it." It was, "Yes!" Because this was one of my goals, and who knew if the opportunity would present itself again? This was happening. I jumped in with two feet, without fear, without hesitation, and with confidence. Because I aligned my identity, I was prepared for the opportunity. Luck is when opportunity meets preparation.

We've aligned our toward values and our away values, and we've made rules that make it really easy to meet values we want and hard to feel values we don't want. Now let's understand the simple but powerful statements that sum up our beliefs and ultimately create lasting change.

CHAPTER 19

IDENTITY:
THE POWER OF I CAN,
I WILL, I AM

*The value of identity of course is that
so often with it comes purpose.*

—RICHARD GRANT, JOURNALIST

I came across an interesting study that explores issues of identity called "The Psychology of Self Defense: Self Affirmation Theory." It explains that in major league baseball, players can have a long and productive career by getting a base hit *only* 30 percent of the time. "A great deal of money could be earned, and fame accrued. Yet the other 70 percent of the time, this player would have **failed**."[43] Still, these players, even with so much failure, are able to *believe* in themselves and *feel successful*. Why?

The study goes on to compare this phenomenon to the experiences of people in contemporary society. People feel failure all the time. This includes "substandard performance on the job or in class, frustrated goals or aspirations, information challenging the validity of long-held beliefs, illness, the defeat of one's political party in an election or of one's favorite sports team in a playoff. . . . rejection in a romantic relationship . . . the loss of a loved one, and so on."

The study discusses how identity is so ingrained that we protect it at all costs, to the point of lying to ourselves about the truth, manipulating past and current events, taking credit for the positive, and blaming others for the negative. We do things to protect our perceived identities to the point of hurting ourselves. We'll self-sabotage, cheat, and steal to protect our images. How many of us know "perfect" families but find out later how many serious problems they have? It almost seems like a shock to hear about their troubles. Maybe there was abuse, drug problems, infidelity, or financial distress. The members liked to keep their "perfect" family identity intact. Their need to protect their identity as the perfect family overpowered even their highest values like honesty and love. Some people value honesty and truth above all else but will lie to their closest friends about what's really going on to protect the image of their identity. Some people value being loved over everything and yet when love disappears, they will sacrifice love to protect their perceived identity. The *idea* of love, honesty, family, and loyalty become want they want most. They are even willing to lie to protect the illusion that they have these things, even though the more they stray from those values, the less they truly have them, ultimately leading to despair, resentment, and pain.

Perhaps you have also done things to keep up appearances. Maybe when you had a fight with a loved one and someone asked how you were, you portrayed an "everything is all right" attitude. Or maybe you've run into financial difficulty and live paycheck to paycheck, but to protect yourself so no one else knows, you continue to go out with friends and spend money, even though you should be saving every penny. The extent to which we will go to protect our identities is quite amazing.

How do baseball players have so much success with only a 30 percent success rate, while we expend massive amounts of energy to protect our identities when we're having about the same success rate? It has to do with the stories we tell ourselves. Like baseball players, we can choose to tell ourselves, "I am great at what I do" for batting a .300, or we can tell ourselves, "I am a failure," for missing 70 percent of the time. The choice is ours. Positive or negative self-talk dictates our successes and our failures.

The difference in the success rates of baseball players, according to this study, came down to self-affirmations or incantations. Those who were more successful said incanted phrases about who they were that empowered them. They said to themselves, "I AM great at what I do."

The Power of I AM

Do you say I AM great, or I AM a failure? Maybe it's not that extreme, but you use softeners that allow you to say you want something but presuppose you can't have it.

I was out with friends recently and we got into a heated discussion. We were talking about goals and a friend said, "I wish I could do that." They wished they could start their own business or pursue their dreams and goals. Why wish it? Why not just do it?

"I hate *wish*," I said to them. "I'm not just calling you out on it; I'm calling myself out on the word *wish*. Fuck *wish*. It's such bullshit. Instead of wishing for it, work for it. If we want something bad enough, we can find a way to make it happen. I'm in control of my life. Replace *I wish* with *I can*. You've got to believe it's possible. When you say *I can do something*, it becomes possible. You don't even have to know how it's going to happen; you just need to know you can find a way to make it happen."

As you move through different stages of life, and explore realms outside your comfort zone, limiting beliefs that you never even realized you had will creep up on you. They have for me many times in my life since mastering Emotional Fitness. Every time you hear yourself say you can't do something, replace it with *I can*. The word *impossible* literally spells *I'm possible*. So, start with *I can* and make it real by committing to it. You can commit by starting with I *can*, then shifting to I *will*, and finally ending with *I am*. Way before Muhammad Ali was a success, he was often quoted as saying, "I *am* the greatest. I said that even before I knew I was." He said it and he became it. An amazing shift happens in your brain when you say the words **I am** before a sentence. *I am* is tied to your identity; you become whatever you say after "I am."

Instead of, "I *wish* I could be confident," say, "I can be confident." Once you believe something is *possible*, you can achieve it. Then say, "I *will* be confident." Finally, integrate yourself into it by saying, "**I am** confident." Reinforce this with incantations of "I am confident" until confidence *is* you.

Here are some sample I AM statements:

- I am love.

- I am confident.

- I am happy.

- I am a successful business person.

- I am capable of anything.

- I am resourceful.

- I am focused.

- I am courageous.

What are some I AM statements that you want to use? Who do you want to become? Who do you want to be? At this stage, we're no longer talking about what you *will* do or *can* do; we're talking about who you *are*. This loving, successful, happy person becomes your identity and you're now able to do anything.

Think of the opposite: who you aren't. Think of how your

negative words show up physically. When you say, "I am worried," "I am angry," or "I am a nobody," it shows in your body. Maybe after years of negative reinforcing self-talk, someone you haven't seen for a while shows up and they've aged a lot. You need to protect your identity from the negativity. If you can shift the way you describe yourself from, "I am an abuse survivor" to "I am a beacon of light for others," you can accomplish so much more. Even after people no longer drink, they still refer to themselves as recovering alcoholics. They define themselves by this disempowered state; they live within the powerlessness. If you say, "I am a recovering alcoholic," it becomes your identity. I believe this is one of the reasons some people relapse.

We've all heard the stories of millionaires who get to the top and go bankrupt, and then somehow, they become millionaires again. "I am a millionaire" is part of their identity.

How is it that people who make millions go broke and make millions again? Your identity is determined by your values, rules, and beliefs. If you truly believe that anything is possible and that any goal is achievable as long as you work hard and never give up, then you will get resourceful and work hard and smart to get back that goal as quickly as possible. **You become what you believe.** People who are "big-boned" always have trouble losing weight, while people who consider themselves "athletic" are always in shape. Your thoughts become your reality. This works for you in the positive but can also limit your ability to change.

Resetting the Thermostat for Success

Who you have been for the last year and the last ten years is all you know, and we are all comfortable with what we know. As you begin to try to change and improve yourself, you start to reach the edge of your comfort zone. Think about it like the thermostat in your house. A thermostat regulates the temperature. If you set the temperature to seventy degrees, it's most comfortable at seventy degrees. If you start to heat up and improve your life, you might go up a few degrees, but the thermostat doesn't turn on the AC right away. You get some success, and then all of sudden you hit seventy-five degrees and the AC kicks in and lowers the temp to seventy. You've reached so far outside your comfort zone that you don't feel comfortable getting that "hot" and so you self-regulate back to what's comfortable, back to what you know.

This is the classic example of yo-yo dieting. Someone sets their thermostat for their weight for, say, one hundred fifty pounds. In their mind, one hundred fifty pounds is comfortable, like seventy degrees on a thermostat. If they gain too much, say, go up to one hundred sixty, their thermostat kicks in and says, "Hey, we need to go on a diet." They lose some weight and go back to the preset one hundred fifty pounds. They loosen up, gain some weight, and go on another diet, losing the same ten pounds over and over again. In the same way, this thermostat keeps you from going too far in a negative or positive direction.

If you want to step up your life, if you want to turn up the heat in every area of life, become the happiest, healthiest, and wealthiest version of yourself, you have to raise the thermostat, raise your standards, and shift who you are. Remember, the thinking that got you here will not get you to where you want to be. So, you have to upgrade your thoughts, your beliefs, your rules, and your values. You have to raise the temperature of the thermostat of your mind. To do this requires training. It requires Emotional Fitness.

Think of an incantation you'd create for your new identity: *I am a millionaire. I am a confident, successful entrepreneur. I am a beacon of light. I am healthy, fit, and strong. I am courageous. I am resourceful. I am loving.* "I am" allows you to *become* whatever you want to feel. Watch how using positive words can create a positive identity that shows in how you look.

Pick your top three I AM statements and write them below:

1. I AM _____

2. I AM_____

3. I AM_____

Every day for the next ten days—while you're driving to work in your car or going for a run—do your incantations and chant your I AM statements out loud. Remember to fully engage your body, mind, and voice. Get into it and *feel* your power grow with each I AM statement. This is training your Emotional Fitness. You only need to do this for five to ten minutes a day and you will start to feel different.

The BIG Question about Identity[44]

Studies show that our lives are often driven by certain questions. As we know, better questions get better answers. What are common questions asked by humankind in general and what is your specific driving question? We all ask the big questions about our lives and identities. These are often questions that have persisted since the dawn of time. Questions like,

- Who am I?

- How shall I live my life?

- What is my future?

According to John D. Mayer of the University of New Hampshire, "Big questions are defined here as those questions that are simple, important, and central to many people's lives. . . . At a personal level, big questions emerge from our curiosity, wonderment, and awe in response to the world. Such curiosity likely is functional and serves to direct people to consider what matters in their lives. For example, the questions often arise out of the specific issues a person is grappling with.[45] The way the questions ultimately are answered—in terms of constructing models of others and the world—will guide our interaction with others."[46]

Asking the big questions is an age-old phenomenon. A common one is "Why am I here?" A few thousand years ago, the Greeks had Delphi, a temple erected to the god Apollo. At its entrance, carved into a column by the Chiron of Sparta, was the command "Know thyself."

Throughout his dialogues, Plato has Socrates discuss self-knowledge. Socrates states he is interested in self-knowledge above all else.[47] Big questions have filled the minds of writers, poets, artists, statesmen, and philosophers throughout the existence of humankind.

Today, for most of us, big questions still fill our minds. Throughout this book, you have found ways to answer your big questions. By understanding your values and beliefs, you come to know who you really are and can answer the question "Who am I?"

The question "how shall I live?" was answered when you wrote down the values and rules you want to live by to become who you want to be. By writing down your goals and putting together an action plan, you are now designing your future with intent. With Emotional Fitness, you have the ability to never quit, to be resourceful, and to find a way to accomplish your goals no matter what.

And yet when it comes to long-term change, these BIG questions about our identities can be the Achilles heel to our Emotional Fitness training programs. Remember we said that all thinking is the constant asking and answering of questions? What if there's one question that you tend to ask more often than any other question? What if this one question was asked so many times throughout the day, you didn't even realize you were asking it? Or worse, that you were answering it?

Remember, the power of questions, how we ask questions, and what words we use all affect the very answers we get. Many people tend to ask one big question that governs their lives and how they interact with people. A big question is likely so ingrained into your habitual thinking that, just like everything in this book, you aren't even aware it exists. But the question drives the answer *and* your life.

If your big question is negative and disempowering, the training you've done will be in constant battle inside you because of the questions you ask yourself. Examples of negative disempowering questions are as follows:

- Why is life so hard?

- Why can't I change?

- Why am I such a failure?

- How come I'm not successful?

- Why am I so miserable?

- Why am I so depressed?

- Why does something bad always happen to me?

- Why do I always struggle?

- Why can't I ever be loved?

Use Pre-Framing to Shift Your Big Question

How do we shift these questions to help us in life, to empower us, and to strengthen our Emotional Fitness? We do this by PRE-Framing our questions.

Remember RE-framing? How powerful framing was in

shifting the meaning of our lives? How shifting the frame of context around an experience can dramatically shift the meaning of that experience?

PRE-framing is the process of introducing a perspective or attitude—a "frame"—that will predispose the answer that follows to give us one that we want. We do this all the time with our questions to other people. Someone may ask me, "Should we go out to party tonight or just be lazy and stay in a watch a movie?" I might not want to party or watch a movie but would like to go for a walk on the beach, but the question presupposes that I will answer with one of the two options presented.

"Would you like to buy this car in red or black?" In sales, we are always pre-framed so that we stay within the salesperson's frame. The salesman doesn't care what color of car you buy, but by asking this question, they pre-frame you. Thus, in order to answer the question with the color red or black, in your mind, you have assumed you are going to buy the car, which is what the seller wants!

We even pre-frame our thoughts. Look at the examples of the negative disempowering primary questions. "Why do I always struggle?" You didn't just ask why you struggle, you presupposed that you *always* struggle, and therefore you pre-framed yourself to give a negative, disempowering answer. This is disastrous when it comes to shifting your identity.

"Quality questions create a quality life.
Successful people ask better questions, and
as a result, they get better answers."

– Tony Robbins

These big identity questions can override our thoughts and actions. If a question dominates all other questions, and its answer drives the majority of your actions, it is known as our **Primary Question**, a phrase coined by Tony Robbins. Most of our primary questions revolve around insecurities or fears. Deep down, we fear not being loved, not feeling good enough, or that our lives don't mean anything.

Is your primary question, "Why am I not good enough?" Look at its pre-frame. Your mind will want to answer the question of why you aren't good enough and give you a negative answer. It's difficult to break the frame, especially when you pre-frame yourself negatively. Instead of trying to break the frame, try asking a different question that consciously uses pre-framing to give you a better, more empowering answer.

The way we pre-frame the question involves using the formulas below:

- "How can I feel [insert positive empowering emotion] **even more** right now?"

- "How can I appreciate **even more** [insert positive empowering emotion] **right now?**"

These questions ask *how* you can feel something positive, which presupposes you are able to find the answer. When you add the words *even more*, the question presupposes the most important thing: that you already do feel the emotion in your life and you just want more of it. Finally, by saying "right now," you empower yourself to feel that emotion immediately. This is an incredibly empowering question.

My old primary question used to be, "Why is life so fucked up?" Every time I asked that question, I found reasons why life was horrible, miserable, and fucked up. Then I shifted my primary question to, "How can I appreciate even more the opportunity life has given me to help people, to love, and to enjoy life right now?"

Questions fill our mind with answers. By changing the

wording of our primary question, we can pre-frame ourselves to give a more empowering answer and experience more success, love, and enjoyment right now.

Write down your *old* primary question below:

_____

_____

Now let's create your new empowering primary question. Use this formula:

• How can I feel even more [insert positive empowering emotion] in my life right now?

Write down your *new* empowering primary question below:

_____

_____

Incant your new primary question daily. Don't worry if your old question pops up a lot in the beginning. Remember, bringing awareness is the first step. Be proud that you identified your old disempowering question and then replace it with your new empowering primary question. After you've asked your new primary question, answer it and take action.

CONCLUSION

*Knowledge is of no value unless
you put it into practice.*

—ANTON CHEKHOV

Breathe. You've just been given a lot of powerful information to digest. Take some time to let it all integrate. This is transformative work. The very wording and structure of this book are meant to rewire your brain. Are you feeling the burn? Good. I've just given you the keys to everything you've ever dreamed of!

First, let's take a moment to celebrate finishing the book. You've come so far in mastering Emotional Fitness. Just by reading this book and learning the tools, your life is changed forever. Once a mind is stretched to new horizons, it cannot go back to its old dimensions. You have begun the process of mastering Emotional Fitness. However, learning something once does not train you for life . . .

Train your Emotional Fitness Daily

You can't go to the gym once and expect to be physically fit, and you can't use these tools in this book once and expect to be emotionally fit. This book has given you the knowledge. But knowing is not enough. Knowledge alone is not power. Action is power.

Your first action was reading this book and doing the exercises. You've learned the tools to train your mind and emotions.

Your next action will be to condition yourself daily to make it all a habit, ingrain it into your belief system and into your identity. You must train your emotions every single day. Becoming the best version of yourself takes hard work.

Remember, emotions are the very fuel that drives us. Emotions motivate us to accomplish our goals, but emotions can also be our downfall, our limitation, and stop us from living the life we were meant to.

History is filled with Emotionally Fit people who despite all odds, succeeded. One of my favorite biographies is Nelson Mandela: Long Walk to Freedom. Mandela was wrongfully imprisoned for more than 27 years in South Africa because he was a black man fighting for racial and social equality for all. In his time in prison, the guards tried to break him. They even offered him his freedom early if he would concede to the injustice. Mandela refused to be let go unless all innocent men were freed.

Later, he was asked, "How did you survive prison for all those years?"

He replied, "Survive? I didn't survive. I prepared!"

He prepared to be a leader. Using Emotional Fitness he turned 27 years in prison to become the leader his country needed. When released, Mandela became the first black president and put an end to apartheid.

History is full of people who had to deal with the emotions of negative experiences and those who shifted these emotions into motivation to accomplish their goals. They had to align themselves internally so that no matter what happened, they kept moving forward. And you can too.

I was not always happy. I struggled for years. It was only once I discovered Emotional Fitness that I realized I had a choice to change. I went from a depressed orthodontist hating my career to a happy entrepreneur living my dream life. I accomplished every goal I ever set, made more money than I ever imagined, helped more people than I ever felt possible and more importantly, I found love, happiness, fulfillment, and purpose along the way. I owe all of this to Emotional Fitness.

The truth is, you can tell yourself now what to believe. You can tell yourself now what you value. You can use incantations and engage your mind *and* body to become who you want to be. Use awareness, language, focus, physiology, power moves, anchors, emotional flooding, incantations of your new beliefs, values, rules, I AM statements, and primary questions to train your new identity with Emotional Fitness. *(See Appendix C for a complete day-by-day Emotional Fitness training program).*

Each one of these tools and strategies is powerful enough to change your life for the better. Use them all at the same time, consistently, and you will be able to accomplish anything you want in life.

Everlasting Persistence

One of the fundamental laws of life is that we are either growing or dying. In order to grow, you must be pushed outside of your comfort zone, which means your level of Emotional Fitness will always be evolving, updating, and improving. The only constant in life is change. Mastering Emotional Fitness will prepare you not only to survive anything that comes your way, but also to thrive! With Emotional Fitness, you can start living the life of your dreams now.

Emotional Fitness is a multi-layered process. You'll work through a few beliefs, shift them, improve your life, and accomplish your goals. And as you go through different stages of life, new challenges arise professionally and personally that require even more Emotional Fitness. With each stage, as you move outside of your comfort zone, you may come across another belief that needs to shift that you weren't even aware you had.

Emotional Fitness is not something that you reach, and you're there. It's not something that stops; it's a dynamic, living, ongoing growth process. If we do not consciously choose to train our Emotional Fitness, our unconscious survival mechanisms run in response to the external world, for better or worse. Therefore, every day, you must train your Emotional Fitness. Because every day you'll want to be the best version of myself, able to handle anything that is thrown at you, able to take advantage of any and all opportunities.

Once you achieve one goal, you're ready for the next. Maybe it's growing your business and maybe it's starting a family. Either way, being emotionally fit helps you accomplish more and enjoy it all along the way.

Since I started this process, new opportunities have appeared that I would've never imagined. And each successive stage requires a stronger, more emotionally fit me. Just as in physical fitness, I am continually pushing myself to grow further, and as I reach one goal, other doors, and other desires open up, requiring an even better me. This is the nature of life, and this is what Emotional Fitness trains you to take on.

As you grow more Emotionally Fit, you might notice some of your friends or family are, like you used to be, stressed, frustrated, sad, angry, upset, alone, distraught, depressed, or stuck in life. Refer them to this book so that they too can join the journey to Emotional Fitness mastery. Give them the gift of knowing how to master life, to accomplish their dreams, and to love life while doing it.

You're going to start to notice, as you follow this program, that life becomes easier. Once you align your values, you will no longer self-sabotage. You will find more passion, energy, and motivation in life. Your health will get better. Business decisions become easier. Relationships thrive, with more love and laughter. Life magnifies and explodes with happiness. Emotional Fitness not only helps you accomplish your goals, but it also helps you become you who want to be, who you were meant to be.

Most believe their *actions* and *decisions* from the past define who they are. The past cannot be changed, but your future can be. Who you *were*, does not have to be who you *are*. What you did five years ago, five months ago, or even five minutes ago does not have to be who you are now. The truth is that the past only becomes your present and your future if you live there. You can decide now who you want to become.

You can choose new habits, new empowering beliefs, new values, and a new identity—a new you. If you believe that, then you can do anything you want, and become anything you want to be. You can design the life of your dreams. With Emotional Fitness, you can accomplish any goal, whether it's to make a million dollars a year, have six-pack abs, find the love of your life, or create a movement to change the world for the better.

Who you are now is based on your decisions. Who you become in the future is who you *decide* to be *now*. **You have the power to decide who you want to be.** Now is your time. We can never change our past, but we can change our future—**by using Emotional Fitness.**

This is the ultimate gift that Emotional Fitness gives you, the ultimate power to be the creator of your life and your destiny. Master Emotional Fitness and you master your life.

The Emotional Fitness Guide and Course
(For Free!)

Many of the exercises in this book require you to write down a few things and refer back to them often. To help you get the most out of this book, I created a **free** online tutorial and course complete with downloadable worksheets, bonus video content, and a daily journal workbook to help you master Emotional Fitness.

Although it's not required, I highly recommend you access the free course and worksheets to help you maximize your success with the content of this book. Just visit the following address to sign up:

www.MasterEmotionalFitness.com/course

Once you sign up, you'll find the material in the same order as the chapters and sections of this book to help you easily master Emotional Fitness. There's additional bonus content beyond what is shared in this book, and I'll be adding more bonus content over time. Make sure to visit the website address below and get free instant access to it now! See you inside!

Visit the link to get free access to your

Emotional Fitness bonus materials now:

www.MasterEmotionalFitness.com/course

ACKNOWLEDGMENTS

I would not be the man I am today without the direct and indirect influence of all those around me. I am forever grateful to all of you.

To the love of my life, Chelsea. Thank you for always supporting my audacious goals, even while knowing the path ahead is not an easy one. With the countless hours of hard work and sleepless nights that may lie ahead, I find comfort in knowing you have and always will be there. Thank you for staying up late and listening to my rehearsal of keynote speeches. Thank you for entertaining my rants of goals, Emotional Fitness, and life. You truly are an amazing human being, filled with love and compassion. Thank you for all your support and love. I love you, Chelsea.

Thank you to my family and friends. I love all of you. I am so grateful to have such great people in my life. All of you have influenced me in many positive ways. Specifically, thank you to my two amazing sisters, Shaina and Carli. To Carli, you have such a big heart, and I am grateful for all the love and support you've given me. To Shaina, thank you for always trying to help me, even if I wasn't ready to receive it. You always show me a different perspective and expand my mind. To both of you, no matter what happens, the three of us will always have each other. You've been there for me, even in my darkest moments. And in those tough times, you filled my life with exactly what I needed, love and laughter.

To my mom, Abby, thank you for giving me unconditional love and support as a child. Thank you for your unwavering optimism towards life. With your optimism, you lead by example. While I was stubborn well into my twenties, I now know the true power of your gift.

To my dad, Greg, thank you for showing me the values that I live by. You taught me what it was to be a man. You raised me to go after my dreams and instilled in me a work ethic that I only hope I pass on to my children. You showed me how to conquer my fears, to stand up for myself, and never give up. I would never be who I am today without you.

I love you ALL!

And then, of course, thank you to the talented and hardworking book coach Caroline Allen with the Art of Storytelling for helping me turn my vision into a reality. Thank you for putting up with the hectic schedule that was my life, for being patient and fully invested in Emotional Fitness.

Thank you to the many inspiring people and mentors, who impacted my life either personally, through books, speeches, or other avenues. Some of you have helped me in my deepest moments of despair, and others have shown me what is possible in life. I thank you for raising the standards of our society and constantly pushing to do more with your own lives. Thank you, Larry Tenebaum, Tony Robbins, Tim Ferriss, Stephen Covey, Richard Bandler, Jon Grinder, Viktor Frankl, Charles Duhigg, Dale Carnegie, and Pat Flynn.

And finally, thank you to all of you who have followed my journey, who read this book and share it with others. In search of my own success, I realized that the only way for me to be truly fulfilled was to empower others to do the same. I truly believe Emotional Fitness is the secret to success in any area of life. Knowing that this will help even one person, inspires me to do more.

Appendix A: References

1   "S07psy4002 (Pdf)." - Dominican University of California, 2015, www.dominican.edu/academics/lae/undergraduate-programs/psych/faculty/assets-gail-matthews/S07psy4002.pdf/view.

2   Kraftman, TL, and SD Pressman. "Grin and Bear It: The Influence of Manipulated Facial Expression on the Stress Response." *PubMed.gov*, Department of Psychology, University of Kansas, Lawrence, 14 Sept. 2012, www.ncbi.nlm.nih.gov/pubmed/23012270.

3   https://link.springer.com/article/10.1007%2Fs10826-018-1096-2.

4   https://www.cdc.gov/vitalsigns/suicide/index.html.

5   Ekman, P., Levenson, RW., & Friesen, W.V. (1983). Autonomic nervous system activity distinguishes among emotions. Science, 221, 1208-1210.

6   Ekman, P. (1989). The argument and evidence about universals in facial expressions of emotion. In H. Wagner & A. Manstead (Eds.), Handbook of psychophysiology: Emotion and social behavior (pp. 143-164). London: John Wiley & Sons.

7   Levenson, et al in "Voluntary Facial Action Generates Emotion-Specific Autonomous Nervous System Activity." Psychophysiology, 27, 1990.

8   ibid.

9   Ekman, P.I, Levenson, RW., & Friesen, W.V. (1983). Autonomic nervous system activity distinguishes among emotions. Science, 221, 1208-1210.

10 Ekman, P. (1989). The argument and evidence about universals in facial expressions of emotion.

> In H. Wagner & A. Manstead (Eds.), Handbook of psychophysiology: Emotion and social behavior (pp. 143-164). London: John Wiley & Sons.

11 Goleman, Daniel. *Emotional Intelligence*. New York: Bantam Books (2005).

12 The limbic system and emotions: R. Joseph, The Naked Neuron: Evolution and the Languages of the Brain and Body (New York: Plenum Publishing, 1993); Paul D. MacLean, The Triune Brain in Evolution (New York: Plenum, 1990.

13 Excerpt from: Daniel Goleman. *Emotional Intelligence*.

14 Reference https://www.youtube.com/watch?v=IdTMDpizis8.

15 Ophira, Eyal, et al. "Cognitive Control in Media Multitaskers. National Academy of Sciences. 25 Aug. 2009, journalistsresource.org/studies/society/social-media/multitasking-social-media-distraction-what-does-research-say/.

16 Carr, Nicholas G. *The Shallows: What the Internet Is Doing to Our Brains*. W.W. Norton, 2011.

17 http://www.logotherapyinstitute.org/About_Logotherapy.html.

18 https://www.sciencedaily.com/releases/2016/03/160330135623.htm.

19 Schroeder, Jules. "25 Marketing Influencers to Watch In 2017." *Forbes.com*, Forbes, 29 Nov. 2016, www.forbes.com/sites/julesschroeder/2016/11/29/25-marketing-influencers-to-watch-in-2017/amp/.

20 http://psychclassics.yorku.ca/Maslow/motivation.htm.

21 http://www.logotherapyinstitute.org/About_Logotherapy.html.

22 https://www.health.harvard.edu/mental-health/the-power-of-the-placebo-effect.

23 https://www.nationalreview.com/corner/
roger-bannister-john-landry-better-runner/.

24 https://www.bitebackpublishing.com/books/twin-tracks.

25 https://www.nytimes.com/1987/02/03/science/research-affirms-power-of-positive-thinking.html.

26 https://www.ncbi.nlm.nih.gov/pmc/articles/PMC5072593/.

27 https://dash.harvard.edu/handle/1/9547823.

28 https://news.uark.edu/articles/8933/angry-breathing-beats-venting.

29 https://greatergood.berkeley.edu/article/item/
do_mirror_neurons_give_empathy.

30 Goleman, *Emotional Intelligence*.

31 https://www.webmd.com/heart-disease/features/
rein-in-rage-anger-heart-disease.

32 https://blogs.psychcentral.com/nlp/2013/01/chronic-anger-damage/.

33 http://amhistory.si.edu/onthemove/themes/pdf/autosafety_candace_lightner.pdf.

34 Baumeister, et al. (1998). Ego depletion: Is the active self a limited resource? Journal of Personality and Social Psychology, 74(5), 1252–1265.

35 http://www.andrewnewberg.com/books/words-can-change-your-brain-12-conversation-strategies-to-build-trust-resolve-conflict-and-increase-intimacy.

36 https://www.ncbi.nlm.nih.gov/pmc/articles/PMC2486416/.

37 http://oem.bmj.com/content/62/2/105.

38 https://www.ncbi.nlm.nih.gov/pmc/articles/PMC2568977/.

39 Franklin, Benjamin. *The Autobiography of Benjamin Franklin*. New York: American Book Company (1896).

40 ibid.

41 Erikson, Erik. *Identity and the Life Cycle*, New York City: W.W. Norton& Company, Inc (1980).

42 Appiah, Kwame Anthony. *The Lies That Bind: Rethinking Identity*. New York City: Liveright Publishing Corporation (2018).

43 https://people.psych.ucsb.edu/sherman/david/advancesshermanco-hen.pdf.

44 Mayer, John. Imagination, Cognition and Personality. "The Big Questions of Personality Psychology: Defining Common Pursuits of the Discipline." Vol. 27(1) 3-26, 2007-2008.

45 Alexander, 1942; Woodhouse, 1984, p.4.

46 Kelly, 1955; Mischel & Shoda, 1995.

47 Griswold, 1986, p. 68.

APPENDIX B:
EMOTIONAL FITNESS DAILY TRAINING

Morning Routine: Wake-Up Assessment and Emotional Fitness Workout

How are you feeling this morning? Are you excited about the day? Tired? Unenthusiastic? Angry at the alarm clock? Sad? Happy? Content?

Write down any specific emotion or range of emotions you feel right now.

_____

How strong is this emotion? On a scale from one to ten, with ten being the strongest and one being the weakest, circle how strong this emotion is to you.

1	2	3	4	5	6	7	8	9	10

Does this emotion help you or hurt you? How?

_____

If you feel a negative disempowering emotion answer the following questions:

1) What are you focusing on? Is it in your control? Is it about you or other people? Is there something else you could focus on that would make you feel different?

_____

_____

2) What does this negative disempowering emotion *mean* to you? Is it possible it could mean something else? Can you shift the meaning to something positive? Can you find the good in it?

_____

_____

3) Are you reacting to this emotion? If so, how can you shift it to act with purpose?

_____

_____

If you need to get out of this negative emotion, do your power move!

If you are already in a good mood, do your power move anyway! It will reinforce and anchor your positive emotional state.

Gratitude and Goals!

Start your day with gratitude. Write down three things you are grateful for today. Be sincere, be honest, and feel each one. They can be big or small.

1) _____

2) _____

3) _____

Review your top three goals. Do they still align with what you truly want? If they don't, change them here. If you have accomplished one of them, replace it with a new goal!

Rewrite your top three goals.	Why are they important to you?	What action are you going to take today to get closer to your goals?

Who do you need to be to accomplish these goals? What values and emotions do you need to show up today to help you be your best self?

Do incantation exercises for the following:

Your declaration of self and purpose:

_____

_____

After each incantation, anchor the feeling in by triggering your chosen anchor (e.g., clenched fist, hand over heart, pressing your finger into your hand).

What are your top three empowering beliefs?

1) _____

2) _____

3) _____

After each incantation, anchor the belief in. Keep saying it louder and with more conviction than the time before. Now, double the intensity and anchor it again. Now, double it again until you feel it in every cell of your body, and anchor it again. By anchoring these beliefs, we are able to call them back to our minds immediately.

This entire exercise should take you less than ten minutes. If you have more time or are early in your training, pull out your Emotional Fitness Master Plan and do incantations for all of your values, your declaration of self, your dominant driving question, and your empowering beliefs.

Daily Check-ins

Do a quick daily check-in on your emotional state twice a day. You can do it more often if you'd like, but midday and right when you get home in the evening are great times to check-in.

If you are having a bad day or experiencing a negative disempowering emotion, immediately check in with yourself. Do the exercises below, followed by your morning routine, power pose/move, gratitude, goals, and incantations to get yourself out of a funk and empower yourself to finish the day strong!

Midday Check-in

Write down any specific emotion or range of emotions you feel right now.

_____

How strong is this emotion? On a scale from one to ten, with ten being the strongest and one being the weakest, circle how strong this emotion is to you.

1	2	3	4	5	6	7	8	9	10

Does this emotion help you or hurt you? How?

_____

If you feel a negative disempowering emotion, answer these questions:

1) What are you focusing on? Is it in your control? Is it about you or other people? Is there something else you could focus on that would make you feel different?

_____

_____

2) What does this negative disempowering emotion mean to you? Is it possible it could mean something else? Can you shift

the meaning to something positive? Can you find the good in it?

_____

_____

3) Are you reacting to this emotion? If so, how can you shift it to act with purpose?

_____

If you need to get out of this negative emotion, do your power move or an incantation with your empowering beliefs. If you are already in a good mood, trigger your anchor for this feeling to reinforce this positive emotional state.

Nighttime Check-in and Self-reflection

Write down any specific emotion or range of emotions you feel right now.

_____

How strong is this emotion? On a scale from one to ten, with ten being the strongest and one being the weakest, circle how strong this emotion is to you.

1	2	3	4	5	6	7	8	9	10

Does this emotion help you or hurt you? How?

Write down three positive empowering emotions you felt today.

1. _____

2. _____

3. _____

Write down three negative disempowering emotions you felt today.

1. _____

2. _____

3. _____

Pick at least one disempowering emotion and answer these questions:

1) What are you focusing on? Is it in your control? Is it about you or other people? Is there something else you could focus on that would make you feel different?

_____

_____

2) What does this negative disempowering emotion mean to you? Is it possible it could mean something else? Can you shift the meaning to something positive? Can you find the good in it?

_____

_____

3) Are you reacting to this emotion? If so, how can you shift it to act with purpose?

_____

4) What did this emotion cost you today? Did it cause you stress? Problems? Did it stop you or slow you down from reaching your goals?

_____

_____

5) What is one thing you learned by doing exercise today?

_____

6) What is one action you will take to improve your Emotional Fitness tomorrow?

_____

Do incantations for your I AM statements and your top three empowering beliefs.

Now, pull out your top three goals. Review them and make sure they are still what you want.

Now, visualize achieving them. Visualize who you will become to achieve them. Visualize how you will act (strongly), how you will talk (with confidence), and how the world looks when you achieve these goals. Remember, Emotional Fitness helps you reroute any obstacle, tackle any challenge, come back from any failure, and be successful.

APPENDIX C:
EMOTIONAL FITNESS QUICK GUIDE SUMMARY

1. **Awareness**

    A. What's your story?

        i.   What do you tell yourself life is about?

        ii. What helps you?

        iii. What stops you?

    B. What's your emotional experience?

        i.   Examine your external world (people, places, things, the past).

        ii. Examine your internal world (the decisions you're making, whether your emotions are in control of if they control you).

        iii. What do you feel like you are in control of?

    C. What are your decisions of destiny?

        i.   What are you focusing on? What else could you focus on that would change your experience?

    ii. What meaning do you attach to the thing you're focusing on? What else could this mean if you look at it from a different point of view?

    iii. What was your reaction to this focus? Or what action can you consciously choose to take?

D. What are your limiting beliefs?

    i. What are some old limiting beliefs you have about yourself and your life, relationships, business, money, finances, love, and health?

2. Conquer Your Goals

A. What are your top three goals in life right now?

    i. Why have you not accomplished them yet?

B. Remember to raise the BAR (Beliefs, Action, Results).

C. What limiting beliefs have stopped you from accomplishing your goals?

    i. If you had a different belief, how would that change the actions you take and your results?

    ii. What is the belief you want to have?

D. What is your fear vs. faith loop?

    i. What are your fears about your goals?

    ii. What is distracting you from these goals?

       iii. What are some statements you make that show you have faith in your ability to accomplish these goals?

   E. What action do you take towards these goals?

       i. Visualize your success.

       ii. Write down exactly what you want to achieve. Be very clear about your goals. Go back to them each day. Visualize what it will take to achieve your goals.

       iii. Commit to taking action.

       iv. Each day DO THE WORK.

Now that you have a plan, what do you do when you fail? Emotional Fitness training helps you keep pushing no matter what happens.

3. Change Your Emotional State in a Moment: Simple Exercises

   A. Shift your focus with the power of questions.

       i. What are you focusing on right now?

       ii. What are you truly in control of?

       iii. What can you learn from this?

       iv. What is one positive thing that can come from this?

B.   Shift meaning with the power of words.

  i.   What words should you delete from your vocabulary (i.e., *can't* or *try*)?

  ii.   What words should you shift to empower yourself? From good to great, OK to fantastic, failure to a learning experience.

C.   Use the power of re-framing.

  i.   What is one thing you can reframe right now (e.g., losing a job, being unproductive) to change its meaning?

D.   Shift your physiology using a power pose or power move.

  i.   What is your power move? This is a move that radically shifts your physiology and prepares you for the day.

  ii.   Do your power pose for two minutes to create a physiological shift. Use anchors to create the same physiological shift. For example, while power posing, you can clench your right fist, then when you clench your fist, you will trigger the anchor and shift your physiology.

E.   Do breathing cycles.

  i.   Do focused breathing: four seconds in, four seconds hold, four seconds out, four seconds hold, and repeat.

      ii. Do relaxation breathing: normal inhale and slow, lengthened exhale. With each breath, keep lengthening your exhale. Do this for two minutes to reset your nervous system and relax.

  F. Use the power of peers.

      i. Who are the five people you spend the most time with?

      ii. Are they the people you want to be around the most? If not, change it.

4. Examine your habits and behaviors.

  A. What is one of your emotional habits?

      i. What is the cue that starts this habit?

      ii. What is the habit or routine that you go through?

      iii. What is the reward that you feel this routine gives you?

      iv. Replace the routine with something that is better for you.

  B. What are some anchors that you can use to trigger a positive empowering emotion (e.g., power posing, hand on heart)?

      i. Stack your anchors.

      ii. What are two experiences you can stack to create a more powerful anchor?

C. Find your emotional home.

    i. What is your old emotional home? This is your go-to emotion that you revert to in cases of extreme stress or discomfort.

    ii. What is the NEW emotional home you want to have?

D. Do an emotional flood.

    i. What is one positive emotion you want to do an emotional flood for (e.g., love, happiness, confidence, courage)?

    ii. What anchor will you use to trigger the feelings of the emotional flood?

    iii. Practice doing an emotional flood.

E. Use the swish pattern.

    i. What is one habit you will break with the swish pattern?

    ii. Take the old habit you want to break and make it into a dark, dim, fuzzy, small picture that is far away.

    iii. Take the new habit you want to replace it with and make it big, bright, moving, and loud, so it feels as real as possible.

    iv. Take the old image in your left hand and the new image in your right hand. Push the old image far out into space as you bring the new image close to your face. As your two hands pass each other, make them collide. As they do, the old image shatters into a million pieces, and all that is left is the new image.

F. Use single dissociation

    i. What is one negative emotion that you want to get rid of?

    ii. Use single dissociation exercises to scratch the record and remove the power of this negative memory and emotion.

5. Examine your beliefs.

A. What are your beliefs about life, love, work, happiness, money, freedom, family, God, kids, friends, travel, health, fitness, failure, success, and time?

    i. What are your positive empowering beliefs? How do they help you?

    ii. What are your negative disempowering beliefs? How do they hurt you?

        a. How did your negative beliefs help you at one point in time? What purpose did they serve? What are they costing you now?

B. Replace with empowering beliefs by creating incantations.

    i. Repeat your incantations with your body, mind, and voice to make it real.

6. Examine your values.

A. What are your current moving toward and away from values?

B. Are your values a means value or an end value?

C. What do you believe must happen to meet these values? What are your rules for these values?

7. Address your internal struggle.

A. What is the order of your values?

    i. Is this how you truly want to live your life?

B. Are any rules in conflict, causing your actions and what you want to be misaligned?

8. Create your identity.

A. What are the toward values that you WANT to live by?

    i. What order do you want your away values to be in?

    ii. What are the rules you want to live by? Remember to make it really easy to feel these toward values.

B. What are the away values that you *never* want to experience?

    i. What is the order of your away values?

ii. What are the rules that you made for yourself? Remember to make it really hard to feel these away values.

C. Declare yourself. Who are you?

    i. Practice your I AM statements.

    ii. What was your old Primary Question?

    iii. What is your new Primary Question?

        a. Remember to use the power of Pre-Framing so your new Primary Question empowers you.

ABOUT
UNLEASH SUCCESS

Unleash Success (www.UnleashSuccess.com) is a podcast and resource founded by Corey Corpodian that helps to break down the secrets of success into real tools and strategies that get real results. On this website you can find interviews with millionaires and fitness experts, as well as marketing strategies, mindset tools, and resources to help you unlock your true potential.

Unleash Success is dedicated to pushing the limits of human potential to maximize success in every area of life. If you are looking for motivation or to join a community of people who want more out of their own lives, go to www.UnleashSuccess.com/TakeAction to sign up. When you sign up, you'll get new strategies for unleashing success in your professional and personal life, plus recommended tools and programs to speed up your journey to the top.

Cheers to your next level of success! We will see you there!

Visit

www.UnleashSuccess.com/TakeAction

ABOUT THE AUTHOR

Corey Corpodian is an orthodontist turned entrepreneur, motivational speaker, and podcaster. He is the founder of Unleash Success. A high energy and impactful speaker, Corey Corpodian has given keynotes internationally for personal development seminars, businesses, and the U.S. Marines. His mission in life is to push the limits of human potential, redefine what we think is possible, and empower others to become the ultimate version of themselves. He lives in Newport Beach, California.

Made in the USA
Columbia, SC
24 September 2019